Marco Preshevski was born in 1971, in Luton, United Kingdom. After spending his childhood and adolescent years in the west of England, he attended the University of Bristol, graduating in 1993 with an honours degree in Chemistry. Marco worked for almost twenty years in healthcare, marketing communications before moving to Australia. Marco lives in Sydney, New South Wales, Australia, where he spends as much time as possible raising his daughter.

For my amazing daughter E, who gave me more reason and inspiration to write this book. I love you more than words can say, and I am incredibly proud to be your father.

A huge thank you to my mum, Sue, for keeping me focussed in everything I do. Love you lots Mum.

Marco Preshevski

THE TIME THIEF

AUSTIN MACAULEY PUBLISHERS™

LONDON • CAMBRIDGE • NEW YORK • SHARJAH

A CIP catalogue record for this title is available from the British Library.

ISBN 9781398427570 (Paperback)
ISBN 9781398475991 (ePub e-book)

www.austinmacauley.com

First Published 2022
Austin Macauley Publishers Ltd®
1 Canada Square
Canary Wharf
London
E14 5AA

To all my family, friends and acquaintances: thank you for your continued support and encouragement while I was writing this, my second book, particularly my sister, Jules, in London, my good friend, Leonard, from Wales/London and lastly but not least, my bloody good mate, Kurt, in Sydney. Also thank you to the team at Austin Macauley Publishers, in London.

Prologue

This book is not a self-help manual for people who have been diagnosed with Parkinson's Disease (PD). It is the story of Marco Preshevski, an ordinary man who was diagnosed with this challenging medical condition surprisingly, at the age of 30 years old and the effect this had on his livelihood, his future career prospects and essentially, his ability to gain and retain employment. It discusses some of the difficult career-oriented decisions that were made in what seemed to be a continual battle with PD where 'time' was literally being ripped out from under his feet, making him question whether or not he would be able to achieve his life goals.

Fundamentally, it is an access-all-areas insight into the world of someone who has endeavoured to maintain and preserve his quality of life and perhaps more importantly, his 'quantity' of working life. That is, how much time he has to devote to generating an income after PD has stolen its non-negotiable share. With the debilitating symptoms of a serious long term medical condition ever present, Marco tells us about his relentless quest to extend his career and keep his mind and body active by engaging in gainful employment. It becomes clear that having PD is not the only direct challenge to achieving this goal – external factors, influenced by PD that are beyond Marco's control, are also brought to light. The overall outcome is the irreversible loss of time and the need for continual re-evaluation of his life goals.

The book recites how this ordinary man dealt with everything that PD threw in the way of furthering his career. Moreover, it conveys the importance of self-motivation to keep moving forward, albeit in the face of constant adversity from PD. It is peppered with colourful anecdotes of the author's real-life work experiences, which remind us that 'life' happens to us all and a sense of humour is required for the journey. On the whole, it makes for an honest, amusing story that defines the ebb and flow of employment, with the added complication of a long-term medical condition thrown in for good measure.

Marco Preshevski's first book, *Drivin' Daughters and Parkinson's*, discusses the impact of being diagnosed with Parkinson's Disease two weeks after turning 30 years old, how it affected his life, how it affected the lives of the people around him and what kept him pushing ahead. With Marco's commitment to return to his career in advertising, his second book, *The Time Thief*, takes a detailed look at the effect Parkinson's Disease had on the development of his career, how this was affected and what changes he made (and continues to make) in order to achieve his life goals.

One

If I never have another job interview, I will have achieved one of my life goals.

---|---

My first proper job interview was with The British Secret Service.

I was eighteen at the time when I was invited to attend an 'informal interview' at my sixth form college near Bristol. I was in the upper sixth preparing to sit my A level exams, in my second and final year. I had secured a conditional offer to read chemistry at the University of Bristol, with my course deferred by one year.

It was Wednesday afternoon. I was in the middle of a chemistry lesson when I noticed Mr Porrin, head teacher of the entire school, including the sixth form, striding towards the demountable buildings where the lesson was being delivered by Mr Mackay. Mr Mackay was single-handedly responsible for inspiring me to read for a degree in chemistry at the University of Bristol.

I watched as Mr Porrin made a beeline for our class…up the steps, through the outside door and wiped his feet on the mat. With another class taking place next door, there was a 50% chance of him coming into our class. *Right or left, which way will he turn?* I wondered.

Mr Porrin turned to his right. *Oh shit, he's coming in here,* I thought. *What does he want?*

The head teacher hesitated in the open doorway, not wishing to disrupt the lesson.

Mr Mackay stopped writing on the chalkboard. "Come in, Jim," he called. "What can I do for you? Have you come to join the lesson?"

Mr Porrin stepped into the room. "No, no, no, no…my sincere apologies for this intrusion, I just need to borrow…umm…Marco, for a few minutes, if I may?"

"Sure, take as long as you need," said Mr Mackay. "Marco…sounds like you're in trouble? Wave goodbye to your friends…" Some of my classmates laughed.

Fuck, I thought. *What have I done now?* I couldn't think of anything that I had done recently that I might get into trouble over. *Hang-on…shit…this is about Donny and me bunking off last Thursday afternoon, it must be.*

I stood up and followed Mr Porrin as he went back outside and down the steps.

"Mr Porrin," I said. He turned his head momentarily towards me. "Sir, is this about Donny and me bunking off an afternoon last week? We only did it because he wanted to get some things off his chest about his mum's new boyfriend. Donny's been through a lot recently – we won't do it again."

Mr Porrin said nothing. We walked to the middle of the large empty playground.

"Marco, you do know that the rules changed when you moved from high school to sixth-form?" Mr Porrin said. "Attending sixth-form is entirely your choice, you don't need an absentee note from your parents…you could take every afternoon off next week and I wouldn't be able to do anything, apart from tell you that your work might suffer as a result."

"Oh," I said, "that's…useful to know."

I looked around. The playground was empty. I looked at the head teacher – why had he brought me over to this playground, instead of his office?

"Did you want to talk with me about something, sir?"

"Yes, as a matter of fact I do, Marco. Before I get into that, I want you to know that this conversation is private and confidential. You cannot talk about anything we talk about with anybody. That means no discussions with friends or with family. Is that clear?"

I was mystified. What was Mr Porrin going on about?

"Wha…?" I squeaked out. Then I coughed to clear my throat before I spoke.

"Yeah, sure…what's this all about?"

"This morning, I took a phone call from a man in London who works for, shall we say, well…let's just say he works for the government…in recruitment. Anyway, this is the time of year when they start looking at what resources they need and he's interested in meeting you."

"Why?"

"Well, they have a particular 'character' profile that they need to fulfil for this type of role, your background, you know…umm, like, with your parents being divorced, you are going to university, which puts you in the above average academic achiever category, you are fit and healthy because of the rowing that you do, you told me that you like some extreme sports, like climbing mountains…"

He paused for a second.

"It's not any one thing; it's a mixture of different aptitudes, that makes you a potential candidate for this type of role."

"Okay," I said, pausing briefly to collect my thoughts. "What type of role are we talking about and why do you know so much about it?"

Mr Porrin looked over my shoulders and glanced around. There were very few people around. There was nobody close enough to hear us.

"Our college profiles well for covering an area of the population which has a higher than average number of people who are well suited for this role," he said. "I've been involved in this for donkeys' years; there are only half a dozen or so colleges in the country that correlate as well as ours, for people who are potential candidates for this role."

"Mr Porrin," I said. "Sir, with respect…you have said that four times now. What type of role are we talking about?"

Mr Porrin looked straight at me. I stared back directly at his eyes. He crossed his arms and coughed.

Then he spoke. "This role is in intelligence…the type of job is an intelligence officer."

I stared at the head teacher for a few seconds longer. For a moment, I forgot I was at the college, forgot that the man in front of me was my head teacher.

"You want to recruit me to become a spy?" I said stifling a nervous laugh. "A spy? James Bond, in real life, eh?"

"No, I don't recruit for the role, a Mr White and a Mr Green who work for the government do that. Every now and then, a student pops up who shows potential. I should tell you that even though suitable candidates are rarer than hens' teeth, the majority don't make it. After a thorough background check, which covers many parameters, I can put you forward for the role as a candidate. This is where my involvement ends."

"Who are Mr White and Mr Green?"

"Well, it's easier if you just think of them as recruitment officers. If you want to take it forward, I will make arrangements for you to meet Mr White and Mr Green on Friday this week. Just wear what you are wearing now; you don't want to arouse any suspicions by wearing a suit. Come to my office at 12.30 pm on Friday. You don't have to tell anybody anything about where you are going beforehand or where you have been afterwards."

"Are you being serious? This is not a wind up, is it?"

"Marco, do I look like I have the time to fuck around with this shit?" said Mr Porrin. "No, I am not winding you up."

Now I knew that this was for real.

Mr Porrin continued. "I do know that they look favourably upon you if you defer entry to university for a year because you can begin training in your gap year and your vacations. As you might expect they will also look after you during your university years and then pick up your training when you leave university."

He lowered his voice. "This is the last time you and I will ever discuss this even though you still have three or four months until your exams are through. After Friday, you must do exactly what Mr White and Mr Green tell you to do. Bear in mind that this interview is just the first stage of the recruitment phase and the majority of suitable candidates don't make it past this stage."

Mr Porrin took half a step back from me, coughed again and folded his arms.

"What's it going to be then, sport? Are you up for it?" he asked.

---|---

The door to Mr Porrin's office was dark blue. His name and job title were on the door, made up from individual letters printed on self-adhesive plastic squares and stuck on the door. Somebody had removed the plastic squares which formed the word TEACHER and presumably the same person had used the pointed end of a pair of compasses or some other sharp, pointed instrument to carve the word GIVER in its place. So, the wordage on the door read as:

MR J PORRIN
HEAD GIVER

Why doesn't he get a proper name label made up? I wondered.

I glanced at my watch; the time was 12:29 and 32 seconds. I watched the remaining digital seconds as they disappeared one after the other, forever lost. At 12:30 pm precisely, I knocked on the door seven times in a row, as instructed by Mr Porrin. Then, I heard the sound of the door being unlocked. Subsequently the door swung open into the office, the hinges crying out for lubricating oil.

From where I stood, I could see a man sitting on the edge of Mr Porrin's desk. *Mr White,* I thought. *Or Mr Green?* I stepped into the room and he came forward, arm stretched out as I took a couple more steps into the room. He shook my hand with a firm grip, and even smiled momentarily.

"Mr Preshevski, how do you do? My name is Mr Green and this is my colleague…" He gestured behind me. "Mr White."

"Mr Preshevski, it is a pleasure to make your acquaintance," said Mr White as I turned around to shake the hand presented to me. He also smiled momentarily.

"You must be the doorman," I said as Mr White closed the door and turned the key. Then, we were very much alone. Mr Green and Mr White stood in front of me. I looked at Mr White, then turned slowly to look at Mr Green, then back to Mr White before my gaze came to rest on Mr Green. I smiled briefly and re-set my expressionless facial expression. Mr Green spoke.

"Something…wrong, Mr Preshevski?" he asked.

"Or maybe you find something…amusing, Mr Preshevski?" asked Mr White.

"Neither, actually," I said, keeping my voice level, steady and my gaze locked to theirs. "I was just wondering how your parents can tell you apart from one another?"

"Please take a seat, Mr Preshevski." Mr Green gestured towards the round table with six chairs arranged in pairs. I took the right seat of the pair on the left; Mr White and Mr Green shared the pair directly opposite me.

"What made you ask that question…about our…parents?" asked Mr White. "Are you assuming that we have the same parents?"

"How could I?" I said. "Despite the fact that you look like identical twins, you both have different surnames…so, how could you be brothers?"

"Appearances can be deceptive, don't you agree, Mr Preshevski?" questioned Mr Green.

"Sometimes," I said. "But you don't have to look too far before things start to unravel. I pity your parents, Mr Green. And yours too, Mr White. I would imagine that there have been, over the years many opportunities for all four of your parents to meet and mix the two of you up. I mean, you do look very much alike…I can't think of a pair of identical twins who look like each other to the same extent as you."

"Water, Mr Preshevski?" asked Mr White, picking up a glass and the glazed clay jug in the middle of the table.

"Yes, it probably is," I said. "But I think we have already dealt with the fact that appearances can be deceptive. It could be acid – after all, glass, from the glazing when the jug was fired in a kiln won't dissolve in acid – unless it is a fluorinated acid, of course."

"Ah, I see," said Mr White.

"So…after you, Mr White. But let's just go back to the issue of how much alike you both look. You may go to the same hair stylist, you obviously employ the same tailor and to get those moustaches whisker perfect, both of you must visit the same barbershop. However, Mr Green…the vertical red stripes on your necktie are only about two-thirds of the width of those on Mr White's necktie. A very subtle point of difference but definitely a point of difference, none-the-less. I'm impressed."

I sat back in my chair and spread my fingers on the edge of the glass table top.

"I mean, bespoke woven silk neckties with sewn in errors? They must have cost you a fortune. How much does the government pay you?"

---|---

The interview progressed with Mr Green and Mr White's double act, trying to throw me off kilter just to see if and how I reacted. I just kept reminding myself to adopt my expressionless facial expression, offer only just enough information to answer their questions, keep emotion out of it. I knew what they were doing – they were trying to work out if I could be trained to withstand interrogation by an enemy. I threw questions back at them throughout, as we discussed my political leanings, religion, my upbringing, breast-feeding and my views on taking someone's life.

"You mean, could I kill someone? Yes, if it was going to keep me alive."

Mr Green said, "Mr Preshevski, do you think you think you could kill someone by holding their head in a powder pile of illegal drugs, forcing them to choke to death on say, cocaine or heroin?"

"Yes, I wou…"

"What if it was a woman, Mr Preshevski?" Mr Green interrupted me. "Could you kill a woman this way before she pulls a firearm out of her vagina and shoots you?"

I didn't hesitate. "That's quite an unusual holster, but, yes of course. In principle, she deserves to die for misuse of a body part."

Then the interview came to an end. I stood up to leave and moved towards the locked door.

"Mr Preshevski, it has been an absolute pleasure to meet you," said Mr Green. "Thank you for your time today."

"Thank you. I enjoyed meeting you too."

"Mr Preshevski, what will happen next, I hear you ask?" said Mr White. "You may receive a phone call in the next two to three months if you are successful at this stage. The caller will tell you what the next steps are. Or you may not receive such a call. Here – can you write your home phone number and the area code please…thank you very much. Well, enjoy your life, Mr Preshevski. It was nice to meet you."

"Goodbye," I said, shaking hands with them. Mr White unlocked the door and opened it. I slipped into a cascade of students heading towards the common room to get my bag and then I went on to my biology lesson, while stuffing a packed-lunch sandwich in my mouth.

Needless to say, I didn't receive a phone call.

Selecting employees is a brutal process. There is a lot to be said for the 'One life, one job' approach to employment which is embraced by countries like Japan. This approach breeds loyalty into the ranks and traps knowledge as well as creative expertise within the company. It makes perfect sense to attempt to retain your workforce by putting mechanisms in place that make it difficult for employees to leave. After all, why invest huge amounts of cash into your workforce and then find yourself five years later, with half of your employees resigning, taking their skills, expertise along with their sense of *job satisfaction* to your competitors?

I know, I know…the job interview is something of a necessary evil. But when you are 'compromised' in some way either physically or mentally, your attempts to 'get ahead and stay ahead in life' become more and more challenging to manage.

How I coped with the constant stream of rejections from failed job applications, when my Parkinson's disease (PD) was fairly advanced, to this day I am still not sure – and getting constructive feedback has been just as difficult to procure, in an attempt to evaluate why 'the other guy' always beat me to the finishing tape. As time went on, it became normal for me to feel that the outcome was inevitable; I just *expected* to be rejected with every application that I made. This way, a positive response would always feel *special*. However, it seems success was almost always just out of reach.

Between 2010 and 2020, I applied for at least four-hundred jobs. From this, I may have attended fifteen or twenty interviews, none of which resulted in an actual job. These jobs were the type that would have allowed me to further my career in advertising (client handling, team managing roles). On so many occasions, I have done my research and prepared quality questions to ask my future employer to prove I could think for myself, only to be told at the beginning of the interview, "We're looking to see who is on the market just now to see if you would be a good fit for our business – there isn't an actual position available anymore…"

What I really want to say to the interviewer is, "So, you've got me here under false pretences, knowing that I have gone out of my way to get across the city on a Friday afternoon to come to a hollowed-out, half-baked interview for a non-existent job? I'm sorry – I wasn't aware that your time was any more valuable and important than mine. Of course, I'd be delighted to work for you, given that you have so spectacularly demonstrated to me how well you treat people who don't currently work for you, but I'm sure you have the utmost respect for the people who do. Or maybe not, who knows?"

It is an extremely stressful process to go through. The psychological game that PD plays with you as it eats away at your self-esteem channels you into thinking that maybe you hold no worth, you're no longer of any value to anyone or any endeavour and this is why you aren't having any success with nailing a decent job. I had to continually tell myself to keep going, ignore PD's negativity, sooner or later something would happen which would be exciting, good for my self-esteem, my self-confidence and would challenge me, like my career in advertising did in the early years.

With a forthcoming interview, the first consideration I need to make is how much information do I have to impart in order to maximise my chances of getting this job? Two scenarios can be played out here: Do I walk into the interview room, wait for my time to speak…then put the cat amongst the pigeons and, admit to the interviewer(s) that I have Parkinson's disease, 'which is really well controlled, by the way, and it doesn't require any adjustments to my working environment'. This is the 'cards on the table approach', I have nothing to hide and I'm telling you about this medical condition because I want to be open and transparent from the start. It's a very proactive, risky approach. Proactive, because it is not an easy subject to discuss 'openly' with a bunch of people you met a few minutes ago; risky, because it means that employers are going to have to take a chance on an unknown quantity like PD. I have seen interviewers of potential employers, on hearing that I have PD, quietly close their notebooks *seconds* into the interview and continue to watch me, looking for clues as to how PD affects this person. All of a sudden, I feel like I am there purely for the entertainment value, the potential employer having decided somewhat prematurely that I'm not the best candidate for the job. It's impossible for them to know if my presence 'on the team' is going to have a positive or negative impact on the business and its clients. Over time, this has drastically eaten away at my confidence, because they have essentially 'written me off' before I've had a chance to demonstrate that I can do this job, standing on my head, whilst playing a flute…

The alternative scenario is where I choose not to divulge any information at all and hope that my unwanted bodily movements are not as obvious as I might think and 'yes, the drugs *do* work, they are maintaining control of my symptoms and disguising the fact that I have PD'. This is a lot to ask of the medication, particularly in the more recent years; I can't honestly say I've ever felt that the meds I take for my PD have worked so well that I feel like I no longer have PD – even for a short period of time, like the quantity of time that would allow you to make it through an interview. It's more about compromise – and expectations – i.e. how close to completely symptom free are you willing to aim for or how much of your symptoms are you willing to have on show?

In this scenario, potential employers will see that 'there is something not quite right about this person'. The problem is that the interview could descend into the potential employer becoming distracted, trying to work out during the interview what it is that is 'not quite right' about you, instead of working out if you are suitable for the role for which you are being interviewed.

This is not a proactive approach; it is by far more risk-laden simply because there are more unknowns to deal with. In this scenario, the employer draws their own conclusions about why there are question marks hanging over your head. They may never find out that you have PD, but for the time being their view of you is tempered by the conclusions that they form during the interview. As an employer, it is far easier in the absence of any evidence to say 'no thanks' to the person with the most question marks even if ultimately, on paper, you might have been the more appropriate candidate.

So, it is possible that as an outcome of the interview, you may have a potential employer, who knows you have PD because you have admitted to it early in the interview. They can then relax because you have forewarned the interviewer that they may observe some unusual movement in the form of dystonia (muscle stiffening) or dyskinesia (wriggly movements, due to overstimulation from medical treatment or deep brain stimulation treatment). In any case, your cards are on the table and are facing up, which indicates that you are comfortable in your own skin.

I thought that this 'bare all and sundry' approach might be received in the manner in which it was intended, with the virtues of transparency and honesty written all over it but it seems I was wrong. This approach yielded no more or less successful outcomes at job interviews than when I didn't tell the potential employer that I have PD. In fact, the additional information that I gave may have helped to make the employer's mind up faster than usual!

Or you may find, because you didn't feel comfortable enough to have an initial discussion about the fact that you have PD, that you have an uninformed potential employer with so many queries hanging over you, it is an easy decision to undertake. It makes sense to choose the candidate with fewer 'unknown quantities' – why make the decision any harder than it already is?

These are scenarios that I have found myself in on many occasions at interviews in many organisations. The vast majority of these interviews wound up without a successful outcome. The fact is that PD tends to dig its claws in deep and I feel, based on nothing but my own experience and awareness that in both scenarios described above, the proactive approach and the riskier approach are equally as in-effective as strategies for job interviews because neither one nor the other leaves the potential employer 'comfortable' with their decision.

Both outcomes still have unknown quantities, whether you have or have not admitted to having PD at the interview and putting myself in the shoes of people who have to make these decisions. I suspect that in both scenarios, their decisions can be justified by saying, "It is possible that there are candidates out there whose experience and knowledge are more closely aligned to what we specifically need and for this reason we should continue to look for candidates of this nature."

Which, unfortunately, doesn't make getting a job any easier if you have PD! For me, the continual, at times heart wrenching rejections drove me to choose to re-train and work in a totally different industry. At some point, you have to ask yourself why is this not working and you have to be honest in your answers you cannot live in denial with this or you will eventually end up deceiving yourself and those around you. To say nothing of the effect on your sanity.

I hit rock bottom when I applied for a fabulous job (in the past two years), which in actual fact was a brisk ten-minute walk from my home. I had bucket loads of the right experience and I spent a whole day refining my CV and writing a very detailed covering letter to make sure I answered every question that the potential employer had asked in the job advertisement. I emailed my application towards the end of the day, absolutely convinced that I would be at the head of the interview queue.

Less than ten minutes after I emailed my application, I received a rejection letter from this potential employer. I was completely shocked; it had felt like the job was created with me in mind. I could not work out what vital piece of information or experience I had missed out of my application. I was very disappointed to not even get to the interview stage – but mostly, I was really annoyed with myself for having spent a day's worth of time applying for that damn job!

At an interview in 2013, I felt the discussion was progressing nicely – I had done my homework for this one and I knew the potential employer's business inside and out. Again, I felt like this job was my destiny like it had been made for me. I couldn't fail to get this job and make it a massive success.

I found it hard to take when I was rejected. I decided to give the interviewer a phone call, to find out why I had been pushed out of the line of suitable candidates for this role.

The interviewer was more than happy to give me feedback which I did not want to hear. "We really liked you and you had some great ideas. But there was just one problem," said the woman who had lead the interview.

"What was that?" I asked.

"Well, it was just that we found it incredibly difficult to understand what you were saying during the interview," she said. She went on to say that my speech was slurred and they were concerned that I had been drinking prior to the interview. Oh, Lord…!

I discussed this with my future ex-wife Jayne and she said to tell the interviewer that I had PD to see if that made a difference. I managed to speak with the interviewer the following day. Whilst she was grateful for my call to let her know why my speech was in the state it was, they had already selected a suitable candidate for the role.

This interview had taken place approximately one year after I had the Deep Brain Stimulation (DBS) procedure, which improved some symptoms of my PD and adversely affected others. The voice is one of the things that may suffer as a result of DBS.

It was this feedback that convinced me to undertake the Lee Silvermann voice training which is specifically aimed at patients whose voice is adversely affected by this type of procedure. I wasn't convinced that just by speaking at an elevated level, you could experience a dramatic improvement in the volume of your voice; to me it felt like a temporary fix, like a Band-Aid underneath a loosely wound bandage when what is actually needed is a rock-hard Plaster of Paris cast. Some medical professionals swear by it; I am not a medical Professional, however, sceptical I remain. Nevertheless, I went through the whole program, but at the final session, I couldn't take any more of the shouting and yelling and had to excuse myself from the course.

Looking back, if my voice was as incomprehensible as the interviewer claimed it was then it was likely my voice quality, its low volume or lack of clarity could have been responsible for many more interview failures than previously realised. I am aware that in stressful situations such as interviews, my throat tightens; it feels like someone is applying pressure to my larynx, as if I am being strangled, making it difficult to get the air to cross my vocal cords, which makes them vibrate, then channel the noise it makes though my upper throat into my mouth and nose, where the tongue and other muscles are used to shape the way the air moves through the mouth to create different sounds as the air exits my lips. All under pressure from my diaphragm. How effective each of these elements are at developing and maintaining the sound has a bearing on the overall quality, clarity and volume of your voice.

Here's a thought. Could it be that the reason I was not so readily employable was down to the way I sound? I find this challenging to believe; after all, approximately only 7% of inter-human communication is by verbal means while the remaining 93% is supposed to be communicated by our body language. Body language has 'volume' too; it can be 'subtle' as well as 'loud', in much the same way that verbal communication is.

My own personal opinion is this: I think Parkinson's Disease disrupts the natural rhythm of our verbal communication by affecting the nerves and muscles employed in making 'our voices'. Likewise, for our body language, PD affects the nerves and muscles that are used to hold our body shapes together and the 'language' our bodies impart. Any form of disruption to the body's natural rhythm – like that caused by PD – could have an enormous effect on the messages that are communicated by the body's natural 'body language'.

These ideas and the conclusions reached have not been tested in a controlled environment. It is merely a way of explaining the outcomes of a decade of interviewing that failed for some reason. These are my own views based on 20 years of living with PD. As can be seen in the pages to come, I wasn't always this unsuccessful at interviewing and employment – something must have changed! I am convinced that there is some merit in 'communication on a deeper level' that in my situation can be used to explain why I was so unsuccessful in my pursuit of gainful employment in the years since I arrived in Australia.

---|---

"I've got some work for you, if you're interested in making yourself some money and you don't mind doing a bit of grafting…"

"Work?" I said, unable to suppress the surprise in my voice. I was in the Nut Tree pub drinking lager shandy with Andy, a long-term family friend of my maternal grandparents and my mother. I was fourteen years old but at maybe an inch or two shy of six feet, I could get away with being mistaken for sixteen years old. Technically, I shouldn't have been drinking anything with alcohol in it as I was more than three years under the UK legal age limit. I had doctored my paper doctor's card to show I was born in 1969 rather than 1971. It was simply a case of using a scalpel blade to gently scrape away the daisywheel dot matrix printed '71' and using a light grey felt-tip pen to dot in the '69' in the dot matrix style. *Et voila!* Some non-photographic proof of age ID. So, if push came to shove, at fourteen, I could 'prove' I was sixteen. Moreover, when I turned sixteen I celebrated being able to 'prove' I was eighteen.

Andy wasn't really a stern up-keeper of the law in general, certainly not where drinking alcohol was concerned. Drinking was his hobby. My mum would have lynched me *and* Andy if she found out I was in the pub drinking. But it was just one of a bunch of activities that I could have been lynched for.

"Yeah, you know, work…what people do to get money to buy stuff with," Andy replied. Then he said, "Do you want another drink? Same again, lager shandy, is it?"

"Yeah, thanks Andy," I said. "What kind of work do you mean?"

"The kind," he continued, lowering his voice slightly as he leant closer, "that could make you some decent money, give yourself some independence and might get you a leg over with a horny granddaughter or two, you never know your luck."

"A leg over? Andy, you do know that I'm only fourteen, right?" Andy was probably three times my age and always getting involved in some hair-brained scheme or another. "Do you mean real employment, this time? I'm not handing out any more bloody leaflets for your mate's water skiing school like last summer. I nearly died of hypothermia down on the sea front!"

"I mean, cutting grass, weeding, just general gardening stuff," Andy said. Then he paused and narrowed his eyes as he looked at me. "You do *like* girls, don't you?"

"Course I like girls," I said curtly. "I just never thought I'd hear the words 'make money' and 'leg over' used in the same sentence…not for a few more years, anyway."

He continued. "My elderly lady friend over on Sherwood Crescent just came out of hospital – she's got heart problems and can't over-exert herself. The council come and cut the grass every couple of weeks, but they do a shit job and never trim the edges or collect up the grass cuttings. Here you go…"

Andy handed me my half-pint of lager shandy. "Thank you," I said.

"Is he eighteen, Andy?" The full-figured barmaid nodded in my direction. "Two pounds, please."

"Eighteen? Of course he's not…what are you, like seventeen or something? It's only a lager shandy; he could buy it off the shelves in Tesco…thanks sweetheart." He handed the barmaid a five-pound note, as he took a gulp of his pint of ale.

"Three pounds change," said the barmaid. "I'd be surprised if he's a day over sixteen."

I turned so my back was facing the bar. "Maybe I'll just have a Coke next, Andy," I said.

Andy continued, "My elderly lady friend asked me if I knew a reliable school kid who wanted a couple of hours work at the weekend, just to run the mower over the front and back lawns, trim the edges, do a little weeding…I thought of you."

Andy often asked me to get 'involved' in various schemes. The previous year I'd spent four Saturdays in a row down on Weston sea front, freezing my nuts off in June handing out leaflets to holiday makers for water skiing lessons. There was no actual money exchanging hands but I would get free water skiing lessons in return for my time distributing leaflets. Down on the seafront, my teeth chattering in the summertime breeze, I began to wonder why I had ever agreed to do Andy 'a favour' for his mate who taught water skiing. It was the last thing I wanted to learn – particularly in our Arctic style summer.

"So, what do you think? Do you want this work? I reckon this might turn into a nice little earner for you. Everyone knows everyone else's business in Sherwood Crescent – it won't be long before you are mowing half the lawns in the street."

I didn't have anything else to do with my time on the weekends, apart from hanging out at the 'mugs' (the video game arcades) in Weston town centre with my mates Mark and Paul, so I agreed to the idea. Andy arranged for me to go round to Mrs Parsons' bungalow home the following Saturday at 11am. I cycled over to Sherwood Crescent which had the Nut Tree pub at the lower end and my grandparent's flat at the upper end on the crest of the hill. My grandparents would have preferred the pub to be where their flat was and their flat to be where the pub was – it would be much easier to stagger home downhill after an evening at the pub.

Number 14. I knocked and Mrs Parsons opened the door. For a split-second, I thought she looked just like the Queen. Not that she was wearing a crown and a long robe encrusted with gemstones, it was just her facial features, spectacles and hair resembled that of the Monarch's. I thought maybe I should bow to her but instead I just spoke words.

"Mrs Parsons, Andy said I should come and talk to you about mowing the lawn," I said politely.

"Oh yes, come in Marco – it is Marco isn't it, that's the name Andy gave me," she said.

"Yes, that's right. He said you needed your lawns cut, it would be a pound an hour..."

"Yes, that's fine, you will probably need a couple of hours to do the front and back, once a week I was thinking. It grows so fast in the spring and summer."

"Okay, sure, I can do that. Is now a good time of day to do it?" Mrs Parsons showed me the garden shed and the lawn mowers inside. There was an electric lawn mower and a manual, rotary mower. I knew from watching my dad mow the lawns at home when he lived with my mum, sister and I that the manual mower with its heavy roller would be the equipment of choice to get those nice parallel lines like the Wimbledon tennis courts. However, I could see that I was going to need to use the electrical mower initially to get the growth under control.

"Now is a good time for me, if it's okay with you," said Mrs Parsons.

"How often do the council come to cut it?" I asked.

"Once every two or three weeks – if we are lucky," she replied. "And they don't trim the edges or clean up the grass cuttings, they leave it in a right state."

"Okay, well, I guess I'll get cracking then," I said.

"Thank you, Marco."

I was tempted to ask if she had a granddaughter in the third or fourth year at school, just to see if Andy's theory about getting some girl action out of this venture held any water, but I thought better of it. Just keep your mouth shut and mow, I said to myself...

---|---

For the first couple of weeks, I mowed Mrs P's front and back lawns with the electric mower, just to get the grass down to a level that was manageable. On the third weekend I used the heavy manual rotary mower on the lowest setting; almost an hour later, my skinny arms aching with lactic acid build up in the muscles, the front lawn resembled Centre Court at Wimbledon. The weight of the roller forced the blades of grass to lie in one direction; it was down to the weight of the roller. I was so proud; I ignored the pain in my limbs and forged ahead with the back garden lawn which was the same width as the front, but twice its length. Another hour and both lawns looked spectacular – and I had no feeling left in my arms. Mrs P was ecstatic; she said the lawns hadn't looked so good since her late husband looked after the gardens.

The front lawn acted as a kind of advertisement to other elderly residents on Sherwood Crescent, and some families. People commented as they wandered past the front garden, while I was working, doing some weeding, or while I was trimming the edges of the lawn to give it a full manicure. My grandparents would walk down the hill and cajole me, my grandfather pointing out playfully where I was going wrong. Mrs P's lawn was in a very good condition which made it easier to make it look spectacular. Her next-door neighbour, Mrs Brown, did not resemble a Head of State, but her eyes looked massive under the very thick glass lenses of her spectacles. Mrs P and Mrs B had front lawns which joined seamlessly so it seemed logical to cut both lawns as one. Mrs P said I could use her equipment; I spent a couple of weeks cutting Mrs B's front and back lawns with the electric mower before I brought in the 'Heavy Equipment' to create the 'All England Tennis Club' lawn effect.

It might sound fairly straight forward but it was a meticulous operation, quite slow and laborious. Much of the time was spent lining the rollers up with each section of lawn to be cut and rolled, which needed to be accurate to the millimetre.

Mrs B didn't have a lawn in her back garden, it was all patio stone slabs. I was making £3 a week from numbers 14 and 15 of Sherwood Crescent and that suited me fine.

After five or six weeks into building my gardening empire, I was approached by a timid, elderly lady who lived in the bungalow directly across the road from Mrs P. She asked if I could drop into her and her husband's house after I had finished up with Mrs P and Mrs B. As I had taken to starting at 9am instead of 11am, I said I would be over just after midday to see Mr and Mrs Sanderson.

I knocked on the door and Mrs S opened it almost as I finished knocking – she must have been waiting on the other side of the door. She ushered me into the kitchen and asked if I wanted a drink; I said, "I'll take a cup of tea, thank you…" I asked where Mr Sanderson was. "He's in bed…he's not too well," she said. Mrs S took a packet of chocolate bourbon biscuits from the pantry, opened them and put them in front of me. I was starving; I didn't need to be told twice to get stuck in. I asked what was wrong with Mr Sanderson.

"Well," the elderly lady said, "he's got an illness called Parkinson's Disease – I doubt you've heard of it? It's an old people's disease, where they can't stop shaking." Even though I was in my third year of science lessons, I couldn't say I knew anything about the illness.

Mrs S continued, "The medicines they use aren't all that good…" I noticed how tired and weak she looked, how frail she was, how the years of caring for a sick husband had obviously taken their toll on her.

"He's also got diabetes, which makes things more complicated." Then, Mrs S went on to tell me how shortly after they had married, they had lived in the East End of London in Bethnal Green during World War 2 and The Blitz. When they came up from the protection and sanctuary of the London Underground station after a particularly long, merciless night of bombing by the German Luftwaffe, they discovered that their house had been flattened along with most others along their terrace during the night. They were told that an incendiary bomb had landed on their house which had exploded in a ball of white flames, setting the terrace and surrounding buildings alight. As they were both civil servants, they were given a subsidised room in a hotel near Whitehall until a replacement home could be found. Fortunately, the bombed-out house was owned by the council, rented by Mr and Mrs S – so while it was an incredible nuisance, they hadn't lost a 'family home'.

They stayed in London until they retired, then they moved to Weston and eventually were given the bungalow that they were currently living in by the local council, in Sherwood Crescent which in the early 1970s was brand new. Mr S started to show symptoms of Parkinson's Disease in the mid-1970s and symptoms of diabetes started to show several years ago. Mrs S hadn't mentioned having any kids or grandchildren so I assumed they had none.

"But that's all in the past now." She chuckled to herself. "Anyway, you'll be wondering why I asked you to come and see me. Well, you see, my husband is no longer well enough to leave the house, let alone mow the lawns. He's been watching your work across the road and he asked me to ask you to mow our lawns. Would you be willing?"

I thought about it for a few seconds, trying to swallow the fragments of biscuit in my mouth. "The problem – with your front lawn at least – is that the turf is too shallow where it meets the concrete of the paths and driveway, it's about an inch or two short. I can cut the grass and trim the edges, so that they are straight, that'll improve it a lot. But there will be gaps where the concrete and grass don't meet."

I picked up another chocolate bourbon, mildly embarrassed as I realised there were only two left in the packet that I'd been munching away on.

"That sounds good, my husband just wanted to say hello, is that okay? He's a bit shaky but apart from that he's okay." I said that it was fine with me. I drank the tea and she took me down the hall to Mr S's bedroom door which was partially open. Mrs S pushed the door wide open.

"John, this is Marco, Marco…John. John, Marco has agreed to tidy the lawns up for us."

Mr S was wearing blue and red striped pyjamas, lying on his left side in bed. He looked like he was shivering violently. The window was open and a breeze wafted in through the opening, but it wasn't cool enough to be *that* cold. As I followed Mrs S into the bedroom, Mr S turned to look at me. His mouth was partially open, his lips trembling and he had a mop of silver grey hair on his head. *So, this is Parkinson's Disease,* I thought to myself. It was my first encounter with the condition.

"Hello, Mr Sanderson," I said.

"'ello, my san." Mr S's south London drawl was as clear as a bell.

"I'm going to tidy up the lawns for you, I've agreed with your wife. The front is quite a steep lawn and there's that annoying electrical supply box in the middle of it, but once the edges are sorted out, it should look fine." They owned a Hover Mower which would be ideal for the steep front lawn.

"Tha-tha-thank you, my boy, I've been watching you wo-wo-working across the road, hope you don't mind, I ca-ca-can see you-you-you work hard f-f-for the money." Mr S stammered and shook his way through the sentence.

Some people might have found this quite confronting and an awkward, uncomfortable situation to be in, but I didn't see a sick elderly man…I just saw an old fella, who was probably craving the company of someone other than his wife (no disrespect to Mrs S) as he battled with Parkinson's Disease. It brings to mind the time when my maternal grandfather was hospitalised in the mid-1970s after he suffered a brain aneurysm. I drew dozens and dozens of pictures to send to him while he was in hospital for several weeks. I understood that he was very sick and he might not make a full recovery – in hospital he was barely able to speak. He was lucky to be alive and *did* go on to make a full recovery, re-learning how to speak and walk again. In spite of my grandmother's terrible cooking, heavy smoking and an occasional epileptic fit, he lasted another twenty years before developing bone cancer.

I made a mental note to have a look in my parent's encyclopaedia to see if there was anything about Parkinson's Disease (there was still a solid fifteen years or so until the likes of Wikipedia became available!).

I told the couple that I would be come over on Saturday afternoons around one pm–two pm to do a couple of hours work a week. My earnings had now reached £5 per week. I decided that it might soon be time to increase the size of the work force if more lawns came on-stream.

In the weeks that followed, I was approached by another four people from four properties who needed similar help with the green stuff in their front and back gardens. They had been impressed by what they saw down the hill and wanted a piece of the action. Only now, with eight or nine lawns to mow, I really needed some help.

I asked a friend of mine, Charlie, to come and help me on Sundays. That way, I could do the lawns of Mrs P, Mrs B and Mr and Mrs S on a Saturday keeping the weekly £5 to myself. Charlie and I would work together on the Sunday, splitting the earnings 50:50. The new clients were all at the top of the hill, near my grandparent's flat and two of them had a seamlessly joined front lawn and separate back lawns.

It was only a couple of hours work on Sunday. But bringing Charlie on would be a decision I would live to regret.

Two

The day on which I was diagnosed with Parkinson's Disease (PD) at the Midland Hospital in London, is not a hazy memory of a windy March day two decades ago. Most of what took place that day still rings true in my mind and the memory is as clear as a bell. From taking the Underground train to Tottenham Court Road, arriving at the hospital, taking note of its incongruous surroundings, meeting the two doctors and the attractive nurse who would take me through the DaT scan diagnostic procedure.

I had celebrated my thirtieth birthday two weeks before this day.

The actual diagnosis of my condition is still fresh in my memory; it is as if it had taken place yesterday. After putting together the outcomes of the procedure and cross-referencing this with the symptoms I had been experiencing for the past two or three years, I was given the diagnosis: Adult Early Onset Idiopathic Parkinson's Disease.

This day was pivotal for me; perhaps it was the most significant day, or the most important day of my entire life. That may sound slightly over the top and I might get accused of being overly dramatic…but it was a very dramatic day. The outcome of this diagnostic test was nothing short of life changing. From start to finish, it took around four hours to conduct, collect results, match with symptoms and offer a final diagnosis of a condition which I believe started to exert an effect five or six years prior to the DaT scan. It was almost like I was making the 'movie of my own life' where the various cast members arrived, played their part and then left, making room for others as different scenes unfolded with the plot getting thicker by the minute.

It feels odd to say this but if I am ever asked to name a *benefit* of having PD, I would probably say something like 'I'm not sure if it can be attributed to having adult, early onset, idiopathic PD but my long-term memory seems to have improved and is detailed, clear and lucid…but ask me what I had for dinner last night and I might have to get back to you on that one…' So far, this appears to be the only 'benefit' that I can report on in two decades of experience with PD.

Or maybe it can be viewed as a side effect of medication, who knows? Either way, it has been extremely useful to have a 'well-functioning long-term memory' over the past couple of years…and long may it last.

Things start to get a bit cloudy towards the end of the day on which my diagnosis was made with the help of an unknown quantity of beer and accompanying multiple gin chasers. I think that many, if not all *ordinary* people, on being told something as 'life changing' as 'You have Adult Early Onset Idiopathic Parkinson's Disease…' just two weeks after your thirtieth birthday would resort to a similar course of action: to *start living in denial* of this diagnosis, beginning with a healthy bout of consuming as much alcohol as was humanly possible – as did I – whilst smoking as many cigarettes as my lungs could take. After all, I was young and indestructible – it would be something I would deal with and that's just how it is! I wasn't going to let PD get in the way of living my life! However, over the years I learnt through bitter experience that PD is non-negotiable – it doesn't strike deals. Moreover, it does not just go away, as if by taking a pill you could make it disappear. It needs to be managed. PD isn't 'fair' – there are no rules to govern the extent of its effect on dopamine production. It is a relentless, unstoppable force that stops the dopamine producing cells in the brain from doing what they do best: to keep you moving. PD prevents these cells from producing dopamine, the absence of which has many effects on the body as well as the mind.

But with time and strength of mind, I found I could manage it.

All this happening at thirty years old? Surely not, this is what old people get isn't it? This is the critical point to remember – I had just turned thirty years old two weeks prior to my diagnosis, yet even now it is an important detail that I often fail to mention when I find myself in a situation where I am going to tell somebody that I have PD. It is the point of difference that makes this whole fascinating story so much more dramatic and important to share with the world.

The only thing about being younger than most people who got PD is that the condition is a great deal slower in terms of progression.

When I was diagnosed, I was between jobs which was unusual for me. I had a perfect vision of where I wanted to work and the kind of people I wanted to work for. I had already met my future employer, an advertising agency called JNA. I had been interviewing with various healthcare advertising agencies in

London and had been fortunate enough (although, some would say unfortunate) to have an offer of a Freelance Senior Account Manager position with one agency called Nearblack. I had agreed that I would start my new role at Nearblack on the Thursday of that week, the day after my diagnosis at the Midland Hospital. This was changed to the following Monday, which was fine with me; I had been offered a second interview with JNA. This interview had been pencilled in for Friday afternoon, two days after my diagnosis day; during this second interview I had to explain what actions I would implement as a result of having been set an advertising task to complete in time for the interview.

Therefore, it is true to say that I was heading for the bottom of a bottle on the evening of that fateful day in March 2001 and this seemed to be wholly justifiable. I wasn't compromising any of the job opportunities that had come my way; I had accepted an offer of work and was still within my rights to take further interviews. But I was glad that I had a day to get my head clear for the Friday interview which I had been told would involve the Creative Director and Senior Copywriter. I would need to turn the charm on to be in with a chance of getting this job, now that there were potential colleagues involved in the interview.

But right now I just felt confused, lost and crap about life in general. My mind was racing in many different directions all at once; it would be a while before it slowed down and allowed me to climb aboard to take up the controls, what few there was of them, anyway. I knew it would be some time before I could even consider gaining the upper hand on my PD. Besides, PD doesn't play by pre-set guidelines or rules. If this was the case, how on Earth did I think I could control it? It would be like trying to control a runaway bull elephant with a remote-control unit housing a joystick. With the batteries removed…

Actually, it wouldn't matter if the batteries were removed. Or installed correctly. They could be brand new, full power, copper-coloured top batteries…you still wouldn't be able to control the beast. Why not? Because there is no way of communicating with it, no way of negotiating with it. Its sphere of existence would be so vastly different from our own it would be totally uncontrollable.

In the days that followed my diagnosis, I didn't really take much time out to sit down and really think about how the diagnosis could affect my life. There simply wasn't enough time to do this. I was relentless in my search for a job that would propel me into the advertising world. I needed to come across as ambitious, capable of leading a team, with boundless enthusiasm and energy for advertising. I had been doing all these things in my most recent role at Promosign albeit using different promotional media. Wherever it was that I would end up working, I knew I would have to switch my mind off from the fact that I'd just been diagnosed with PD. At least for the short term.

I needed to look happy, raring to go, with a big soppy smile slapped across my face. I practiced smiling in the bathroom mirror the day after my diagnosis, the day before my Friday interview. I wasn't convinced; you could stretch my lips into a smile and show off all my teeth – but the eyes never lie. When we are truly, unreservedly happy, we smile from our eyes. One of my friends, 'H', had already had some of the photographs developed from my thirtieth birthday at the Electric Ballroom in London, just over two weeks ago and she had sent some to me…yep, sure enough, in the photos I was all smiley eyes, oblivious to the forthcoming diagnosis and the devastating impact that it would have on life as I knew it.

I had to prepare myself in this way for the Friday interview as well as doing some extensive background reading on the brands I would be working on in the new job that I was starting on Monday. My new boss, who was more of a salesperson and less of an advertising man, clearly had big plans for me to have more of a sales-oriented role, which, if I was not careful could take me away from the creative side of the business, something that I was very keen to avoid. As this gradually dawned on me, I realised that my days at *this* agency were already numbered…I knew instinctively that Nearblack was not destined to be my 'forever' employer…

---|---

Charlie's overall contribution to my grass-cutting empire was to unravel the reputation that I was building. True, I wasn't by any stretch thinking of doing this kind of work full-time for a living, but it was relatively easy work and it suited me for the time being. I had developed a taste for enjoying work without having a boss looking over my shoulder. But, just as the global economy was destined to crash on Black Monday in October 1987, Charlie single-handedly managed to bring our business down, crashing and burning all around us, losing half of the work we had built up in just one day.

In asking Charlie to work with me, I had overlooked the fact that he was a pyromaniac-in-training, having set his own garden on fire more than once in the short space of time that I had known him. That should have set the alarm bells ringing for a start. So, it was hardly a surprise when he managed to set fire to one of our client's outdoor dustbins during his smoking break. Ignoring the 'NO HOT COALS' warning on the heavy lid, he pulled the lid up and flicked his still burning cigarette butt into the dustbin instead of stubbing it out before putting it in the dustbin. Within a few minutes, the dustbin was smoking like a chimney. I panicked and began racing around the garden, trying to find a hosepipe. Charlie hadn't closed the lid properly and this helped the fire to 'breathe'. Another couple of minutes and it was fully on fire. I found a hosepipe in the shed, wound onto a wheel, not yet connected to a water source, but I knew where the garden tap was. The client was by now watching from the window, her hands held to her face in disbelief, observing the chaos outside as I rapidly unreeled the hosepipe, attached it to the garden tap and turned the water on. Charlie was holding the business end of the hosepipe and as the water began to flow, he aimed it at the blazing dustbin. The bin lid had melted in the intense heat of the flames and did nothing but add fuel to the fire. Charlie doused the flames with water until all that was left was a char-grilled metal dustbin, and a pile of soggy, partially burnt newspapers. With the fire over as quickly as it had started I turned the water off at the tap and as Charlie lay the hosepipe on the lawn I confronted him.

"What the hell were you thinking, Charlie?" I picked up the wheel and wound the hosepipe back onto it.

"I didn't think there would be much to set fire to in the bin," he said.

"So, you just tossed a lit fag into a dustbin?" I asked, shaking my head. "You idiot."

He just shrugged his shoulders. The client, a staunch anti-smoker relieved us of our services on the spot.

But Charlie was not finished with destroying my reputation that day. After the Towering Inferno had been dealt with, we had one other front and back lawn to cut. I asked Charlie to mow the back lawn; it was flat and shaped like a tennis court, with a small shed and vegetable patch at the end of the garden. I thought nothing could go wrong with such a straightforward lawn. The front lawn was more complicated and on a steep incline, so I decided to do that myself with the client's hover mower.

It wasn't long after I'd started trimming the edges of the front lawn that I heard a commotion coming from the back garden. I downed tools and walked around the house to the back garden. I could hear the owner of the house, Mrs

Foster shrieking, saying things like, 'Get out of here, you filthy animal, go on, OUT'! I walked into the back garden, where Mrs F was brandishing a broom, pointing it in Charlie's general direction. It looked like Charlie was trying to do up the zipper on his jeans.

"What's going on, Charlie?" Could the day get any worse, I wondered.

He looked up at me. "I was just having a piss behind the shed, because I was busting. I couldn't hold it in anymore, so I turned and pissed on the vegetable patch."

"Bloody hell, Charlie, couldn't you just piss behind the shed?" I asked, not sure what answer to expect.

"I tried to but I had a bit of a stiffy going on…I was worried about getting splashback off the shed."

Not the answer I expected. I stared at him blankly for several seconds. "Charlie – what is it about cutting the grass that gave you a stiffy? I mean, it's cutting grass, there ain't nothing sexy about it."

"Oh, I dunno, I was just getting bored and I started thinking about Michelle getting naked." Michelle lived in our street halfway between Charlie's house and mine; she was two years older than us. We both worshipped her.

That would do it, I thought. That'd give anyone a stiffy.

Needless to say, the client gave us our marching orders.

---|---

Meeting Mr Sanderson was my first brush with PD. He was into his 70s when he was diagnosed and according to his wife, it came on all of a sudden, with little warning, as well as being full on with the shakes.

"It felt like things changed almost overnight for him…like he went from being outdoors and active to mostly bedridden and unable to walk safely, because he can't get his legs to work properly," Mrs S told me after several weeks of mowing the front and back lawns. They already looked a lot better; the lawns, that is. Not Mr Sanderson's legs.

I asked if he had a wheelchair that she could use to take him out for some fresh air.

"We do, but he's not keen to stray too far from the house," she said, staring off into space like she was remembering happier times. "Also – and this is quite understandable I suppose – he gets embarrassed with his shaking, because there's no way he can control it. People stare, you know."

"Is there no way of controlling it?" I asked. "I mean, I suppose they've tried different types of medicine?"

"Yes, they have," she said. "He actually takes a medicine called levodopa which takes the edge off the shakes and makes it slightly more bearable for him…but it still isn't working altogether too well and people still notice."

She went on. "The hospital doctors say that there aren't that many options, they usually get some control with leva dopa, but for a lot of people who have Parkinson's, the effect of leva dopa wears off over time."

She was staring into space again. "I just don't know what to suggest to him."

I felt frustrated because I had no knowledge from which I could draw any form of conclusion and offer suggestions.

"I guess the best you can do is just keep him comfortable," I offered. I was feeling a bit out of my depth.

Sadly, Mr S passed away within a few weeks of this conversation with Mrs S. I turned up as usual to mow the lawns to be met at the back door by an exhausted looking Mrs S.

"John's passed away," she said. "On Friday morning. He had a heart attack and then another one while the ambulance people were here…"

I wasn't sure what to say. I had never been this close to actual death before.

So, I said, "Do you still want me to mow the lawn?"

---|---

My teen years were like most other teens: a plethora of many new, 'first' experiences. There was always a new 'first' experience just around the corner. First money earnt, first brush with death, first alcoholic drink, first kiss, first time in trouble with the law…the list goes on.

Like a lot of kids my age, I had my first newspaper delivery round. It was an era of proliferation of the free advertising newspaper, such as the Admag, where everything from joints of meat to holidays to cars could be bought and sold in a phone call.

I was given a newspaper round by Scan newspapers. Their logo was so badly designed; you could have been forgiven for thinking the company was called Scab newspapers. I was paid the princely sum of £1.47 to deliver one hundred and forty-seven newspapers to one hundred and forty-seven homes in a round which began in the next street over from mine and stretched off into deepest, darkest 'bird land' (the unofficial name of the estate on which I lived – each street was named after a bird).

The newspaper van would deliver a slab of papers onto our front garden path, usually around 6pm on a Friday evening. One guy drove the van, another appeared in the sliding door on the passenger side; before it had actually come to stop, sliding door guy was launching a newspaper bomb onto our path. Some weeks, it was just the newspaper that needed to be delivered; on other weeks, there were printed flyers that needed to be slipped inside each paper. I would get an extra 0.5 pence per flyer to be delivered or 73.5 pence in total. *Is it really worth it?* I used to wonder. The back pain alone made it near impossible to complete my round.

I made the round a total of three times. Sometimes I had to split the pile to be delivered into three smaller piles, returning home to pick up pile 2 and subsequently pile 3. After three weeks, I'd had just about all I could take. As a youth, being so tall I had a few spinal 'twinges' and the paper round wasn't helping.

There were some particularly creepy houses on my round, set back far from the road up winding driveways. I recruited my mum and sister to come out on the round with me along with Wingnut, our dog. I don't know why I thought that I would feel less creeped out or safer… because I didn't. It was just to have some company while I pretty much ran the entire round, to try and 'ease the pain'.

I was shoving a newspaper into the mailbox built into the front door of the house of one of the girls at school, Amanda. I already had a crush on her. Suddenly the door swung open and there stood Amanda from my class wrapped in a bath towel from her upper chest down to her knees. In the dying light of the day, I could make out that it was held in place by a twisted corner of the towel, anchored by her ample cleavage. Leaning against the open door, her long, dark, wavy hair was collected and tied up in a bun on the back of her head.

"Hello, Marco," she purred.

I didn't know what to say – or do, so I said the first thing that came into my head.

"Hi, Mandi," I said nervously. "You look like…uhhh, I mean…like you had a…here's your newspaper. And a flyer…Dewhurst's Butchers are doing half-price pork sausages this weekend…"

I glanced down at her breasts. I'd never been this close to a nearly naked girl before, tantalisingly close – another first. So close, I could actually touch her…in my imagination. I also imagined getting my first sharp slap on the cheek for an unauthorised first grope. I wouldn't have known what to do if her bath towel suddenly fell to the ground. I would probably have just vomited with nerves.

"Thank you…for the paper," she said and took a step backwards. "I did just have a bath…a nice hot one. See you Monday." She blew me a kiss as the door closed slowly.

"Yeah, see ya," I forced out in my best falsetto, trying to sound casual. The door clicked as it shut; I stared at it for a few seconds. I think I had just fallen in love, for the first of many times.

My mum said, "Who was that, who came to the door just then?"

"That was Mandi," I told her, smiling to myself. "One day, I'm gonna marry her."

As I continued my round, I began to think I had imagined the episode. Things like this didn't happen to me.

Then, I cringed. *Fuckin' Dewhurst's Butchers…what was I thinking?*

---|---

It didn't take long before the management at Scan newspapers realised that I wasn't delivering their grungy paper advertiser, or any of the associated flyers. I was in fact lining various rubbish bins on my round with multiple copies of Scan. So, I was making my deliveries…just not to the correct places. I like to think that all I was doing was accelerating the process of an inevitable fate for Scan. It lasted for several months before disappearing forever. I used to enjoy reading the 'personals' section. Some of the ads begging for love were quite poetic.

After six weeks in total, the van stopped delivering slabs of newspapers to the garden path on a Friday evening. I took that to mean I had been fired, also for the first time, but certainly not the last.

Three

In the weeks and months following my diagnosis of Parkinson's Disease (PD), one of the myriad thoughts that kept on coming to mind was, *How am I going to be able to support myself financially?* The prospect of slaving away for thirty-five or forty years to get to retirement age was daunting enough to cope with if you are fit and healthy. But imagine having to work in a job that required you to be fairly active on a day-to-day basis, such as being a gardener, or a swimming instructor or a Police officer – and then someone you never met before turns around and says, "Oh, you've got Parkinson's Disease which is going to make doing your job harder than you ever thought possible." This is a fundamental issue that we all need to consider as we grow older but for people with PD it is more important to think about sooner rather than later because the restriction in bodily movement may limit their ability to continue with their job. It is one example where PD really does steal time from the people it affects.

The answer lay in optimising my physical fitness. For many years, I had an offensively overpriced gym membership that was being under used – this was about to change. The aim was to get my muscles, nerves and bones as strong, flexible and supple as possible. A physically fit, flexible and active muscular-skeletal system that was optimised would provide me with the best chance of maintaining my ability to keep my body moving well, which would ensure my muscles and nerves would stay healthy for longer. This in turn would enable me to fulfil the requirements of a job that would help me prepare for the future and to be financially secure. Even though it has been a few years since I cancelled my last gym membership, I still manage to get out running a couple of times a week and do an on-line high impact interval-training workout. I recently taught myself to swim the 'free style' swim stroke. Swimming is such a fantastic exercise. I take my daughter a couple of times a week and get some laps in. This is the way I manage to keep my nerves, muscles and bones healthy. Other people with PD have told me that they enjoy Pilates or yoga as a means of keeping their nerves, muscles and bones healthy and strong.

I decided to get in touch with the Parkinson's Disease Society (PDS), with a view to finding out what information they had on maintaining financial support. I felt that I should talk to them almost out of courtesy, I didn't feel like I needed to talk to them. When I phoned the PDS, I felt like I was apologising for 'taking the car out without permission'. I really had nothing to ask about or discuss with them.

The man on the phone I spoke to had a very negative outlook on my situation, as he spoke he seemed to be wallowing in buckets of doom and gloom. In fact, the only thing I can remember him saying is 'I hope you've got plenty of savings, 'cause you're going to need them…'

Great, I thought. I had none of the above.

I became so concerned about the issue of financial security and support that I began to get attacks of paranoia every time I made a minor error at work; I was absolutely terrified that at any moment, I was going to be called into the managing director's office to be fired.

This is one of many ways in which I found that PD plays a psychological battle with people with the condition; it can destroy the fundamental elements of your self-confidence which can induce paranoia. Everything starts to become magnified when you have PD because you are so aware of your 'self'; you notice even the smallest changes in your physical and mental beings, and you can be in danger of 'making a mountain out of a molehill' or over-analysing your actions. I find this still happens in the present day; through fear of something like losing my job, I over-analyse things which, if I didn't have PD, I probably wouldn't do. I just don't want to miss anything but usually there is nothing to miss, which can take a lot of convincing!

---|---

Another of my big fears in the wake of my diagnosis was that I became concerned about being able to get a quality night's sleep and what the net effect on my performance in the workplace would be. Following my diagnosis, I would I lay awake for hours with the words *Adult Early Onset Idiopathic Parkinson's Disease* going around and around my head. I could visualise these words, as if they were printed on the spinning wheels of a gambler's fruit machine, coming into line three words at a time: *Adult-Early-Onset, Idiopathic Parkinson's-Disease*. The wheels spin again and the lights flash, the jackpot sirens would ring out as the wheels line up: *PD-PD-PD*.

I was desperate to sleep. It is a strange, unnerving feeling, not being able to switch this stimulus off when I wanted to, having no say in the matter. The more I tried to put it out of my mind the harder it would fight to stay. Moreover, I think it is easy to be all consumed by PD in this scenario such is the intensity and insanity of the situation. I feel that for some people it is easy to lose the psychological battle with PD at this early point in their relationship with the condition. You become exhausted due to over-thinking the issue and it just feels so easy to throw in the towel, conceding defeat. Once you arrive at this state, PD really has got the better of you and your mind.

There were still things that I wanted to achieve in my life. I love a challenge and where I felt most at home for several years was in the mountains. I didn't care where, I was happy in the French Alps climbing on the Mont Blanc massif or in the beautiful Lake District hiking up Haystacks, Green Gable, Great Gable and onwards to England's highest mountain, Scafell Pike. I was usually on my own because I would often leave it until the last minute before I decided to drive 250 miles up and across the UK to the Lakes. The weather in the Lakes can change so dramatically in a short space of time so I had to weigh up the risks involved of climbing and hiking at almost 1,000m high, on my own. There was no sign of my PD at this stage in my life – I was in my early to mid-twenties when I was going off on these jaunts. I was at that age where you feel that you can achieve anything and danger is…WHAT danger?

As I descended Great Gable for the first time, there was a steep scree slope to negotiate (scree: a mass of small, loose stones that form or cover a slope on a mountain). I stepped out onto the scree and in a blinding moment of revelation, I realised that this wasn't one of my best decisions as I began to slide down the slope. To maintain my balance, I had to place my other foot lower down the slope but essentially the stones below my feet were now a 'rock surfboard' and I was gathering pace. The stones on the scree slope were sharp, having endured many hundreds of millions of years up on that hill being weathered and worn by the elements of the harsh environment.

I had to get the weight of my body off my feet, so I threw myself into the slope. Using my backpack and my gloveless hands, I started to slow myself down. When I had stopped sliding, I looked at my hands and wrists. It looked like I'd been at the centre of a disagreement with a razor sharp cheese grater. It could have been a lot worse, I suppose. One long cut on my right wrist crossed two veins that are just below the surface of the skin. What would have happened if I had inadvertently slashed a vein up on that hill? I could have quite easily died up there on that mountain if that happened.

I still have the scars to remember this escapade by. I got a scolding from my mother, "You should know better than going off on your own, anything could happen…what is it about you and mountains?" I tried to explain that the sense of achievement pervaded my whole being and I was drawn to mountains – and their personalities. Each was unique, and the more remote and inaccessible the greater the achievement.

So, much to my mum's displeasure, I was 25 when I trekked up the Khumbu Valley in Nepal to the foothills of Mount Everest and had planned to climb one of the many peaks or foothills to Everest called Pokalde, which was just over 19,000 feet high. It was still overshadowed by Mount Everest, another 9,000 feet of skywards altitude. I knew the limits of my abilities and just by looking at it, I felt no desire to climb Mount Everest – no desire at all. It just looked like one big bag of trouble and I wanted no part of it. However, there was weather on Pokalde coming down the Khumbu from the north, so we were forced to change our 20,000 feet peak to one called Nangkartshang, elevating to around 17,000 feet, starting off from 14,000 feet. I was disappointed not to climb to 19,000 feet but you can't tempt fate out there in the Himalayas – the weather is quick, ruthless and occurs on an unprecedented scale. Your sense of judgement of size and distance gets trashed because there are no points of reference out in that wilderness – there is nothing made by humans to give you a sense of scale. There are no roads, street lamps or buildings – just rock, mountains and sky.

It is nothing short of spellbinding.

I was proud of myself and the achievement of climbing to the 'roof of the world' – well, into the attic space of the roof at least. In preparation for this trip, I trained in the gym for strength and out in the mountains of Scotland, Wales and the Lake District for stamina for six months prior to flying to Nepal with the group I had joined for this, the expedition of a lifetime.

---|---

Occasionally, I have found it challenging to accept the unpredictability of PD. I have received no guidance on timings of when things might happen to me – and what these things might be. Like, for instance, when would I have to start taking medication, or how many years of full-time work could I realistically expect following diagnosis? To be honest, I was petrified thinking about having to admit to work colleagues and managers that I had PD. Most people think it is a condition that occurs principally in the elderly. When diagnosed before the age of 50 it is labelled as 'early onset'. To be diagnosed with PD in your twenties or thirties is considered to be extremely rare. When I was diagnosed the incidence was one in twenty thousand – so in a full Wembley stadium, there could be 5 people under 30 years of age with PD (either diagnosed or undiagnosed). With the advertising industry being so competitive, for the first few years I kept it under wraps because I was concerned about challenges from other colleagues. I was actually embarrassed to admit that I had a condition that people who were thirty-five to forty years older than me were diagnosed with routinely. I was concerned that I would be the subject of ridicule. Ultimately, I was scared of being embarrassed and that people would start to notice things that weren't right about me; for instance, my hands tremor slightly when my medication needs to be topped up and are rigid when I perform small, intricate tasks with them. Like doing up shoelaces, for example.

I may have been worrying unnecessarily – I probably wasn't in other peoples' thoughts as much as I thought I was, despite being able to draw attention to myself when it wasn't required.

---|---

My mum told me that a friend from her darts team, Kelvin, had his own landscaping and gardening business and was looking for a Saturday morning boy to be the 'go-for'. I would go-for this and go-for that and generally help out on jobs with Kelvin and the guys who worked for him full time.

I was just fifteen and full of male hormones. It was weekend and school holiday work, working mostly with a guy called Roger who was like a sex-gland; he could talk about nothing else but sex and that he was going to give the missus a 'back scutler' after he finished work. He demonstrated his Saturday lunch time plans for 'the missus' in unnecessary detail with a few elaborate hip thrusts, timed to perfection with gorilla-like hoots and grunts, his facial muscles clenched in a way that made him look like a perfect candidate for the national sex offender registry. Roger just looked filthy, even before he opened his mouth. He would wax lyrical about various sexual positions, such as the back scutler, knee wobbler, donkey punch – the list seemed to be endless. I had only a vague idea of what he was talking about until Paul, Mark and I discovered a pornographic movie in Paul's dad's home video collection. During school holidays, we studied this video in detail and clarified a number of issues, answered questions that had gone unanswered and until now, were shrouded in mystery. If we had put in the level of attention to our schoolwork that we did to this movie, all three of us would have been A grade students in all subjects.

I was now able to talk to Roger about 'giving 'er indoors one from behind' with a small amount of authority and knowledge, on his level. I felt like a man of experience – things couldn't have been further from the truth. I'd had a very limited amount of experience with the opposite sex up to this point in time.

On many occasions my inexperience shone through, particularly when an attractive female passer-by would take a wide de-tour around our work site, unable to escape the leering eyes of my sex-pest-colleague.

"There you go, Young Un, there's one for you…kitchen back scutler for me, what say you?"

"Shut up, she can hear you," I would say, embarrassed. "I'd give her a reverse knee wobbler, followed by a toe touching back scutler…"

"WHAT?!"

"What's wrong with that?"

"A reverse knee wobbler and a back scutler are the same thing, Young Un…"

Every Saturday morning before work, Kelvin would buy us breakfast at the Copper Kettle Café, just outside Weston town centre. I would cycle over to Kelvin's house for 7:15am to meet the guys – Roger, Rob and Shaun, who was Kelvin's younger brother. Rob was quite reserved; he was a music lover and with his long, dark hair, he looked like he should be the drummer in a rock group. He told me stories from the early days of the Glastonbury Rock Festival, when it was originally called the Pilton Rock Festival.

I ordered a big breakfast which would fuel me up for the morning's work. I was in love with the waitress at the Copper Kettle, Tina, a sizzling redhead, who I would gaze at adoringly. Needless to say, I had the shit ripped out of me about Tina by my colleagues; they were brutal when the opportunity to tease me mercilessly arose, but they meant no harm and besides, it helped towards toughening me up. It was around this time that I began to stand up for myself more at high school, having endured several years of bullying and being picked on relentlessly.

I was concerned that I would bump into other students from my school while I was out working for Kelvin. Truthfully, I was a bit of a snob – I used to think that working for Kelvin was below me, or the type of work I did was below me. The last thing I wanted was for someone at school to know what I did for work. Only on rare occasions did I see someone who I recognised or who recognised me. I was a very sensitive teen and I was lacking attention from my father. I needed him to get his head out of the Model Bus Federation (which was all he was interested in / obsessed with) and start being a role model to give me someone to aspire to and teach me how to handle people and life situations. Unfortunately, he was just unable to fulfil this role. This is where Kelvin and the guys who worked for him came into my life and for a couple of years, fulfilled that missing role model, answering the sort of questions that a boy needs to ask his father. I would be sorely mistaken to think that the guys would give me the *answers* that a responsible father would give to his teenage son. Parents give half the answer – these guys went into a level of anatomical detail that you would normally hear only in first year medical school, when it came to discussing sex. They were real salt of the earth 'men' and I was lucky to have them around me.

As previously mentioned, I was fairly good at drawing unwanted attention to myself. My mum told me that there was going to be a jumble sale on Saturday afternoon at the local community hall and I should go and buy a pair of jeans to wear for work. I found a pair that looked long enough and fit my waist, but they were extraordinarily flared in the leg. I decided to cut a large section of material from the legs and re-sew the seams on the outside of each leg. Drainpipe jeans were all the rage at the moment and I was sure I could create the same effect. I turned the jeans inside out so all the re-stitching would be hidden from view.

I was pleased with how smoothly the re-sew had progressed, using my mum's embroidery thread for extra strength. I turned the jeans outside facing out so they were ready to wear. Then I pulled them on.

Now, there are jeans that are slim fitting yet still comfortable to wear all day. These jeans were so tight they could have been mistaken for 'skin' with a denim blue tattoo. I was quite concerned that they might cut off the circulation to my lower limbs as I poured myself into them. I didn't even want to think of the damage they might be doing to my 'family jewels'.

They were so tight, that where I had stitched the material together you could see the skin of my legs, as the thread under tension fought against my legs that were threatening to tear the stitching apart. They were uncomfortably tight *everywhere.*

In today's world, they would pass as a statement of fashion for a top designer clothing brand whereas I just wanted a pair of slim fitting, unvented jeans to work in. As expected, my newfound sense of fashionable work wear gave my work colleagues something new to rip into me about. I took it…like a man.

---|---

A week or so before Christmas, (in my school holidays) Kelvin arranged a day for the annual works party. This was largely just a big drinking session, with the guys he employed, friends, family and members of the darts team all invited. As was tradition, a few of us met Kelvin at the Copper Kettle Café for breakfast to 'line the stomach' with beer-absorbing food. This was viewed as a necessary precautionary measure.

Then, the party moved to the Prince of Wales pub, around ten o'clock in the morning which was when it was officially allowed to open for the service of tea, coffee, cakes, scones and soft drinks. This was also the time at which it unofficially opened for the service of alcoholic beverages. Mayhem ensued.

Each year there was a darts competition. It is never a good idea to mix copious amounts of free alcohol with sharp, airborne pieces of metal with points on the end. Add to this cocktail a measure or two of disagreement, a sprinkling of raised voices and all of a sudden, there's a fight. Actually, at the Prince of Wales, it wasn't so much 'will there be a fight?'; it was more like 'when will there be a fight?' As pubs go, it was as rough as hell. It still exists, and probably hasn't changed a bit.

I usually threw the towel in by mid-afternoon, leaving the warmth of the pub and exiting into the frigid winter air. The amount of alcohol being consumed was ludicrous – I couldn't keep up with these hardened drinkers. Some of them drank two pints of beer at a time. I made my way home where I passed out on the sofa. But not before my mum read me the riot act about underage drinking – again. I used to get a clip around the ear if I was being a smart arse and said something like 'the biggest problem with underage drinking is running out of money too quickly'.

Four

I grew up faster than most of my friends. This is one of the consequences of the breakdown of a marriage; suddenly, I became the man of the house. My mum wasn't able to work because she was on income support. To make ends meet, I often contributed money into the family purse, to make sure there was food on the table for my mum, my sister and myself. My father, who was working full time earning good money as a contract draughtsman contributed a miserly £25 per week as a maintenance payment for my sister and myself. As we grew up, this already meagre contribution to our lives failed to increase. When our father was legally allowed to stop paying this money, on our eighteenth birthdays the amount had not changed from when my sister was nine and I was thirteen despite his earnings increasing over the years.

---|---

As children, we are in such a rush to grow up. This is true of my own daughter; at the age of eleven, she is already thinking about and telling me what she'll be like when she's twelve and – rather scarily – as a teenager a year or so further down the line. I thank her for the advance warnings; I keep telling her to enjoy being the age she is at because it will not be around for long and will be gone before she knows it. Youth is wasted on the young, as the saying goes.

When it comes to the process of aging and PD, there are some distinct differences in 'priorities' between patients who are young and those who are elderly. The younger patient, who may still be of working age, will do everything they are capable of doing to slow down the rate of progression of their PD. It seems to be the case that the younger person with PD may have a slower rate of disease progression being Early or Young Onset patients; this is often seen in this subset of patients. After a few meetings with my consultant in London, known as The Prof, he commented that the rate of progression of my PD was among the slowest he had ever witnessed.

People with PD who are of working age will go to great lengths to disguise their symptoms, or anything which is visible that suggests 'there is more to this person than meets the eye, something about the way he (or she) moves is not right'. I have been shaving my head for a year now, finally giving in to the fact that I was naturally losing my hair. This makes the lumps and bumps from the Deep Brain Stimulation surgery that I went through in 2012 a lot more visible. I wear a baseball cap most of the time, so I don't unnecessarily scare any small children!

To family and close friends, these are the unavoidable scars of DBS. To strangers, potential employers and acquaintances that I don't know well, these are scars from a fictitious road traffic accident that I was involved in during my late teens.

I don't have any feelings of guilt for being economical with the truth in this way – as far as I am concerned, my PD is on a 'need to know' basis – if it is important for you to know that I have PD then I will present you with all the information you need. But if I can avoid 'opening a can of worms' and appear to be as normal as the next guy without feeling the need to disclose information about my PD, that is what I will do.

Elderly people with PD tend to have different priorities than younger people with this condition; they are less concerned about mixing in with other people and disguising their symptoms. They are more concerned with staying upright on their feet, avoiding falling over and causing themselves serious injury, rather than how they look and how they come across as an individual.

---|---

I decided that I was going to be a Veterinary Surgeon. I loved animals and wanted to be able to help them. This was triggered by a newspaper advertisement depicting cruelty to animals overseas, which had a big impact on me. *I can't do much about what goes on overseas,* I thought, *but I could help to look after animals here.*

The only problem was that I wasn't a straight A student, on average, I was at best a B grader in most of my subjects. In a handful of subjects, I was an A grader – like in English Literature, French and Woodwork. But these wouldn't help me get a place at Vet College, competition is fierce and ideally you needed three A grades at A level. After I left high school with a string of 'O level' passes, I went to sixth form to study physics, chemistry and biology at A level. Some people chose to do mathematics at A level, but I thought I would do better in biology. Annoyingly, in my first year at university I had to take maths as well as chemistry. Geology made up the final third of my first-year studies, as I have always been interested in minerals, but I don't really count this as the geology lecturer was clearly insane, encouraging us to 'touch the rocks, feel the rocks, smell the rocks'!

However, when I was asked by my A level tutor what career I wanted to pursue, I replied that I was going to be a vet…and he started to laugh.

"Sit down, you fool," he said, composing himself, taking off his glasses and wiping his eyes. Then he looked at me with his beady little eyes. "Are you serious? Have you any idea how competitive it is to get a place at a Vet College? For a start, you have to be on target for three straight A grades in physics, chemistry and biology. That'll get you over the first hurdle. There are only around 400 places a year in the UK; only six or seven colleges offer it and it's a five-year course. Plus, it helps if you grew up on a farm and you have spent time working with a vet both in the surgery and out in the farms. Why would you want to put yourself through all that just to shove your arm up a cow's arse?" He started laughing to himself again.

I muttered something about making a difference in the world, as well as inaudibly labelling him with the words 'you arsehole'. Probably the wrong attitude to have, but there it was. *Nothing like a bit of encouragement from the teaching staff,* I thought.

To the best of my knowledge, nobody in my family owned a farm but I was so determined to pursue my dream career that I asked our local vet if I could come to the surgery on Saturday mornings to watch what he did, to gain some practical experience.

The practice was made up of three male vets and one female vet. The surgery was always packed on a Saturday morning; I began to wonder if people's pets became unwell in the latter part of the week. After a few months, I asked if I could work a few days in my school holidays. The female vet said I could do the morning surgery with her and then assist with the surgical operations for the day which would often run into the afternoon. These procedures consisted of any urgent ops, then routine ops such as dog neutering.

The female vet enjoyed castrating male dogs just a little too much. In the operating theatre there were two other females – one was a vet nurse, there to assist the vet, the other was a University student. The vet nurse had prepared and anaesthetised the first dog, ready for the chop. He was in another world; the vet nurse started by shaving the scrotum, so it was free of dog fur. Next, the vet took over and cut the scrotum with a scalpel; this made me feel slightly nauseous, I had to sit down in a chair, as out popped the testicle. Then, while looking straight at me, she would yank the testicle and its attached tube. I could literally feel my own testicles receiving that hard yank from the female vet – waves of nausea washed over me. Then, after applying the same action to the other testicle, the tubes were cut and tied. She then stitched up the scrotum, so that it no longer resembled a miniature toast rack, after squirting some antibiotics inside the redundant sac. Clearly, the female vet relished the power she had over our furry friends' sexual status and the nauseating effect a well-timed yank could have on me. Neutering a female dog was much more sedate – no drama involved.

"Are you all right?" asked the female vet.

"Yeah, I think so," I said, "I wasn't prepared for castration being so 'violent', that's all."

---|---

I enjoyed small animal vet science, but I was really keen to get out on the farms. Out on the farms, that was where the Vet reigned supreme. One morning, I was out on the farm calls with the Senior Partner of the practice. We were walking with the farmer who was discussing the state of a pregnant sow, in one of the sheds. Before we got anywhere near the shed, we had to run the 'cow gauntlet' through a cow milking shed of approximately sixty cows, thirty on our left and thirty on our right, their back sides facing the central walkway.

"Keep your eyes peeled," said the Vet.

"For what?" I asked, suddenly worried.

"You'll see…" he replied.

Cow's defecate and urinate a lot of the time. When they are shovelling truckloads of grass down into the first of four stomach chambers, they are pissing and shitting away anything that they cannot digest and absorb.

I looked along the length of the milking shed. Cow shit was being jettisoned from one side of the shed to the other by the methane-propelled rectums of sixty cows. I pulled the hood up of my waterproof to cover as much of my head as possible. I tied the face chord so just my eyes were visible. If I had protective eyewear, I would have worn it. Just as I had secured the face chord, one of the cows on the left side of the shed squeezed one out with enough force to hit the Vet on his upper arm.

"Shit," he said, predictably. "See, I told you, you need to have eyes in the back of your head for this job."

If I had eyes in the back of my head and had been on the Vet's left instead of his right, I would be clawing cow shit out of my rear-facing eyes right now.

It's true – there was no way of predicting from which direction the next dung-missile was going to come from. I just kept spinning left and right, trying to catch sight of the next one before it went ballistic. I watched for the tell-tale signs such as the animal's tail rising. I survived the length of the cow shed unscathed, despite several near misses.

The following night, I dreamt of the cowshed and having to run the gauntlet again, except I was wearing my school P. E. kit – which basically comprised of a white pair of shorts and a white t-shirt. The dream took a nightmarish turn for the worst when I realised the school canteen was positioned at the exit of the cow-milking shed and, yes…lunch was being served. Between my hot lunch and I were sixty cows and the content of their colons. Weighing up my options, I deduced that I needed to spend as little time as possible in the 'danger zone', which meant a sprint to the line. In the nightmare, I got crapped on twice – once on the leg and on my flank. Still, I got laughed at in the canteen, but I was used to ridicule by then. Then I woke up. In my dreams, I never get to the enjoyable parts; it's just about getting through the difficult parts.

That's what having PD feels like in the early days following diagnosis. It's a lot like having nothing to look forward to…and being shat on multiple times by Mother Nature.

---|---

We had one more patient to see at the farm – the huge sow, who was heavily pregnant and in a very bad mood. She was in a shed on her own, she must have been six feet long, maybe longer. She was ready to give birth but was having complications; she needed to be induced. The Vet said, "Get ready to make a run for it." Before I could ask him why, he punched the oversized creature twice on the thigh to temporarily numb the flesh, then plunged a thick needle into the punch site forcing the contents of the syringe through the needle. Still, the pig squealed in pain (I think) or it may have just been surprised. Either way, in a second, it was rearing up on its legs, attempting to bite the hand that was trying to help it. The Vet gave me one almighty shove in the back, towards the door which the farmer held open, which I literally fell through, closely followed by the Vet.

"Yeah, that one doesn't really like needles. Forgot to mention that…and for her size, she can move bloody fast…"

Turning to the farmer, he said, "Let's see how she goes with that today…the next thing to consider is a C-section but we're not quite there yet." The farmer nodded in agreement.

Five

The Nut Tree pub had a lot to answer for, or more accurately the people who were regulars at the pub. I found myself working there in the kitchens for a number of weeks when I was around the age of seventeen, in the kitchens washing up the restaurant crockery and cutlery, feeding most of my weekend wages back into the cash register from the other side of the bar. My maternal grandparents would frequent the Nut Tree probably 2-3 nights a week. It was extremely popular and had a lively atmosphere.

My mum went the Nut Tree fairly 'infrequently' – probably between once a week and once a fortnight, so in her mind she wasn't a Nut Tree regular.

She wasn't a big drinker, either. The problem was that she didn't know when she'd reached her limit. One night she had far too much to drink and by three o'clock the following afternoon, she still had not put in an appearance. My sister and I were getting a little concerned, so we did just what any other responsible offspring would do – we called the doctor, who visited the house and gave mum a jab of penicillin in her butt cheek. My sister and I looked on, enjoying the episode. I like to think that the doctor did this to make *himself* feel better, having wasted his precious time on an out call to a patient with a bad hangover: my mum.

On another occasion, I was annoyed with my mum, who turned up at home way too late and too toasted for a weekday evening. The following day, I heard her get up to use the bathroom, then stagger back to bed.

I decided to confuse and disorientate her; I sellotaped a wall of newspaper sheets to the outside frame of her bedroom door. The next time she got up, she opened the door only to be faced with newsprint nightmare. She freaked out, shrieking, "Oi, Mark you little sod!" At first, she was too scared to put her hand through the paper and was screeching that she was going to vomit. Eventually, she summoned the courage to shoulder charge the newsprint wall and made it to the bathroom with seconds to spare.

I applied for a Saturday job at a popular chain of hamburger restaurants. Working outdoors, for Kelvin particularly in the British wintertime, was getting less appealing as time went on. I concluded that I had fulfilled this part of my working life; I wanted something indoors, somewhere warm and dry.

The restaurant in Weston was managed by two guys called Pete – Pete 1 was the quiet, scary type, Pete 2 was more vocal, a lot less scary. I got along well with both of them. I used to work predominantly on the quarter-pounder grill, making four burgers at a time. While the meat was cooking, I'd split four buns and toast them, put cheese slices on three buns, mustard and ketchup. Seventy-five percent of the quarter-pounders sold had cheese on them. By now, the top part of the mechanical burger grill was lifting, there was probably fifteen seconds before the meat started to burn, so you had to be quick in preparing the buns. I would lift burgers in one go and slide two rows of two burgers onto the bottom buns, sliding the toasted top buns on to finish. Then, it was just a case of sliding the tray of four burgers up to the wrapping area and then wait for further instructions.

The restaurant in Weston was often a target for drunks looking for late night trouble, since it was one of the last establishments to close at night. As I was tall, the management wanted me to work on the door if I was working a long evening shift. I was told to puff my chest up and to look mean. They overlooked the fact that if I turned sideways, I would practically disappear because I was so skinny.

Weston used to get more than its fair share of trouble because it was the first large beach resort that tourists to the South West would encounter as they travelled from Birmingham in the North and London in the East. There was a lot of fighting between Weston's underground gangs – mostly of Greek origin and the Asian gangs from Birmingham.

I once saw a guy from Weston with a small 'axe' embedded between his skull and right ear, as a result of a street fight between gangs. Paramedics took him to hospital to have it removed.

Jesus Christ, I thought, *is this what we've reverted to? Attempting to take the scalp – or the ear – of your enemy?* Had we suddenly travelled back in time to the Wild West, where cowboys and Indians fought over indigenous land rights?

There were regular running street battles between gangs in Weston, there was always some kind of drama taking place.

Phil was the landlord at The Gardens Public House in the centre of Weston, the latest town centre pub to be refurbished. It was an overnight success; a group of young officers from the local Royal Air Force base at Locking were regularly spending a great deal of money there. It was the place to be and be seen. Being a 'corner pub', it had an entrance on the High Street and another on Oxford Street; it made sense to keep the High Street entrance locked when it was quiet; from the bar I could see out to the street through the Oxford Street entrance. Our doorman Ron (who looked like he was physically constructed from cube-shaped and oblong-shaped blocks of concrete) and Phil would then manage the customers through just one door.

Phil was a retired Police Officer with the Criminal Investigation Department. He was married to Sara who managed the restaurant side of the business. The rumours among the staff were that Phil used to work deep under cover and was involved in several high-profile drug busts in the Birmingham area. What was he doing running a pub in sleepy Weston, then? Apparently, the rumours suggested that he was starting to get too well known in the drugs underworld and he came close to blowing his cover which would have had less than desirable consequences. He was told that he could leave the police force or take a desk job to preserve his identity. Phil made the difficult decision to leave the police force, a victim of his own success.

Phil interviewed me and I started working behind the bar at The Gardens two or three months after Phil took over the licence. After six month's work, without a single day off work Phil and Sara decided to take the August Public Holiday Monday off, leaving the pub in the hands of Deborah, the assistant manager. Apart from Ron the doorman who was working on one of the two entrances to the pub, I was the only other male working in the pub that day.

During the early afternoon, I took a call from the manager of the Imperial Bar at the top end of the High Street.

"Hello, The Gardens?"

"Yeah, hi, it's Dave here from the Imperial…"

"Hello, Dave, what's up?"

"Well, I just wanted to let you know there's a coachload of idiots from the Forest of Dean in town. They've just beaten up the desk sergeant at the Police Station then came here. We refused to serve them, so they've turned a few tables over, smashed a few pictures, glasses and ash trays and it looks like they're heading your way…they were last seen heading down the High Street…thought you'd appreciate the warning…"

"Oh great," I said, rolling my eyes looking at Ron. "Thanks for letting us know, Dave, cheers." I hung up the telephone.

"Who was that, what's going on?" asked Deborah.

"That was Dave at the Imperial which has just been smashed up by a coachload of farm hands from the Forest of Dean, and they're heading this way. Phil would never let them in so neither can we."

"Okay," said Deborah. "Ron, lock the High Street entrance. Put that 'Closed For Refurbishment' sign up outside – that'll confuse them if they come that way."

She turned to me. "Marco, get on the Oxford Street door. From now on, the pub is closed to any customers who aren't already inside. Say it's being refurbished – we can only have a certain number of customers and we've reached that number."

Deborah took the bunch of keys from around her neck on a lanyard. "I'm going to lock both doors from the inside. Ron – when you've put that sign out, go to the Oxford Street entrance with Marco. I'll be just inside with the keys in case it kicks off. If these guys come around, just tell them the pub is closed for refurbishment, you don't have keys etc., etc…"

I was shitting myself. Farm hands from the Forest of Dean in Gloucestershire, these guys would be on a mission to procure whatever alcohol they could get their hands on, and then cause mayhem throughout the town. It sounded like their party had already started at the Police Station and I doubted if Ron and I would prove to be much of an obstacle for them. Particularly if they managed to get the doors open; the interior, partially glazed doors that Deborah had locked wouldn't take many kicks from a Forest of Dean boot before the locks failed and the doors were opened.

"Shit, here they come…must've gone down to the beach on their way around," said Ron peering out from the entrance looking towards the beach. I turned to look; I could see between fifteen to twenty heavy set guys, some wearing shirts, others had fashioned makeshift bandanas from shirts or t-shirts. Collectively they looked like they were on an alcohol fuelled beach holiday, spilling off the pathway into the road. Drivers who hooted their car horn at those walking in the road received a flurry of verbal insults and various angry hand signals from the group. They were a mixture of ages, from the late teens and upwards, clearly intent on causing trouble on their walking tour around Weston.

"What the fuck were they doing down the beach?" I wondered out loud. "Building sandcastles, or what?"

"I don't know," said Ron. "Building sandcastles…being arseholes…"

The unruly group were almost at the pub's entrance. Ron and I stood shoulder to shoulder, arms crossed. They stopped in front of us.

"Pub open then, is it landlord?"

"Sorry, gents, the bar is closed, for refurbishment," I replied.

"How come I can see there's people in there then, landlord?" Obviously, he was the smart one of the group.

"Coffee only – for the over 65s – no alcohol served," said Ron.

"Where can we get a few beers, then?" asked the smart one.

Neither Ron nor I said anything. The last thing we wanted to do was recommend another pub no matter how much we wanted to get rid of this group of farmies. We were being forced back into the entrance doorway, as more of the group tried to pressure us into letting them into the pub.

"Is there somewhere we can get a drink, we won't be no bother, like…"

"Come on, Landlord, we've got cash, we just want a couple of drinks…we'll just take our drinks and stand outside."

"Nobody wants to let us in or take our fuckin' money…jus' lerr us in for a couple of swallies, then we'll be on our way…"

I gritted my teeth. "YOU AIN'T FUCKIN' COMING IN HERE!" I said loudly, almost regretting it the second after I'd said it. Ron half looked at me with a startled 'what the fuck' expression on his face.

A moment's silence. *This is it,* I thought to myself, *this is where I get the crap beaten out of me.* I've nowhere to escape to, I literally had my back to the door. The locked door, to be precise.

Suddenly, an arm thrust its way out of the group, between the two farmies closest to me. It was as thick as my thigh and the hand attached to it was the size of an excavator bucket. The hand grasped my shoulder and gave it a shake, followed by a couple of playful slaps on my chest. It felt like the hand was going to break a rib or two.

"Good on ya, son, for standing your ground," said a voice from within the group, presumably attached to the arm and hand that was congratulating me. The voice was laughing while it spoke. "YOU'VE GOT BALLS OF STEEL…"

Then another voice said, "Come on, lads, we'll get some beers from somewhere else."

The group crossed the High Street and ambled along Oxford Street. A police car with its blue lights flashing followed the group from a relatively safe distance. As it passed the pub entrance, Ron and I stepped out onto the path. The Police officer in the passenger seat gave us the thumbs up signal and a watery smile.

"Jesus Christ," said Ron. "I seriously thought we were going to get the shit kicked out of us, just then." He pulled two cigarettes out of the pack he retrieved from his trouser pocket and handed one to me. I was shaking like a leaf as I lit the cigarette on his lighter.

"Yeah…thanks, me too…I think I might have actually shit myself. Or pissed myself a little, you know, like when you get scared suddenly or you get a shock."

"I guess so," said Ron, who was looking at me a bit oddly by now. This was probably an everyday experience for him. For me, it had been a near-death experience.

A Police support unit was brought in to round the farmies up – probably Riot Police from Bristol. They were put back on their coach and given a Police escort to the Almondsbury interchange, some twenty-five miles north of Weston on the M5 motorway.

Six

I was offered a place at the University of Bristol to study for my Bachelor of Science undergraduate degree in chemistry provided I made certain grades in my A-levels. I had glandular fever when I sat my A-level examinations at Sixth Form. I was too ill to take a bus to the exam hall so I took a taxi each way. It cost a small fortune, but what were the options? I didn't have any. My dad helped towards these costs. I could tell it caused him physical pain to part with the cash that would make it more comfortable for me to arrive at Sixth Form in some kind of state that made it possible for me to sit my A-levels, rather than having to sit on a rattling, old bus with worn-out suspension for the best part of an hour and twenty each way. That would have been his preferred mode of transport given his obsession with public service vehicles.

As it turned out, I was graded B in chemistry, C in biology and D in physics. All passes but no chance of getting into vet school then. I had given up on this dream when I faced the facts: I wasn't going to get three straight A grades at A-level – with or without glandular fever. My GP helped me by writing to the University selections body (called UCCA at the time) and explained that I had glandular fever at the time of sitting my A-level exams and could they be lenient enough to offer me a place in the faculty of chemistry at Bristol? He also wrote to the board of examiners and explained my situation.

I think this and the fact that I had opted for a deferred entry, giving me a year out of studying, was what got me a place in the University of Bristol starting in October 1990, which boasted a reputation of being a 'top five' faculty of chemistry in the UK at the time.

At University, I was working in what was widely regarded as the most dangerous building in Bristol, with a multitude of poisons, toxins, flammable and explosive substances stored within its walls, with several hundred underqualified undergraduates mixing them together in the name of science. This was in the days before it was deemed responsible to have safety guidelines for handling dangerous substances; we were told just to wear eye protection at all times in the labs.

Anything considered to be 'dangerous' was handled in a fume cupboard, which operated under negative pressure, sucking air in under the vertical sliding sash window of the cupboard which ensured that no dangerous gases could escape into the lab where we worked. The vertical sliding sash window was made from reinforced polycarbonate, which could take a significant blast should the worst occur. This was re-assuring as we had something in our lab which could explode in spectacular fashion.

We had an ether still in one fume cupboard in our lab. Ether is a highly volatile, flammable liquid, properties which make it exceptionally useful as a solvent. Ether was used in the past as an inhalant anaesthetic, with its aromatic odour and sweet, burning taste. We used it to clean glassware to avoid contamination of reactions.

The 'still' was a glass, round bottom flask which rotated whilst warming ethyl alcohol in the presence of sulphuric acid, the cooled 'distillate' collected as pure condensed ether and ran off to a drawing point. A slight vacuum was applied to lower the boiling point, so the heat used was minimised for safety. Sodium wire was used to 'dry' the ethyl alcohol and sulphuric acid mixture, essentially keeping water from contaminating the ether. At the drawing point there was a glass bung; you removed this and used a hypodermic syringe and needle to 'draw off' some pure ether.

However, ether is about as explosive and volatile as petrol, so only a few labs in the building had ether stills. Consequently, people from other labs would use our ether, which meant throwing up the sash window, removing the glass bung, drawing off some ether with a hypodermic needle and syringe, replacing the glass bung and dropping the sash window for safety. Except on one occasion, where someone didn't replace the glass bung securely and it 'popped out', leaving the ether to evaporate until the reactants in the round bottom flask heated up enough to melt the sodium wire as well as leaving the sash window raised.

This occurred over a lunch break. I had left the building and my supervisor Paul was working in the adjoining office. When I arrived back at the lab, I thought that it was strange that the sash window was raised…and the reaction vessel contained what looked like a suspicious, swirling, gaseous mixture of chemicals.

"That doesn't look right," I said to Paul.

He looked up at me. "What doesn't look right?"

"The ether still," I said, "I've never seen it looking like that…"

Paul was a Ph.D student and supervisor of third year students who were putting together their final year's thesis. He was studious and reserved, shorter than me, but also wider than me. He walked round to the fume cupboard which contained the ether still.

"Shit…shit SHIT SHIT!" I heard him say, watching him slam the sash window down. As he turned the electricity supply to the cupboard off, he shouted: "Marco – this thing could go off like a bomb at any second! We need everyone out of the building – hit the emergency alarm by the door on your way out please."

"Okay, yep, no problem," I said excitedly. All of a sudden, I felt pangs of excitement in my stomach – it was a real-life emergency and I was involved in it! I hit the alarm glass panel, smashing the glass and releasing the alarm bell. Then I left the building, alarms ringing wildly and went over to the emergency gathering point by the library.

The fire brigade was automatically called; the faculty had an emergency line direct to their control centre. Upon arrival, they checked the ether still; they confirmed that it could have exploded at any moment, we were protected by nothing more than the laws of physics. The glassware wasn't reusable, but it had cooled down to a safe temperature for handling. Several changes were recommended, such as using a 'lock' on the glass bung, as well as improving signage to make sure the sash window was left in the down position – never in the raised position.

This was only the second time I'd been involved in calling the fire brigade out…the first time was when Kerry, Paul and myself set fire to the farm access lane near our homes, when I was ten years old.

---|---

Unfortunately, I cannot claim that every job I have had has been a positive experience. Sometimes, I wonder if my errors of judgement along the way were more than purely bad decision making on my part? Was it that I was just very young and very stupid and didn't have the life experience to know what was right from what was wrong? I wish that I were able to attribute this behaviour to the effects of Early Onset Parkinson's Disease, but I have no evidence to suggest that I had the early stages of PD when I was in my early twenties. I do recall being made aware that there was some evidence out there which suggested that children who were deemed to be 'introspective' were more likely to show signs of Parkinsonism in later life. I was quite withdrawn and introspective as a child but to this day, I have not read any of the evidence surrounding this interesting observation.

However, I think it is highly unlikely that I had the early stages of PD ten years before my diagnosis, which clouded my judgement to the point where my decision making and subsequent actions had less than desirable outcomes.

I put it down to poor judgement and a level of arrogance, which made me think I was indestructible. In addition, unusual feelings or activity which is deemed 'out of character' are often associated with some of the drugs used to treat PD as undesirable side-effects and I certainly was not taking any of these medications a whole decade before my diagnosis.

So, as amusing as it is now, looking back thirty years into my past, it is with some regret that my judgement about what is right and wrong was significantly clouded for a period of time. In some ways, I guess it could be seen as a 'wake-up call' before things got out of hand and I found myself in too deep and out of my depth.

---|---

I was in my first year at University, without a part-time job. One of the guys I shared a flat with, Bob, worked at Bristol's largest nightclub, Vermillion. It was located just across the road from the Central Police Station, in Central Bristol. So, if there was any major trouble occurring in the night club, someone from the club just ran over to the station and requested help.

Bob worked security on the door of the club and was a petty thief, like most of his family members; he proudly claimed that he had an uncle who was a bodyguard to the Kray twins, in 1960s London. Bob got me an interview for a job working on the cocktail bar at Vermillion– not that I could make cocktails, but there was a guy on the bar who could.

The club was huge and set over three floors. Working on the cocktail bar was fun; usually every night there was at least one overly amorous couple who would become partially dis-robed in the large soft seating area near the cocktail bar, thinking that nobody could see them, at which point we would phone the Floor

Manager and tell them that an incident was occurring at Bar six, the cocktail bar. A coded call would go out usually by the DJ: "Pat Rafter – Bar six" and all available security personnel would make their way to Bar six. They would pull the couple off one another and eject them from the club taking them down the fire escapes.

Bar staff at Vermillon were given a certain amount of flexibility with how much we could charge for mixers (splashes of Coke, tonic water, lemonade, ginger ale). If the customer wanted just a splash of coke with their vodka, we could charge them 10 pence for the splash. If they wanted a large amount of coke, we could charge multiples of the splash.

Stupidly, I thought I could cream off some of the profit that the club was making without them noticing. I would charge £2.00 for a whisky and coke, or any spirit and a mixer, but only ring through as £1.90. When the cash register opened, I would keep back 10 pence for each drink and I would casually drop the coin into my pocket. I had wrongly assumed that the management wouldn't be able to tally the amount of mixer used to the amount of money paid. This showed an obvious disparity – more mixer was being used compared with that being sold.

I probably did this for a month, each Saturday evening. I guess the management noticed the drop in takings on the nights I worked. Then, one Saturday evening, the bar manager casually mentioned that someone was stealing and that 'undercover investigators' were going around, watching the bar staff. I turned to look at the area of the bar that I had been working.

My blood ran cold; there were two guys just sitting facing the bar, they weren't paying the slightest bit of attention to the club and I could just feel their eyes bore straight through me. I had no idea how long they had been sat there, but they must have been there long enough to see me slip a few 10 pence coins in my pocket.

Shit! I've been fucked, I thought. *Those two guys must be the undercover investigators.*

I considered making a run for it, except I was two floors up and the club was heaving. There is no way I would get to the door. The security staff would have been onto me in seconds and I would probably have come off worse. Plus, I would have to stop at the cloakroom and get my coat, it was freezing outside.

Could I escape down the fire escapes? There was still the 'coat' issue to consider and besides, the last thing I wanted was to run into the club managers in the semi-darkened fire escapes. This course of action would be acknowledgment of the fact that I had been pilfering coinage from the cash registers behind the bar. The club managers could get quite 'emotionally involved' when someone was doing the nightclub a disservice and they weren't afraid to let their fists do the talking. I could handle myself in a one-on-one situation but any more than that would be too overwhelming.

Could I dump the coins that were weighing down my trouser pockets? The only place I could think of in my rapidly panicking mind was the bin. But with five people working behind the bar and customers crowding around it was next to impossible to get any privacy. And after all, I didn't really want my colleagues to see me off-loading coins into the trash can.

Then, Ruth, the floor manager appeared at the entrance to the bar and beckoned me over.

"Marco, would you come with me please," she said. She was wearing her best poker face; I had never seen her smile. I'm not sure if she was capable of smiling. She was a hard looking woman; it was obvious that years of smoking, drinking and nightclub living had taken its toll on her.

"Yeah, sure, what's up?" She didn't answer me.

I tried again. "Is there something wrong, Ruth?" Again, she ignored my question.

I decided that I was going to have to admit the truth and hoped that she would be lenient with me. After all I thought, I hadn't really stolen from the club, I had just overcharged customers on a few drinks…and pocketed the difference…however, stealing is stealing and I knew people in the nightclub business could be ruthless. I just wanted the ground to open up and swallow me…how on earth had I got myself into this situation?

Ruth showed me into a small office on the ground floor. One of the guys who was sat at the bar watching me earlier was in the office.

"What's going on?" I asked. Ruth sat behind the desk and gestured to another empty chair. I sat down; I was nervous and trembling slightly.

"Marco, this gentleman is an undercover investigator, that we use to identify people who are stealing from the club," Ruth said. "Would you mind emptying your pockets onto the desk, please?"

I stood up. I dug my hands deep into my pockets and emptied two fistfuls of 10 pence coins onto the desk.

"Do you want to explain yourself?" asked Ruth, lighting up a cigarette.

I shrugged my shoulders. "I'm a student at the university. I need the money – for bus fare, that's all. My financial situation clouded my judgement. I'm really sorry. Please just fire me and let me leave without making a scene…"

"Can you give me one reason why I shouldn't just go across the road and let the police come over and have them put you in a cell overnight?"

"If I get nicked by the Police, I will probably get kicked out of university…just let me go, please, Ruth."

Ruth inhaled deeply from her cigarette. She thought for a few seconds before speaking, looking directly at me. "Marco, leave this place and never set foot in here again…do you understand me? Get your stuff and go."

I left the room, got my coat and walked out of the club. It was 1.10am. I didn't see Bob before I left.

I felt like I had just dodged a bullet. I walked all the way home to my halls of residence, about four miles away. I had plenty of time to think about how stupid I had been and how lucky I was that Ruth hadn't taken it to the Police.

---|---

The following day, Bob and I played squash. On the way to the squash court, I told him what I had been up to behind the bar of the nightclub. He just laughed.

"Welcome to my world!" he said.

---|---

I needed to take some time out of bar work while I was at university. Working in the nightclub on Saturday evenings meant that I slept until around midday on Sunday. So, I lost Saturday evenings and half of Sunday to work other than working for my degree course.

But of course, I missed the money that working behind the bar gave me. It didn't take long before I stopped berating myself for getting caught and fired from the club. Bob was largely to blame for the development of my amateur career in thieving. Choring – that's what we called it.

We justified it to ourselves by never concealing items. We always had a line ready in case we felt a hand on our collar: "Oh, I'm so sorry, I completely forgot to pay for this." This would have worked well if we were caught choring a set of saucepans from the supermarket by putting them under the grocery basket on the wheel frame of the trolley we were putting our groceries into. We left the set of saucepans there until we were back at the car – so we couldn't be accused of concealing stolen goods. On the short walk back to the car we expected to hear the words, "Excuse me, sir, store security…" But they never came.

Or there was the time we decided we needed new duvets for our beds, when we strolled into a well-known department store and picked up a boxed duvet each and walked out of the door without concealing them – we were hiding in plain sight. Bob would often take chances and slip a pack of batteries in the back pocket of his jeans, but generally, we were ready to feign amnesia to talk our way out of our criminal activity.

As we were both students, we needed to acquire new textbooks for our respective courses every so often. The University bookshops were on Park Street in Bristol, which inclined steeply towards College Green and the Cathedral. The books we needed for our course amounted to hundreds of pounds, but we quickly deduced that most of the staff in the bookshops appeared to be sleepy, part-time, teenage girls. Nobody would accuse us of shoplifting books that were clutched close to our chests as we perused the shelves – we blended in, looking like every other student drifting about in the store, before making an unhurried exit, chored books held tight to the chest. Once again, we were hiding in plain sight, ready to say, "Whoops! I'm sorry, I forgot to pay for this…" if we were caught.

Bob was a mature student, doing an undergraduate degree in engineering. However, Bob's heart was in acting and in particular, being an 'extra' on TV shows. He told me he had no intention of completing his degree. He attended few lectures and even fewer practical sessions. He was one of those annoying people to whom intelligence came naturally.

Ironically, Bob was often seen on TV shows like 'The Bill' and 'Casualty', both of which were made in and around Bristol; invariably he would be playing the part of a criminal. It was cool to know one of my mates was up against 'the Filth' and Detective Chief Inspector Burnside, an icon of 'The Bill'. Evidently, Bob had the life experience and crime family legacy to draw on for these roles. Moreover, he just 'looked' like a criminal. Bob broke into our Hall of Residence Bar and stole, among other things, an industrial microwave oven. He sold the stolen goods back to the Hall bar; nobody complained including the Bar Manager, who happened to be the one of our flatmates, Nathan. Bob had actually used Nathan's keys to gain access to the bar, without him finding out.

I think Bob is up there with my childhood friend Charlie for the amount of laughter that he and I generated in each other. From snowball ambushing the posh students in Will's Hall, up the hill near where we lived, to going hunt saboteuring…he was just great fun to be around. We ended up living with each other for the duration of my course after which we parted. I hear about him from time to time but I've no idea where he is or what he is doing today.

---|---

My mother often said that I have 'champagne taste, ginger beer money'. I must confess to a love of small luxuries, such as Polo aftershave by Ralph Lauren. At another well-known department store in Bristol, a display unit with dozens of expensive aftershaves adorning its shelves was placed literally just inside one of the street entrances and was partially obscured to most of the store. This meant I could be in-and-out before the door I had entered by had closed itself. I never took more than one bottle of aftershave, but I found it difficult to justify to myself why I chored something I 'wanted'. Up to that point, I had limited choring to things that I 'needed'.

I took this to be a choring milestone. It felt like I was at the point where I would start justifying and reasoning with my conscience that it was okay to take things I wanted, rather than just things that I needed. I was at the point where the proverbial 'slippery slope' began, and I really did not want to be going head-first down this path.

My next bar job was at a grungy little Bristol nightclub on Park Street called 'Wedgies' (the name alone screams 'class', does it not?). I finished my exams for the second year and then looked around for work. My other housemate, Sarah, who was also Bob's girlfriend, was about to leave her bar job at Wedgies, having completed her degree, so she asked Stuart the manager if I could take over her shifts.

The name 'Wedgies' goes back to an era when the club was a strip-joint. Often, guys would shuffle in early and ask what time the show began; I would tell them that it was no longer a strip joint but was now a legendary dance venue.

As clubs go, the best thing about Wedgies was the music – the DJ was awesome. He played an uninterrupted blend of House, R & B, Soul/Funk and Hip Hop; he recorded ninety-minute segments to audio cassette for me, with no interruptions, blending the tracks. I would play these on repeat in my Mini, driving around Bristol with Bob or Whendi (who I met in the second year of university) until the tape snapped, wore out or got snarled up in the tape player. It was just great original music to cruise around to.

One of the biggest problems with the club was that it was a target for criminal activity, particularly money laundering. Because the club was quite small, any lighting that was not necessary was kept off. It was so dark, we could not see if we were being given counterfeit bills as payment for drinks. This was a major issue as we worked so fast behind the bar we could neither see nor feel if a money-note was a fake, it was not really possible to see a difference in quality of printing, or compare the paper type. On one evening alone, we took nine fake twenty-pound notes; Bristol was at the mercy of real criminals who were creating a money laundering enterprise in the city. Eventually, Stuart the manager got a bollocking from the club owner and was told to purchase ultraviolet lights to put next to the cash register which would show characteristic differences between the fake and real £20 notes. We were also more suspicious of people buying one drink with a £20 note, obviously they wanted to part with their fake notes, to obtain as many 'clean' notes as possible. I managed to identify one fake note, a badly photocopied £20 note which felt like it had been printed on thin cardboard! While I pretended to get the customer his change, I called Stuart and told him what had just occurred. Stuart called the door and two guys came down to the bar. Before this toe-rag knew what was going on he was sat in the back of a Police car.

The club was also something of a health hazard. I lost count of the number of times that I saw cockroaches scuttle along the bar top, becoming inebriated in the pools of alcohol before taking a dive off the end of the bar. I just hoped that none of the customers ever noticed them.

Seven

Just as I was finishing university, I was offered a job with a company called DMS, the pharmaceutical giant. I was now a medical sales representative, in the southwest of England, selling prescription only medicines to GPs. I was sharing a house in Poole on the south coast with my friend Andi. It was good fun; we used to go to the Black Ball in the winter and the White Ball in the summer. Andi was one of the 'Faces' of the vibrant social scene in Poole and nearby Bournemouth. We never queued to enter a bar or a club, we would just wander up to the head of the line of protesting teeny-boppers. Andi would touch the doorman's arm and mention her name, which was *always* on the guest list. She had been cultivating these relationships for years. As the door opened, she would turn and smile at the 'youngsters' in the queue. She was and still is, to my mind, nothing short of awesome.

I was on the graduate training program, part of the graduate intake for that year which consisted of six weeks learning about certain diseases and products that DMS had developed to treat these diseases.

We were asked to prepare a presentation that we could give to the group, about anything we chose. It was a task to see how our presentation skills were developing.

I chose to make a presentation about a 'tin of Heinz baked beans' – I wanted to make an everyday product a hero. I phoned Heinz and asked them for dozens of facts about baked beans, like the average number of beans per tin, the tin dimensions, average length and width of a bean, nutritional value and so on. I used the average number of beans per tin as a competition during the presentation – everyone had a guess and the person who guessed closest to the average number of beans per tin won…a tin of baked beans.

One of the products I was selling was for the treatment of benign prostatic hyperplasia (BPH) in elderly men, which was basically a non-malignant enlargement of the prostate gland. BPH is responsible for several 'problems with men's waterworks', such as nocturia (excessive toilet visits at night-time), urge incontinence (a sudden need to urinate) and post-micturation leakage (dribbling urine onto clothes after toileting). Our product could reduce the size of the prostate gland by twenty per cent and provide relief from these symptoms. The product had just been launched when I joined the company and the take-up by GPs was slow. GPs needed the guidance of their local hospital to avoid missing a cancerous prostate gland before they would consider using our product to reduce the size of the prostate gland.

It was clear to me that GPs and Hospital Specialists needed to be 'brought together'. Up to the mid-1990s, the GP would refer all cases of BPH and suspected prostate cancer to the Urologist. You could generally rule out cancer with a prostate specific antigen (PSA) blood tst. The current treatment of BPH and confirmed prostate cancer was a surgical procedure called Trans-Urethral Resection of the Prostate (TURP). Under a general anaesthetic, this procedure involves inserting a device into the penis, as far as the prostate gland. This device had a superheated wire loop, that could be moved back and forth, shaving off bits of the prostate, hollowing it out from the inside whilst being irrigated with water. While this worked well to improve the flow of urine, it often brought about problems such as retrograde ejaculation (where patients ejaculate 'backwards' into the bladder) and blockages of the urethra caused by small pieces of the prostate getting washed up into the bladder by the irrigation water; apparently, this blockage is extremely painful.

One of our friendly local urologists offered me the chance to see a TURP performed on a patient. In addition to the TURP, which I observed with great interest, the afternoon's list included raising a woman's collapsed bladder, which I watched without incident. The afternoon concluded with the circumcision of a young boy, during which I almost passed out. I'm not usually squeamish at the sight of blood, but I couldn't believe the amount of blood that there was in snipping off the foreskin. The Urologist said I was not the first person to react this way, observing a circumcision.

Eight

After two and one-half years of being a medical sales representative with DMS, I was browsing through the Guardian Newspaper's list of media and creative job vacancies. One that caught my eye was an advertisement for an 'International Account Manager' as it involved a significant amount of international travel. The company was called Promosign, I hadn't heard of them before but all their work was in the pharmaceutical sector. I was looking for an opportunity to put more distance between myself and the future ex-girlfriend. I had just found the perfect way to achieve this and get out of the relationship.

Anita, who was also an employee of DMS had been pressurising me for an engagement ring for a while now and it was getting on my nerves. I was only twenty-four, just a couple of years out of university and I didn't have particularly strong feelings for her. Well, not strong 'positive' feelings, anyway. Maybe I had more strong 'negative' feelings for her? I wasn't really too bothered about throwing the towel in on the relationship. I told her, on a disastrous camping trip to the Haute Savoie region of the French alps, that if she didn't stop going on about us getting married, we were going to have to go our separate ways. This didn't really register and a couple of days later she resumed her marriage monologue. I wrote a mental note to end this relationship, 'toute suite!' as our charming local hosts would say.

One of the things that concerned me about Anita was that at 26 years old, she was fast turning into her parents, adopting their language and was just aging way before her time. She still lived at home, her parents cooked and cleaned for her. Basically, she had very little motivation to move out of her parents' home and start fending for herself. By the time I was her age I had left home seven or eight years prior. The only thing I liked about our relationship was that she had a number of good-looking friends, which made for a very good social life. Anita's hot girl-mates gave me something to fantasise about during the endless dinner and house parties.

I had ended the relationship at the end of a week's holiday on one of the Greek islands, Rhodes. Unfortunately, she managed to talk me into 'giving it another shot' when I was trying to tell her I was out of bullets. I suffered another three months until I screwed up on a Christmas present to Anita, a monumental cock-up which I didn't see coming at all. I'd asked my mum to help me on this and even she totally missed out on seeing that my good intentions might get misinterpreted and rendered as insensitive and inappropriate.

It was Christmas morning. Anita was sitting up in bed opening presents that I had given her. Her parents didn't mind us sharing a bed in their home.

"What's this?" she asked. I opened my eyes slightly. I was trying to go back to sleep as it was only 7am.

"Ummm…well, it's some really nice smelling…"

"Deodorant," she said, finishing my sentence. "Marco, what the hell are you doing buying me deodorant…for Christmas?"

I turned my head to look at her, my eyes fully open now "Wait, wait…it's just smellies…you remember when I said a couple of months ago…"

She wasn't listening, she was off, out of bed, into her parents room, "Mum…look what he's bought me – for Christmas, for Christ sakes."

I tried to continue, raising my voice '…that there were some better smelling deodorants than the ones you buy at Tesco's… and there's no need to blaspheme over anti-perspirant.

I started to laugh. *Happy Christmas – Where's my cigarettes?* I thought.

Anita stormed back into the bedroom. "What the fuck were you thinking?" she asked. She was by now starting to get the 'wet eye syndrome' – all teary and dusty, like. "You're basically saying that I smell badly, that I don't smell nice." I could hear Anita's dad downstairs putting on Merry Christmas, Everybody! by Slade. "…*So here it is, Merry Christmas, everybody's having fun!…*" Except me that is, I wasn't having any bloody fun. I groaned, all I wanted to do was pull the duvet over my head and sleep.

"No, I never said you smelled badly," I said, trying to figure out how to cap this flaming well and smother the flames.

"I just think you can smell even nicer than you do already – that's not cheap stuff, you know…" I was trying to sound sincere.

"I don't care how much it cost, that just adds insult to injury," she retorted as the tears rolled down her cheeks and the sobbing started. "And for Christmas too…"

"I'm sorry," I said, wondering what the hell I could do to escape this mess. "Maybe I should have given it some more thought…I didn't think you would take it so personally."

"Marco – you gave it to me as a Christmas present – how much more fucking personal could it be?" I lay there wondering what I could say to console her.

"I wrapped it myself," I said in a mildly indignant tone but I don't think it had the desired effect.

By now, I had pretty much given up trying to justify buying her deodorant as a Christmas present. But I had a plan. A plan that would take me away from all this festive misery. I took the doomed twin-pack of spray cans and chucked them in the waste bin by the door. By now, Anita's parents were having a row, "…it's the same each and every bloody Christmas… you always…" Ken's voice got drowned out by that of Slade's Lead Singer, Noddy Holder. I got dressed really quickly, grabbed my bag, went downstairs and then I bolted for the front door, took three leaps up the inclined driveway to where I had left the getaway vehicle. I jumped in and drove 150 miles to my mum's house, arriving a couple of days earlier than expected.

I knocked on the door and my mum opened it. I saw her expression of fleeting confusion. The sound of people emanated from within the house, reminding me that it was still Christmas Day.

"Where's Anita?" she said, trying to see if my soon-to-be ex-girlfriend was behind me. "Shit Marco… you're two days too early!"

"Isn't that what the innkeeper said to Mary and Joseph in Bethlehem?" I replied. "Happy Christmas to you too, Mum! I need a drink…"

A couple of days after Boxing Day, I disposed of the relationship in the same way I had disposed of the offending present. I was supposed to go to a New Year's Eve party with Anita, but I'm sure my name was 'mud' by now, once Anita had told all her friends what an insensitive bastard I was. There was absolutely no way on God's green earth that I was going to that party. I'm fairly sure it would be a Hostile New Year's celebration, rather than a Happy one. So, to add fuel to the fire, with courage and honour…I broke up with Anita on the telephone sometime in between Christmas and New Year. As upset as she was, she said she wasn't surprised.

A month later and I had been talked into trying yet again to salvage the relationship. To be honest, I was lazy and I was missing the social life that came with being Anita's boyfriend. Also, Anita had decided to move out of her parent's home and into a shared house with a friend, which meant more privacy. The relationship pitched and lurched precariously, but it survived another nine months to October 1995 before the Promosign opportunity gave me a solid reason for ending it with Anita once and for all.

I told her I was leaving DMS and was joining a company that meant I would be overseas for anything up to 6 months of the year. I lied and told her that I didn't think it was fair to keep her 'on the dangle' about a future together – it just was not going to happen. Reluctantly, she agreed.

I was now free to further my career by joining Promosign as an International Account Manager, without feeling I had to put the needs of a 'partner' before my own.

This feeling lasted for about three weeks, by which time I had a new girlfriend.

Then, a few weeks after joining Promosign in December 1995, I set out on my month-long Himalayan Trekking Expedition to Pokalde and Everest Base Camp, along the Khumbu Valley in Nepal. This had been planned, booked and paid for ten months before I left the shores of England so there was no problem from the point of view of my new employer. Like my mother, they were just concerned that I made it back to the UK in one piece.

Nine

I wasn't what you would call a 'typical' employee at Promosign; I was quite obstinate and very sure of my opinion being the final call. For this reason, my boss's boss, Cynthia, who was in charge of Account Handling and Project Management had me in her office to give me a dressing down occasionally. I needed it; I was way too arrogant for my own good. Cynthia was barely five-feet high, from Singapore and in spite of her vertically challenged, she was always buzzing with energy. She had some clear ideas on how things should be in the agency and with a touch of the 'rebel' spirit about her, we saw eye-to-eye on many issues. She missed the point occasionally during meetings and occasionally picked up the wrong end of the stick, mostly due to being 'lost in translation' between Singaporean and English.

On leaving the office one evening, she managed to put her car into 'drive' instead of 'reverse' and successfully mounted the curbstones that surrounded the flower beds and marooned her vehicle, because the wheels of her car were unable to gain any traction with the cobble stones of the courtyard. One of the multimedia managers had some ropes in his Jeep, which he used to pull Cynthia's car free of the flowerbed. She had done some considerable damage to the underside of the car, but it was still drivable.

I, too, had an altercation with a company vehicle at Promosign, in one of the minibuses that were used principally by the warehouse staff. I needed to bring something from the warehouse to the office, a distance of maybe two kilometres. At the warehouse, I misjudged the width of the vehicle and managed to reverse too close to a drainpipe that was covered with razor-sharp metal mesh for some reason and sharp enough to take the paint off the nearside of the minibus.

Having reversed in, I had to drive it back out, which helped remove more paint and damaged some of the shape of the panels.

"Oh shit," I said to myself, "I'm going to cop it for this."

I drove back to the office and parked the minibus in the top carpark where it would be out of sight. Then I could discretely tell the personnel officer about my little 'accident'. However, Alec, one of the exhibition designers, saw me limping into the top carpark, the aluminium panels on the nearside of the minibus showing off their new design.

He opened the door to the Projects room, where I worked, at the far end on the left.

"Eh up, Marco." His northern voice boomed in my ears from where he stood in the doorway. "What the fuck did you do to the minibus?"

People in the office looked up from their work, confused at first, looking first at Alec, then down the office towards my desk.

"It's nothing." I was mildly embarrassed. "Just a scratch…"

"Just a scratch?" said Alec in mock surprise, laughing. "Just a scratch? Did you drive it through a fuckin' razor wire factory or something? There's hardly any paint left on it." With that, he left the room, probably off to inspect my handiwork up close.

"What happened, Marco?" various people asked.

"It's nothing, just a few scratches, nothing more than that, just chill…"

Later that afternoon, the personnel officer discreetly telephoned me and asked me to drop into her office to discuss 'Marco's minibus incident' as it was now known throughout the company. For several weeks after, I had to endure endure banter from all sides such as nicknames (Petrolhead, Brake Fluid; apparently this is a good paint stripper, ha bloody ha). Fortunately, the insurance would cover the cost of repairing the vehicle and I heard nothing more about it…except when Alec recited the story God knows how many times down the pub on Friday lunch times., usually to recently joined designers.

Ten

I worked for Promosign for just over five years during which time PD made its presence known, from the first uncontrollable episodes of depression, to the initial physical manifestations of the condition which provided the motivation to see my GP urgently. At this stage, PD wasn't even on the doctor's radar…I was about thirty-five years too young to be considered for this. It was a case of ruling things out one by one, so they started looking at any potential issues with my bones, blood circulation and muscles and nerves. Promosign were very supportive and discrete about me taking a week's sick leave to go into hospital for some 'tests' which were supposed to help with my diagnosis. I was relieved; I was sure that by the end of this week, I would know what was going on and what needed to be done to 'put it right'.

However, the test results came back as 'inconclusive' which was frustrating given the block of time I had taken out of work for these tests. I had nothing concrete that I could tell my employer about what was going on.

From the beginning, it had always felt like it was a problem with the nervous system. This was confirmed in my mind when the initial manifestations that occurred were my left foot curling over while I was out running, a tendency for my arm to assume a position as if supported by an invisible sling and an unruly 'pinkie' finger, which danced around out of control, flicked and folded up on itself. It felt much more sophisticated than a bone problem or a circulation disorder. It feels almost like it was dormant, having been part of me my entire life, waiting for some unknown signal to turn PD from silent to active, granting it the opportunity to wreak havoc.

Was this at all possible? Had PD been a part of my life, all my life? Had I recently created an environment, which allowed PD to switch on and go about its business, destroying dopamine-producing cells?

---|---

I have always felt like I tried to avoid drawing attention to myself but in consideration of the facts, I am probably more effective at drawing attention than I previously thought. This is largely because I have a rebellious streak embedded in my personality, having a tendency to go against the grain particularly if it yielded more of a positive outcome than was previously expected. Sometimes I just enjoyed ruffling a few feathers and there were plenty to ruffle at Promosign; there were egos just about everywhere you looked.

Fun!

---|---

From the moment I joined Promosign, there was talk of moving to larger offices, closer to London and the airports. There were a number of reasons for this: being closer to London meant better access to resources, new staff and clients who were travelling through the UK were easier to meet with. Better proximity to the airports was important as we spent so much of our time in them. But the main reason was to allow the company to grow in response to the amount of business it was handling.

It took the company directors two and a half years to decide on a new base for the Promosign offices, just to the North of London. Deborah, the Personnel Director, had spent the last couple of years tearing around Hertfordshire, Essex and parts of London viewing possible new bases for the company. In the end, she decided to purchase a site that had been a conference centre in recent years, built around a seventeenth century coaching house.

On the day that we were supposed to officially move into the new offices Deborah's assistant Sandra arranged a small, fairly obscure lunch party, with sandwiches, cheeses, a selection of cut meat. It was all but gone within ten minutes of being delivered.

Jerome, one of the senior account handlers and Max, one of the exhibition designers and I decided to go to the pub for some lunch. We jumped in my car and went round to the pub in the village. We had a good lunch and washed it down with a couple of pints before heading back to the office. I half expected to get hauled over the coals for going to the pub for lunch and, as it happens, I wasn't wrong. It came as no surprise when Cynthia pulled up her window blind as the three of us swaggered down the hill from the top car park.

She knocked quickly on the glass and having gained our attention motioned for us to go to her office.

"Shit…" I said. "We might be about to get a telling off here, guys. She doesn't look happy."

"For what?" asked Max. "Just for going to the pub?"

"Yep," I said, "while there was an official party going on…"

"But there was no bloody food left…" said Max in amazement.

Once inside, Cynthia's office we presented our argument.

"We only went to the pub because there was no food left, that's what happens when you host a party in the design department," said Max.

"No, you went to the pub because you wanted to send a message…" said Cynthia, who was fast approaching her tolerance limit of smart-arse comments.

"We've got email for that," said Jerome. "We went to the pub for fish 'n' chips…"

"You're on thin ice already Jerome," Cynthia said. "Marco, what have you got to say? Don't you think it was a bit insensitive to go to the pub when Deborah had arranged some food and drinks here?"

"Probably, but there was no way we went just to cause trouble. We only went to the pub because there was no food left, Cynthia," I said bluntly.

"Marco! People were asking where you had gone," she replied sharply.

There was a brief pause while I decided how to respond.

"Well…it's nice to know that we were missed, for a change," I said sarcastically, unable to hold back the arrogant laugh. Jerome was laughing too but tried to hide it. A cynical smile spread across Max's face.

Cynthia was anything but happy. This was by far the maddest she had ever been with me…

"MARCO!" she hollered, bringing her hand down on the desk. I jumped. "This is not the kind of behaviour I would expect from a team leader! It is unacceptable and is highly inappropriate…"

I expected Cynthia would lose her cool with me at some point. I'd been in trouble recently for winding up Deborah's assistant, Sandra. The problem with Sandra was that she considered herself to be the most important person at Promosign; she had a lot of responsibility being Deborah's Assistant and the Buildings Manager. But she thought that her priorities superceded that of everyone else in the company. She had very little idea what an average day looked like when you were an Account Handler looking after half a million pounds worth of exhibition stand trying to make and retain as much profit as possible. Or as a designer trying to dream up a unique exhibition stand design that would blow the competition out of the water. As far as she was concerned, when she sent an email, she expected everyone to stop what they were doing and respond. She had no idea how busy things could get for us and she would get upset if we didn't reply to any of her 'pointless' emails within an hour of her sending the original.

It took an email from me, warning of a universal shortage of electrons about to reach our solar system and therefore could we only send the most important messages. Everyone knew I was winding Sandra up – playfully, not maliciously – with the exception of Deborah who asked Cynthia if I was serious about the 'electron' situation. Deborah hadn't realised that I was toying with Sandra; reluctantly, but with plenty of laughter Cynthia made me write an apology to Sandra, which annoyed Paul (my boss) so much that he replied to Sandra's email for 'Vending Machine Suggestions' with 'R. Soles Vanilla Crunch Fingers, some Chocolate Covered Ants and some Vandall Guff's Air Biscuits, please'.

We both ended up in Cynthia's office again for a 'mild' telling off…due to more inappropriate behaviour.

But when it comes to inappropriate behaviour, one of Paul's new account managers, Emmett, took the gold medal…

---|---

"Emmett, you're kidding me. *Please* tell me you are joking?"

"Nah man, it's for real. That's my sperm up there on the big screen."

I could feel heat rising from my stomach, into my chest, up my neck and into my head, where it stopped…I rubbed my temples, expecting steam to erupt from my ears like a character from the cartoons. I'd never had to deal with a situation involving inappropriate behaviour. This surpassed all of my experience; I had no idea how I was going to handle it.

---|---

On this occasion, we were working at the World Congress of Fertility in Lausanne, Switzerland, where we had managed the logistics of 'bringing to life' three bespoke exhibition stands, including installation at the congress in four days without a hitch. Each stand had a dedicated project manager from Promosign, who had worked alongside the account handler ensuring that they knew everything about the project. So, the project manager was essentially the producer of a 'given project'; the account handler 'owned' the client relationship.

It worked harmoniously for the most part. If there was ever any tension, most of it arose from the Promosign Exhibition Design Department who felt that they were responsible for driving these projects forward. "No, I'm afraid you are wrong there," my manager Paul told the Head of Design. "In order to drive our projects forward, you need to know what the client is asking for, that is why we have account handlers. As the title suggests, they handle the accounts and are responsible for driving projects forward."

The dedicated project manager of each exhibition stand was responsible for ensuring that the exhibition stand worked perfectly and that any issues that arose were dealt with, most of the time the client wasn't even aware of any issues. A lot of the time on-site was spent managing the client's literature. Most of our clients appreciated our involvement and viewed us as an extension of their marketing team; many of our clients' careers were made on the success of these large, global projects. The exhibition stand being the commercial face of the client company was one part of our client's presence at these international medical congresses, so there was a lot of responsibility resting on the shoulders of the client service team from Promosign in terms of meeting client expectations.

As the three project managers on the exhibition stands were relatively inexperienced, the Promosign directors and senior managers had met prior to the congress and decided that a senior manager needed to be on-site at the congress. The clients were too important to Promosign to risk a major issue occurring and there being no senior manager on the exhibition stands to resolve it. Paul looked over at me, his eyebrows raised in mock expectation.

"Okay, okay," I said, "I'll go…"

"Cheers, Marco, thanks for making that easy," Paul said, "I can't see any major problems occurring; should be a fairly straightforward trip."

"That's what the space shuttle pilot said," I said, standing up to leave the meeting room, "just before it blew up…"

Emmett was the dedicated project manager who was working on the Biofurium exhibition stand at the World Congress of Fertility in Lausanne. This was the first opportunity he had to meet and work with the Biofurium client, Karen Linskill. Slim, attractive, originally from Philadelphia, she was relaxed and laid back. I'd arranged a meeting with Karen at 6pm at the Biofurium stand the night before the Congress Opening Day to introduce her to Emmett and to walk her around the exhibition stand. She asked for a couple of straightforward changes which the installation team made before the walk-around concluded. Karen left shortly after for a meeting with the Biofurium team, followed by dinner with colleagues and a couple of experts in fertility who Biofurium was sponsoring to be at the congress.

Day One of the congress in Switzerland was very busy on the exhibition stands, as expected. I moved between the three exhibition stands, greeting the clients as they arrived. I knew some of them better than others, but I had met them all at least once. I telephoned each client before I'd left London for Switzerland to tell them that I would be on-site, in case of any unlikely major issues and to make sure we had exchanged mobile phone numbers.

The three dedicated project managers seemed happy enough; they didn't seem to be experiencing any issues. "Keep smiling," I said. "Look as if you're loving it!" Exhibition stand management is hard work and was especially hard on the feet. There was precious little time to take the weight off your feet; literature racks needed to be re-stocked, some rubbish needed to be cleared away, the clients needed information on this or that and the project managers were often used to obtain such. There were plenty of distractions both on our exhibition stands as well as on other competitor stands, from branded video games to interactive robots, all competing for the highest levels of stand traffic.

Day Two arrived; it was 9:30 am and I was about to leave my hotel room, having read through my emails and filtered out the important messages from my office from the ones which started with something like 'Mineral water refills available in reception' or 'Vehicle flow direction in staff car park', most of them from Sandra in the office. These messages, obviously 'critical' to the smooth running of Promosign, would have to wait for a while until my razor-sharp wit could create responses that were layered with enough sarcasm to get me reprimanded, at some point in the near future.

My mobile telephone lit up and started to buzz, skating around on the desk. It was Karen Linskill calling. I picked it up and answered.

"Karen, good morning, how are you?"

"Oh, hello…Marco…yes…uh…good morning to you too…" Immediately, I sensed that something was wrong – she sounded tense. I sat down on the edge of the bed, putting my knife-proof Mandarin Duck workbag on the floor.

"Is everything okay, Karen? I'm just leaving to come over to the exhibition hall."

"Um…no, not really, Marco. We've got a situation here on the exhibition stand, something that I've never had to deal with before…"

"Is it something which Emmett can handle, until I get there?" I asked. *What the hell was going on,* I wondered?

"Unfortunately, I think not," Karen replied, "I hate to say it, Marco, but Emmett is essentially the problem and I'm not sure what the best way to handle it is. I'm discussing it with you first, out of courtesy as you are the most senior person representing Promosign here."

I could feel the blood draining from my head. My arms and legs felt like dead weights. I was hoping that Emmett had messed up Karen's Exhibition Stand Literature Distribution Strategy and had given away the limited number of free expensive hardback books on Fertility to a bunch of junior doctors. However, my intuition was telling me it was something considerably more serious. The only way to get to the bottom of this was to be direct.

"Karen, tell me exactly what Emmett has done to make you feel this way?"

There was a hesitant pause before the client started to talk.

"I find this highly embarrassing and difficult to talk about, but first thing this morning just after I'd arrived at the stand, Emmett told me he had something to show me and took me to an adjacent stand where they were demonstrating the power of their microscopes." Then, he said, "Look up there at that screen." And as I looked, he said, "That's my sperm on that big screen."

Five minutes later, I was in a taxi, on my way to the exhibition hall, talking to my manager Paul on my mobile phone.

---|---

"Christ almighty…" was the only thing Paul could say after I'd outlined the situation. He was rarely speechless.

"I know he's a bit odd at times but clearly Emmett has completely taken leave of his senses," I said.

Paul found his voice. "What made him think that to provide a sperm sample to a competitor stand was a good idea, even if they are not a direct competitor? Next – and I don't even want to know the answer to this – where did he go to procure the sample? I'm hoping that he didn't just knock one out in the storage room on the exhibition stand. And lastly; what planet is he on to think it would be a good idea to show the client his sperm on a big screen?"

"Yes, I agree and there is more. Karen thinks Emmett made a pass at her. He was saying something like 'Look at my boys go' and he winked at her. Under normal circumstances, I wouldn't be so concerned – but in the presence of this guy's jizz sample, anything goes."

"Holy shit…NO! Have you talked to Emmett about any of this?"

"Not yet – I just left the hotel, I should be there in around ten minutes. I don't think he can go on working on the exhibition stand. Karen won't be comfortable…she said that I needed to know that she would have to escalate this by telling her manager, Carlton Treswecki, the Business Unit Director. You know him, don't you?"

"Yes, I do." Paul's voice was strained. "Ruthless Ukrainian. He could fire us in seconds flat."

"I would let Deborah and Geoff know about this – just in case Carlton does fly off the handle and calls the office." Deborah and Geoff were the owners of Promosign.

"Yes and I'll let Cynthia know too," said Paul. Cynthia needed to be in the loop as she was the Director of Client Services and Paul's boss.

"Okay, I'm almost at the venue now, so I'll catch up with you in a bit, once I've put these flames out." I hung up and paid the taxi driver. Then I dived out of the silver Mercedes and joined the throngs of people streaming into the Congress Venue. The exhibition hall was located centrally in the congress venue.

I headed straight for the Biofurium stand. As I approached, I could see Karen was at the far-left hand side of the stand, talking to a couple of visitors. Emmett suddenly appeared from behind the door of the storage room, carrying a box loaded with the client's literature to was put out on the stand. He saw me and I beckoned him over, as I walked to the opposite end of the stand from where Karen was in conversation.

"Hey, Marco," Emmett said.

"Got something to tell me, Emmett?" I asked.

He thought for a couple of seconds. His face lit up. "I've got something to show you," he said smiling proudly. He pointed up at the big screen that was positioned about three metres high on the adjacent exhibition stand.

"Emmett, you're kidding me. Please tell me you are joking…"

"Nah man, it's for real. That's my sperm up there on the big screen."

"Are you out of your mind?" I said. "I took a phone call from Karen this morning; she wasn't at all happy. Do you have any idea what the re-percussions are of you showing the client a sample of your sperm; the word 'inappropriate' doesn't begin to cover it. What the hell went through your head to make you think it was a good idea? You've no idea how serious this is."

"Ahhh…shit…Marco, I'm sorry. The guys over there were just looking for subject matter, they had used blood, hair, I asked if they could do anything with sperm, they said that would work perfectly. They asked if I would be willing to bang one out, in the interests of medical science…"

"Bang one out? Bang…one…out?" I repeated. "That just about says it all, Emmett. Are we at a brothel? On another note, people are wondering why you had your mind on the needs of another exhibitor and not on the one that is paying your salary."

"I didn't think it was that big a deal…"

"The client obviously did. Emmett, you took Karen over to this exhibition stand, and showed her your sperm on screen. I assume you 'banged one out' in your hotel room, and not anywhere around here? And then you made some comment to her which makes her think that you were hitting on her."

"I only said, look at them sucker's go…they gave me a sample bottle." I held my hand up, my palm towards his face.

"Spare me the details, please. And you winked at Karen?"

"Okay, maybe I shouldn't have done that. But it was just for a bit of fun…I wasn't trying to be offensive."

"Emmett, you were quite obviously hitting on Karen and being inappropriately suggestive, to the point where the client has put in a formal complaint about this incident. Any incident that involves an element of sexual misconduct is taken more seriously than a general complaint and for this reason, I can't let you work with this client. Can you please go and get anything that belongs to you from the stand and come back over here, please."

"Am I in trouble, then?"

"It's not good, I'm afraid. I've got no choice but to put you on a plane back to the UK this afternoon. You should phone Anita-O at the office to book a flight and arrange a pick-up from the airport. You might want to think about going to the office first, before going home; otherwise, this shit storm will only get bigger. Paul will want to talk to you about this sooner rather than later. We could potentially lose the account if Karen's boss gets involved so they are taking it very seriously back at the office."

---|---

As expected, Karen's manager Carlton Treswecki did get involved, firstly demanding an explanation from me, then from Geoff, one of the owners of Promosign. An intense workaholic in his mid-thirties originally from The Ukraine he never stayed in one place for more than a few seconds. So, I was surprised to see Carlton sitting with Karen at one of the tables on her exhibition stand, drinking coffee. Obviously, she was telling Carlton what a wanker Emmett had turned out to be…literally.

Shit…I didn't think an hour ago, that I'd be walking into such a frosty environment as this, I thought to myself.

"Hello Carlton, hello Karen, sorry to interrupt…" I began.

Carlton interjected, as expected, words laced with his thick accent. "Marco, what the hell is going on… I come down here this morning, expecting the utmost professionality, and Karen tells me that the stand manager from Promosign has got his sperm all over another exhibitor's screens…"

At any other time in my life, I would probably have wet myself laughing at this particularly as Karen's eyes widened momentarily. But not this time…I buried the bomb of laughter that was floating to the surface somewhere deep inside me and adopted my concerned-about-business expression.

"Yes, I understand it is incredibly inappropriate, and it's difficult to talk about, but I think that Emmett really thought he was just helping out…it's the manner in which he offered his services that leaves a lot to be desired," I said. "I have sent him back to London, as I don't think you, particularly you, Karen, would feel comfortable working with Emmet."

Karen nodded. "Thank you, Mark, who will manage the exhibition stand this week then?"

"I'm afraid I will have to be that person – sorry!" I said with a hint of self-deprecation, just to ease the tension in the atmosphere.

"I'm happy to hear that, but I will still have words with Geoffrey at your office…" said Carlton.

"Well, I can tell you that he is due to fly out here this afternoon. If you are around and free, maybe we can take you both for dinner this evening?"

Clients were always busy at these congresses, but Geoff, co-owner of Promosign considered himself to be something of an international professional diner and loved nothing better than taking clients to the best restaurants in town. It was not unusual for us to see him sign off restaurant bills of £2–3,000. Clearly, we needed to lavish attention on Biofurium so I called Geoff's assistant who made his dinner bookings; she said she would come back to me with a venue and a time.

"Very good, that sounds good." Carlton had calmed down considerably. "For now, let's just make sure we don't get any more sperms on our competitor's screens, huh, okay, Marco?"

"Yes, I agree with you, Carlton." I spluttered, almost choking on the words.

I knew exactly what he meant.

---|---

Despite my best efforts, I found it difficult to get along well with Deborah, Geoff's wife and founding partner of Promosign. She was very full of herself and I just thought that she was so aloof; she liked to think that she was super-intelligent, yet I never heard her say anything 'original' or something you couldn't get out of a textbook. She had a reputation for 'going psycho' when pushed beyond safe limits; I was always quite wary of saying the wrong thing in front of her. Or when her back was turned.

I had an idea that she might put in an appearance with Geoff in Lausanne that afternoon. She would occasionally appear if there was some crisis taking place. Maybe she had been told that she was good at finding satisfactory outcomes in difficult situations; she appeared to have believed them. I knew she was looking for problems that didn't exist by the way she rushed over to me and insincerely asked me how I was doing. Dinner that evening was entertaining. Geoff's assistant booked a table at an appropriately expensive Italian restaurant. Carlton ranted and raved for several minutes about the seriousness of the Emmett situation before Geoff managed to talk him around, making Carlton see that it was an extraordinary error of judgement on Emmett's part and that it was his personality that was responsible for this situation. They agreed that I had taken the most appropriate course of action in removing Emmett from the exhibition stand and flying him back to London. Fortunately, Paul (my boss) had managed to get to Geoff and Deborah before Carlton spoke with Geoff and therefore was able to give the owners of Promosign a heads up on what had occurred. Deborah made a point of sitting between Carlton and myself; I knew she wanted to quiz me on what had happened to check I had followed the appropriate procedures. I pointed out that there were no procedures for dealing with colleagues' sperm samples at high magnification; at least, not to my knowledge. Would it come under biohazards, I wondered? I told Deborah, somewhat sarcastically, that I'd be happy to draft something for the company's policies and procedures file.

Unfortunately, we had to let Emmett go from the company as it was agreed he was too much of a liability. It was difficult to make him see the error of his ways when sitting face-to-face with him after the congress in Lausanne. He just kept arguing the same points from his point of view. He wasn't able to see things from the client's perspective…for some reason, he couldn't see why this mattered so much. In addition, there was some concern over confidence in his abilities and trusting him to carry out the duties he had been assigned to whether alone or in a team environment. In the fragile world of Global Pharmaceutical Marketing, the competition was intense and huge sums of money exchanged hands with high levels of expectation attached to them, so it was deemed appropriate to minimise our level of risk exposure by making Emmett's position redundant.

Eleven

I have been fortunate to spend a lot of time in and around Rio de Janeiro, Brazil, for both personal and professional reasons. From a young age, having seen a photograph of the city in an atlas, I wondered if I would ever get the chance to visit what looked like 'Paradise on Earth'. I was enthralled by the beautiful looking beaches, the spellbinding clear azure blue of the ocean and the mountainous backdrop covered in tropical rainforest greenery.

Working at Promosign had given me a lot of opportunities to collect passport stamps at some fairly exotic and far-flung destinations, such as Hong Kong, New York and Vancouver to name but a few, but when the World Congress of Cardiology (WCC) was announced for April 1998, to be held in Rio de Janeiro, Brazil, everybody at Promosign wanted to go.

Professional people who took part in global medical congresses preferred going to congresses in destinations where the local population could benefit financially from an injection of cash into the local community, particularly when the divisions of poverty and wealth were clearly 'on display' This is the reason there are not many congresses in the tax havens of the world.

In the last few months of 1997, we were approached by a number of existing clients as well as several potential new clients to create exhibition stands to represent their company and relevant medical products at the WCC. Since the WCC was held once every five years, clients were willing to throw money at these projects to ensure they had a strong presence and were viewed as global leaders in their 'therapeutic areas of interest'. As a company, we had a strong reputation for creating highly 'interactive' exhibition stands. At Promosign, we had a multimedia division, the people in this part of the company were tasked with creating exciting and medically relevant interactive exhibition stand projects as well as stand alone projects.

We secured four exhibition stand projects and a hospitality suite/meeting area/media zone project. With the help of Helen, a junior account manager, I was preparing two exhibition stand projects, one for RPR and one for Schering. Both clients were unnecessarily demanding and challenging to work with in the months and weeks leading up to the WCC in Rio. The other exhibition stand projects were with BMS-sanofi and BMS USA. We had to be really careful about how we managed representing BMS-sanofi and RPR as they had competing products. This was handled by explaining to clients that each client is serviced by a bespoke team during the development of the project and there was no crossover or leakage of information. In addition to this the BMS USA project was handled by people in our office in New Jersey, USA.

I was tasked with overseeing the BMS-sanofi projects which included the WCC as I had been involved in the original sales pitch for the business. The design of this exhibition stand was the brainchild of Lynda, one of the senior designers at Promosign. It was more of a sculpture than an exhibition stand, with five-metre high intertwining tusk-like structures, that cost £25,000 for each pair to manufacture, using a complicated fibreglass process. Jerome, a middleweight Account Manager at Promosign handled the account with a great deal of expertise after we had won the business.

Along with Jerome and Helen, Cath, the BMS USA Account Manager, would be joining us in Rio de Janeiro, in addition to a team of designers from our UK office and a technician to set up and manage the computers, screens and content on the BMS-sanofi exhibition stand. To make life more entertaining, I had been having a turbulent 'relationship' with Cath for a few months, since she made the unusual transition from client-side to agency. We weren't exactly together, even though I'd agreed to the finance director's request that we share a hotel room at the WCC 'just to keep some costs down'. This didn't go down with Cath, who got on the phone to Cynthia (who was also the finance director at Promosign) and had a very terse conversation about her accommodation needs while in Rio, pointing out that the clients usually allocated rooms for the agency staff, because it cost a fraction of the regular rates.

---|---

The ideal first step in designing an exhibition stand on the scale that we were working to was to undertake a site visit to the venue, to look at the block of air that would one day be replaced by an expertly designed and constructed masterpiece of multi-density fibreboard and off-white paint. To put it in simple terms, a site visit is a form of insurance policy to review the exhibition space to identify anything that may have an impact on the design. This could be the column in the middle of your exhibition stand space which is not shown on the congress organiser's floorplan, or the position of electrical/running water supply outlets. Or there might be an overhead gantry that reduces the regular build height from five metres to three metres? The objective of the site visit is to identify anything that could pose a problem – as well as an opportunity – when it comes to installing the exhibition stand.

A good designer can see things that initially might pose a problem and spin it around to become an asset. At one congress in Berlin, just before I joined Promosign, it turned out that the organiser had failed to mark-up a concrete stairwell on the exhibition floorplan that reached the floor of the exhibition hall, in the middle of the client's exhibition space This was a major omission, so Promosign negotiated a deal to dress the entire stairwell in the client's brand colours, carpets and logos. The designer integrated the stairwell into the exhibition stand and cleverly channelled potential customers from the floor above, down the stairs and onto the exhibition stand where there were a team of hostesses promoting the client's exhibition product quiz. More hostesses worked the stairwell and floor above to maximise the number of visitors to the client's exhibition stand. By the end of the congress, over 95% of the registered doctors had visited this stand and taken part in the product quiz.

It naturally fell to me to undertake the site visit in Rio with Alec, one of the more experienced designers. I did my utmost to conceal my delight about going to Rio – in early January too, leaving the UK for a week in the middle of winter. We took business class flights to Rio with Lufthansa via Frankfurt on-board an Airbus A340 and arrived the following morning, appreciating the fact that we had left the European winter five or six thousand miles away. We went through customs and then picked up our gear in the arrivals hall. We had brought with us a regular video camera to record the site visit as well as a highly sophisticated camera which could show the exhibition stand design shown in situ as it would appear when installed at the venue. Clients loved this technology.

Alec and I had already had a chat about security and the fact that this was Rio and we were going to stick out like a sore thumb to any number of local thieves, who would think nothing of threatening you with a blade if you didn't handover the expensive camera hanging around your neck.

"But I'm not talking about these cameras," I said to Alec who was in the front passenger seat of the taxi that was driving us through the morning rush hour in Rio. I sat directly behind him, as he sat with the window wound down, his right arm balanced on the remaining inch of glass window that wouldn't wind down. The air blowing in through his window was deceptively cool and refreshing…the heat of the day hadn't arrived yet, but it was definitely in the post.

"What are you going on about, then, for fuck's sake?" he asked.

"Well, I read in the not-so-distant past that an air hostess wearing a Cartier watch and a diamond ring, travelling by taxi into Rio from the airport, much like we are now, pulled up at a red stop light with her arm out of the window, much like yours is now…when some thieving toe-rag ran up to the taxi, grabbed her arm and chopped it off with a machete, taking her watch and diamond ring…"

Alec turned to face me. "Are you fuckin' serious?"

"I never joke when there's a chance that limbs might be compromised," I told him, struggling to maintain a straight face. "You're not going to be much use to me out here unless you've got a full complement of arms and legs."

Alec wound the window back up at breakneck speed.

In less than thirty minutes, we had checked into our hotel rooms, changed into swimming shorts and tee-shirts, ordered some breakfast to the outdoor pool deck and jumped into the pool. Lush green rain forest covered rocky outcrops creating a tropical backdrop to the hotel, and beyond that one of Brazil's largest and most notorious Favelas came into sight. Across the road, the beachfront promenades were made up of patterned white and black stones and beyond that the beach, ocean, mountains and sky.

It was eight o'clock in the morning. Finally, after all these years, I had made it to my 'Paradise on Earth'…even if, technically speaking, I was at work.

---|---

We were due to meet the WCC organiser's exhibition manager the following morning at the venue and Jose from a company called Certame (an exhibition stand builder that we had used previously on a project in Argentina) the day after tomorrow. We had the day to explore some of Rio, which after breakfast meant Alec buying the loudest Rio de Janeiro t-shirt he could find, from one of the shops in the hotel. It was offensively loud…so loud in fact, that I couldn't find one to match or come anywhere close. "Fuckin' champion…" was all he had to say about his tee-shirt…he was from the North of England. I settled on a tee-shirt that was 'noisy' but it didn't make you want to spontaneously vomit, like Alec's. So much for our conversation about security and blending in. It had become clear to me over months of working with Alec that he couldn't string a sentence together without the word 'fuck' (or one of its derivatives) included in some way. For this reason, I tried to keep clients out of his vicinity as much as possible.

During the afternoon, we took a taxi directly to Sugarloaf Mountain, which was a spectacular way to see the city. Alec was like a small child, going from one side of the cable car to the other. With our tourist t-shirts on, we should have written 'Please Mug Us – We're English Tourists' on our foreheads, we looked like easy targets for would be thieves.

However, nobody at all ever approached us in a threatening manner in Rio. It might have been the fact that both Alec and I were both well over six-feet tall, maybe we looked like too much of a challenge. We didn't have obvious cameras or mobile phones hanging around our necks which might have made us a less than savoury choice to rob.

---|---

At the venue site visit the following day, we were amazed to find that the exhibition hall was essentially open air. It seemed crazy but the organiser told us that it meant the venue didn't want or need to pay for air conditioning, which would cost a small fortune in such enormous spaces. Air conditioning was left to the exhibitors to pay for – clearly, any exhibition stand with an air-conditioned meeting room was going to be a popular choice when the Rio daytime temperature soared to thirty-five degrees with 100% humidity. Working in that kind of heat was the only thing I wasn't looking forward to about this project; I was in shorts and a tee-shirt recording the site visit on the video camera and was sweating profusely. What would it be like with full-length trousers and a shirt on, managing the exhibition stands?

We used thick rolls of masking tape to identify the ground area and boundaries of the four exhibition stands that we were working on, so that clients would be able to see the space their exhibition stand would occupy in the video site visit report that we would prepare for them.

"I bet you get some big spiders in here, what with it being open air an' all," I said to Alec. I was still videoing him as he set up the other camera we had brought, which could show the individual exhibition designs in position at the venue…

"Spiders?" he exclaimed. "Where? I fuckin' hate spiders…"

I glanced up at the ceiling. "Up there…on the ceiling, I would imagine, crawling in from the Brazilian jungle to take shelter from tropical storms," I said. Sure enough, right above us on the six-metre high ceiling was a huge spider, at least the size of my palm.

"Jesus Christ, look at the size of that thing," I said, swinging the video camera upward to zoom in on the spider. With its eight black and yellow striped legs, it looked less than friendly. Alec tipped his head back, looking up from under his baseball cap.

"Fuck me sideways," he said in his gruff, northern tone. "That is fuckin' huge…I shit you not."

"Be careful, mate," I warned. "With that tee-shirt on, he can probably tell that you're not local, he might fancy a change from eating frogs and birds…and he looks like a jumper!"

"Fuck off, you're joking right?" he said nervously.

"Only telling you what I read in the immigration material on the plane…probably best not to stand directly underneath it, Alec, it might be hungry." Even though he was physically large, Alec was clearly perturbed by the Brazilian spider and could move quickly. Even though I was just winding him up, I wouldn't know a jumping spider from a crawling species so I made a point of avoiding the area directly below it. I marked the spot with a masking tape 'x'.

For dinner on our second evening in Rio, we made a reservation at a restaurant that was recommended by the hotel. It was a first-rate, table served, Brazilian barbeque restaurant. The trick is to go for the better cuts of meat, by sending away the early offerings. As we were finishing our meal, the heavens opened and we were treated to the sights and sounds of a tropical storm complete with a flash flood.

It happened so quickly; one minute we were chatting to the restaurant owner, the next we were looking at the rivers and lakes where there used to be roads and parks. The deluge continued to pound the streets of Rio – worryingly, there appeared to be fewer taxis operating than normal, and those that were still driving appeared not to be going in the general direction of our hotel.

Alec was getting paranoid; I was winding him up again. I told him about an article I'd read where a couple had been chopped up at a restaurant and put in the freezer, because they were having a disagreement about the bill. They were stopping the restaurant from closing. They were then fed to unsuspecting future customers as items off the menu.

I've never seen him look so relieved to see a taxi pull up outside the restaurant when finally the flood waters had subsided enough for normal traffic to resume.

---|---

As the WCC congress loomed closer, I started to get the feeling that this was going to be a very stormy ride. It was something of a poisoned chalice…yes, it was in a far-flung, somewhat mysterious destination. But I had enough experience to know that on difficult, intense projects, all you saw of the location was your hotel room, the taxi and then the congress venue.

The warning signs were written on the wall; both my clients seemed to have taken a personal dislike to me, for reasons better known to themselves. No matter what I actioned, I could get nothing positive back from the two clients.

The site visit had yielded no surprises, so there were no problems there. In fact, my manager, Paul, had another client who was going to be in Rio at the WCC, working on a product that was not in our remit. As they had not visited the venue, they were eager to see our video report. Paul began a meeting with this client and the marketing team at the client's office in Philadelphia and kicked off with our video footage of the WCC venue. However, Paul chose to use the unedited, raw footage of the venue and because he hadn't reviewed the footage himself, he was mortified when the camera swung upwards and zoomed in on a spider, accompanied by my colleague's and my highly vocal 'excited' commentary. Red-faced and embarrassed, Paul apologised about our colourful language; apparently, the client just laughed and congratulated Paul on having such a thorough site visit team.

---|---

Flying out to Rio wasn't as smooth going as it should have been. We all had business class tickets, but Jerome somehow managed to convince his driver that the flight was out of Terminal four at London's Heathrow Airport, when in fact the flight departed from the North Terminal of London's Gatwick Airport. So, my mobile phone started to buzz in my jacket chest pocket as my driver pulled into Gatwick.

"Jerome," I said. "How are you, mate?"

"I'm slightly delayed," he replied with uncharacteristic tension in his voice. "I thought the flight was from Heathrow, but I've since found out that it leaves from Gatwick, is that right?"

"Yes, didn't you check the itinerary?" I said. Stupid question, I thought, as I was getting out of the car. I scanned the drop off points for my colleagues; I could see a couple of the designers. "We are at Gatwick's North Terminal. Where are you?"

"Just leaving Heathrow," he said with a nervous laugh.

I rolled my eyes skywards. "Okay, well hopefully, you will get here in time to catch the flight...rush hour is over now, so you probably will be okay."

"I've also got a flat crate full of vinyl cut lettering and logos, that needs to go on as oversized luggage."

"How big is that then?" I questioned. This was typical on a large complex project or multiple projects. The designers always left the arranging production of logos and lettering until it was too late to put them on the truck/in the shipping crate with the rest of the exhibition stand materials. Invariably we ended up hand carrying the logos and lettering.

"Oh, it's about my height and width," he said.

"Does it weigh as much as you?" I asked sarcastically.

"Probably not far off, it's got a wooden frame, with plastic covering."

"That's going to cost a fortune to get on the plane," I said. "Okay, well, I'll wait for you at the drop off point."

Jerome arrived after forty-five minutes, looking somewhat flustered in his purple crushed velvet jacket. The crate was as long and wide as a coffin, but not as deep. Nonetheless, it cost almost £5,000, the price of a return business flight from London to Rio de Janeiro to put it on the plane.

The madness had started.

---|---

We had an on-call minibus taxi to ferry the whole team about in Rio. We hired a couple of 'mobile phones' in Rio that were in fact satellite phones; within two days we had run up charges of £10,000 and were told by the Finance Director at Promosign not to use them anymore. I can't say I was surprised – every time I saw Jerome speed walking through the exhibition hall he had one of the satellite phones glued to his ear. We were spending money like water, to the point where our company credit cards suddenly stopped working, while we were trying to buy essential services for the exhibition stands. On the other side of the exhibition hall, Cath was in tears trying to buy essential services for the BMS USA exhibition stand; she was trying to purchase electrical power to the exhibition stand but her credit cards, like everyone else's, would not allow us to complete a sale.

All of our company credit cards had been sensitized, mainly due to our satellite phone costs. None of our cards seemed to be working. I phoned the Promosign office and spoke with Cynthia the Finance Director, who told me she had just requested a complete release on the credit cards.

To make it a day to remember, Clara, the Head of Design, decided to take her troop of designers to a shopping mall to buy overpriced wastepaper baskets and penholders for the exhibition stands, when they should have been on site positioning logos and vinyl cut lettering. I was more than slightly annoyed with her when she told me that she'd taken the design team out to lunch and then to a beach afterwards, for a swim. Meanwhile, the rest of the team, who had been working long hours to get the exhibition stands ready for the congress remained working vigilantly. I told the Head of Design it was insensitive to take the design team out to lunch – particularly as it was company policy to have a designer on site to take responsibility for positioning all vinyl lettering and logos, which was needed at this time.

The exhibition stands were completed on the penultimate day of the installation period. This meant all we needed to do was clean and tidy the stand, get literature and promotional 'giveaways' into the storage facility on each stand and present each stand to its respective client, all of which we would do on the final day of the installation.

I'd heard about a bar in Rio called the Rock in Rio Café, which was loosely based on the well-known Hard Rock Café. I asked the concierge to book a couple of large tables for this evening. We were taking the four guys from Madex, who constructed the BMS-sanofi exhibition stand in London, shipped it to Rio and had flown out to install the exhibition stand. Like the Promosign agency staff, they enjoyed a drink or two…

Two hours into the evening and chaos had joined the party. The Rock in Rio Café was essentially a nightclub with an attached restaurant. The two tables I had reserved each had a beer tap in the centre of the table – a crazy idea. I swiped the card reader of both, which meant you could refresh your drink when your glass was empty – there was no need to go to the bar. The net effect of this was to make you drink as much beer as was humanly possible in as short a time as possible. On top of this, people (myself included) were drinking caipirinhas, a deceptively strong cocktail made from limes mixed with sugar cane spirit and crushed ice.

Chaos descended into carnage. There were comatose bodies of designers and account managers strewn around the Rock in Rio Café. People sat on the floor near the bathrooms blocking the entrance to the facilities, cradling their heads; no doubt, they were feeling the effects of excessive alcohol consumption. It was either that or they were thinking about how hard the following day was going to be with an almighty hangover. Nonetheless, a lot of people with legs that still functioned were enjoying themselves on the dancefloor.

Eventually, the Rock in Rio Café closed at some point in the small hours and their staff attempted to move us all out of the building, towards the taxi rank. I was with Cath, Lynda (one of the senior designers) and Jerome. Somewhere in the surrounding crowds were our colleagues. Although I had valiantly attempted to drink the bar dry, I was mostly craving sleep.

"Let's just sit down here for a minute," I said.

"Good idea – when this crowd has thinned out a bit, we'll get a cab," said Jerome.

---|---

Cath, Lynda, Jerome and I literally just sat down on the curb and passed out. When we eventually came around, it was impossible to know how long we had been sat there…but scarily – the entire area was deserted. The Rock in Rio Café was closed. We were sitting outside where earlier there had been a large crowd of people, who had been in the Rock in Rio Café and other places.

While we sat there, we became aware of a rapidly repeating, 'clicking' noise…rather like the sound that a tiny horse galloping towards us would have made. We stood up looking down the road towards where we thought the noise was coming from. We could make out something moving toward us…

It was a crab, scuttling along the road on its claws. It was a fairly large crab too, mostly red in colour. When it saw us, it stopped, reared up on its claws and raised its large front claws in defence.

"Where the hell did that come from?" asked Jerome.

"Well, we're not too far from the sea," I said as the crab lost interest in us and continued on its way. "I'm more concerned about where it's going…he's heading away from the sea."

Lynda spoke, "Look, let's walk down to that main road. I can see there's a petrol station, we might be able to get a taxi from there…"

"Yeah, let's get out of here, it's not a good idea to hang around out here…we could be murdered by a wide variety of people at any time," I said, feeling quite vulnerable all of a sudden.

We were out in the middle of nowhere and I really wanted to be back in the safety of our five-star hotel, so we walked briskly to the main road, which was the main route between Rio and Barra. It's one thing to be out in Rio's central district during the day but walking around these deserted suburbs at night is very unwise. As luck would have it, an empty taxi heading in the right direction came our way and pulled over, following some enthusiastic arm waving by all four of us.

We made it back to the hotel in one piece.

---|---

Despite the presence of many hangovers, at 10am the following day the team were on the minibus, ready to go and finalise the exhibition stands. Armed with antihangover coffee and therapeutic doughnuts, we began work.

Client materials were loaded onto shelves in the storage rooms. The surfaces were cleaned and the carpet protective plastic covering was cut away on each exhibition stand.

The client from RPR didn't come to the stand before the congress opening morning. I hoped and prayed that she didn't want any changes made, but she seemed happy enough with the exhibition stand. She even cracked a smile (which I would call 'progress'), I had started to think she was unable to achieve this. Her stand was quite straightforward, with a bunch of graphic panels, an air-conditioned meeting room and a coffee bar which was run by a couple of hostesses. One of these hostesses, Helena, was destined to become my girlfriend and eventually my fiancée. When we met on the exhibition stand, some might say there was chemistry between us…I would say it was pure electricity. We were drawn to each other like industrial magnets. Of course, we remained professional at all times, particularly as I was still involved with Cath, who was often close by.

The client from Schering continued to treat me with contempt, even while I showed her around her exhibition stand. But Helen, the junior Promosign account manager, was making progress with her and she seemed to be warming to Helen. *Best leave her to it,* I thought. *You can't expect everyone you meet is going to get along with you!*

The opening day of the congress was steady in terms of traffic around the exhibition hall. Usually this is the busiest day of the congress, but for some reason it never reached a point where we were running low on coffee, pens or fluffy toys. I was happy with this – I wasn't keen to hoist boxes of client literature around in thirty-degree heat.

---|---

It was close to midnight when the phone in our hotel room started to ring. It was Jerome but something was wrong. His voice was trembling.

"Jerome, what's the matter?" I asked. "Are you alright?"

"Just about," he said. "I just got mugged out on the street in the Copacabana night market."

"Are you hurt?"

"No, but they took my wallet, my UK phone and my passport. I managed to keep my briefcase and satellite phone."

"I suppose you were wearing a suit as well?"

"No – well, not really, my velvet jacket. I just had dinner with my client and couldn't get a taxi, so I thought I'd walk back to my hotel."

"This is what I was saying, we should all be trying to blend in, don't make yourself a target." I sighed. "We'll need to go to the embassy tomorrow to get a new passport…have you cancelled your cards? Your personal cards?"

"Yes, I have. Look," he began, "I can go to the embassy alone, no point you wasting your morning too."

"Fine," I said. "Just as long as you're okay, mate."

"I'm okay, thanks, just a bit shook up, that's all."

---|---

The following evening, it was Michael the exhibition stand technician's turn to get mugged. His assailants were a midget and an eight-foot high, stilted man; Michael barely made it to five-feet high but he towered over the midget. The stilted man occupied Michael's attention by grabbing the technician's genitals, while the midget went straight for his pockets and pulled his wallet. It happened at the Copacabana Night Market again, where Jerome had fallen victim to street thieves the night before.

Twelve

It was the last night in Rio for most of the team, Cath and I had booked to stay a couple of extra nights at the hotel. We needed a break. The projects in Rio had surpassed the clients' expectations so it was seen to be a great success. But we were exhausted. It was on this weekend stayover that I experienced what I believe to be one of the early signs that I was developing Parkinson's Disease.

For the last couple of years, from early 1996 onwards, which was around the time that I started working at Promosign, every few months I would go down with a bout of extreme depression. Happening every 4–6 months without warning, it took my mood down to levels beyond rock bottom. I was never able to identify a 'trigger' for these episodes but the symptoms were really debilitating. I could barely develop the motivation to move while the depression was at its most intense. Then, after a couple of days into the episode it was gone, leaving me with an intense headache for a day or two afterwards.

Cath attempted to ruin our weekend by describing what she could see in me. "You know, to me it looks like some kind of depression, you are in such a negative space…" I asked her to stop stating the bleedin' obvious, it was only adding to the burden of what I was trying to claw my way out of.

Promosign staff were very sociable, so I socialised with them often. On one occasion, I was suffering with one of my depression episodes but I had agreed to go to the cinema as planned, despite wanting to go home and stick my head in bucket full of iced water. I sat through the entire movie, just staring at the screen, not really sure what was going on, not taking it in. By the end of the movie, I could not tell you what the general plot was, or its name.

The movie was 'Independence Day', where aliens attempt to take over the world. It could have been 'Singing in the Rain' with Frank Sinatra; in my current state of depression, I wouldn't have known the difference.

---|---

With my diagnosis confirmed as 'Adult Early Onset Idiopathic Parkinson's Disease' surprisingly, there came a 'sense of relief'. The period of time that I was unsure of what was going on, had now been and gone. At least now I was aware of what my internal adversary, was, what it had already done to bring my condition to the state I was in, and I knew roughly what the future 'might' look like. Even if it was tough to look at my possible future, it had to be done because I knew I could do one of two things and these were pretty much the only options I had:

- I could give up and let it consume me, letting myself go and throw the towel in conceding defeat.

Or

- I could face it and become resilient to the onslaught of my adversary, resisting all its efforts to take over control of my life.

I didn't really have much of a say in the matter; my future had already been decided. I had nothing to give up with; I didn't have and still don't have a couple of million GB pounds lying around that could pretty much see me through if I used the money carefully and didn't buy too many Ferraris. The only way I could think of getting my hands on that amount of money would be if I won the lottery. However, since I rarely bought lottery tickets I think my chances were significantly lower than regular lottery players.

So that was it; I was going to have to lace up my gloves and get stuck into the fight.

Sometime after my diagnosis, I found myself living in a 'state of denial'. I tried to trick myself into believing that this was all a hoax, albeit an elaborate one. I tried to make myself believe that because my symptoms were reasonably mild at the moment, they would always be that way. Living in denial was just a coping mechanism – I was just treading water, keeping my hair dry – mostly, anyway. It gave me some 'time out' from the condition and allowed me to formulate a 'plan of sorts' that I could use in protecting myself, most of which was built upon the need to keep a positive outlook. But the psychological battle in the early weeks, months and years was relentless. PD never let me put much distance between us and if I did for one moment forget that I had PD, it was always there, ready to jump back into the front of my awareness:

"Don't forget you've got PD, you don't deserve to have nice thoughts – you've got to put me before everything else in your life – and if you don't, well, I'm never going to let you forget I'm here so you had better start getting used to it…"

It wasn't just nice thoughts that I wanted to have; I wanted to have a productive and worthwhile existence in my employment. I had no time for this game of cat and mouse, being made to feel guilty and undeserving of a pleasant thought about an upcoming event, or a positive thought to do with work. But with thoughts like these continually popping up in front of my eyes I began to wonder if there was enough brain capacity for both PD and what I needed to be successful in my work? Could I work around this madness and retain my own precious sanity in order for me to do my job to the requisite level?

Living in denial is the best route that I could take given the circumstances, in order to 're-live life before PD' and introduce the sense of a 'life of normality' that this brings. It allowed me to tell certain people that I had PD, in a certain way; I would tell close friends in a very casual, off-hand way. For instance, as I was driving, pulling away from the stoplights, I would say something like, "Oh, by the way, you know those tests I was going for? Yeah, turns out I have Parkinson's Disease…" Like I'd overlooked some detail or another and then try and move the conversation off onto a different subject.

My theory was that if I can show that I'm not too worried about having PD, treat it like I had no time for it and it was just a minor inconvenience that I had no time for, then hopefully my friends wouldn't be too concerned about my diagnosis. But then, I'd forgotten – many of my friends were in healthcare communications and many of them were a great deal more intelligent than me; it was obvious that I was having difficulty facing this condition. Perhaps some of my friends had direct experience working with people who have PD, or maybe they were working on a drug for the treatment of symptoms of PD. But mostly they were just concerned with how I had delivered this important news, in such an off-hand, casual way, which had all the hallmarks of living in denial stamped right across it.

By living in denial, I was attempting to try and convince myself that this wasn't such a big deal after all, and that the condition wouldn't interfere with my life. The pressure would never get to a level where I would crack. I could continue with my lifestyle, one that I had worked so hard to create. I had a very immature approach to the condition, when really, I should have been taking it a lot more seriously.

The truth of the matter is that I was embarrassed having developed a condition that was usually seen in the elderly. 'Parkinson's Disease – isn't that a disease old people get? Why had I been given a disease that old people get? Something had gone wrong somewhere – I had just turned thirty, not sixty! From an employer's point of view, would they feel like they were recruiting someone who on paper was thirty years old, in a sixty-year-old body? Would I have the stamina to do my job?

PD made me feel vulnerable on so many different levels. Ultimately, I felt like a failure, like I had missed boarding the boat to an ordinary, happy life by milliseconds of it pushing away from the dock and now it was impossible to get on it. So near yet so devastatingly far, I felt like I had brought my family name into disrepute, as if I had personally failed my parents. This was part of the reason why I didn't – or couldn't – tell my parents for three months following my diagnosis. I was scared how they would react to this news; the last thing I wanted to occur was for them to feel responsible for and think that they had given me PD (even though at the time of my diagnosis, there was little evidence for PD being a hereditary, genetic condition). But being a parent myself, when you love your child as much as I love mine, you would do anything to remove something that has a negative impact on their life.

Perhaps one of the worst ways that PD made me feel about myself, was that I was unworthy of happiness, satisfaction and that I was unworthy of being in the company of other people who didn't have PD…like I was a fake and I didn't possess the right to share their company, I didn't belong, I was isolated, almost segregated. This doesn't surprise me; dopamine is a pre-cursor to some of the brain's 'happy molecules'. It makes sound scientific sense that a reduction in dopamine should result in fewer of these happy molecules knocking around and consequently with PD in full swing, you are going to feel less happy, more of the time.

But the feelings of unworthiness and social isolation, being so much more than straightforward happiness like I have nothing to contribute to this life, cut really deep. At this point in my life I had managed to surround myself with a circle of friends that I felt were on my wavelength. These feelings of social isolation made it difficult, or more stressful whenever I was introduced to someone I haven't met before; as well as this I used to have severe anxiety when surrounded by crowds of people, such as at busy train stations.

The anxiety would affect me so rapidly that I would literally 'freeze' on the spot and I could be stuck there for any amount of time until I could call someone who would 'walk me out' of my frozen state. It should be noted that the feelings of unworthiness, social isolation and anxiety, were at their worst when I was finding it difficult to control my PD with oral medication as well as before I started to take medication, in the early months and years after diagnosis. The consequence of not being able to control my PD and the symptoms I experienced with oral medication meant that in 2012, I underwent Deep Brain Stimulation surgery as a more permanent means of symptomatic control of my PD; without doubt, this had a positive effect on these negative feelings of unworthiness and social isolation. I cannot recall a complete 'freezing up' episode this side of the DBS procedure.

---|---

When I joined Promosign, my line manager Paul was the account handler for what became one of the largest accounts handled by the agency. He had developed this account over a couple of years picking up a project or two from different divisions at the client's marketing headquarters on the East Coast of the USA, which, by proving we could deliver a first-class service turned into another five or six projects, maybe more. He had demonstrated the agency's key strengths: excellence in design and superlative project management. Clients were very happy with the efforts of Paul and the team working with him.

It is fair to say that most project managers and account handlers enjoy the early stages of a given project the most – matching the needs and objectives of a client, coming up with a few very strong ideas that meet the brief and delivering these ideas to the client – for us, this is the 'fun time' of the project. From the point of view of a designer, there is no doubt that working up their designs so that they become more than figments of their imagination is the motivating force behind the designer, these are the 'good times' for the designer. They have the challenge of constructing something which looks a lot like what was presented to the client in the recommendation meeting, where the original design was sold to the client. This is still an interesting part of the project for account handlers and project managers – there are usually a few challenges that need to be overcome, just to make sure the project can be delivered on time.

Once the installation of the client's exhibition stand is complete, it is in the hands of the Project Manager to provide the client with on-site management of the exhibition stand. This can be the toughest part of the project through lack of tasks to complete. It is hard on the brain, hard on the feet…just, well…hard.

---|---

"If I never have to set foot on another exhibition stand again, it will be too soon," Paul said, stamping his feet back to life on the carpet area of his client's exhibition stand. We were at the European Congress of Clinical Oncology, in Vienna. It was rare to see Paul doing stand duty, he only did it a couple of times a year, just to keep in touch with one or two clients. I was managing the exhibition stand of another client.

"My feet are killing me. Come on, Marco, let's go and get a cup of tea over at the message centre and have a sit down."

We were bored out of our minds. The 'thrill' of being in charge of exhibition stands that were fairly passive and not really all that active had long since passed. Even managing stands that were highly active, with multimedia stations scattered around didn't hold that much more interest for us because by the time the multimedia content was signed off, we would have viewed the entire content at least ten to fifteen times, meaning it wasn't new to us. Good for the doctors…and that's what drove us forward, seeing all that fantastic information end up in the right brains of the people who can act on it and perform acts of medicine that were akin to miracles.

Paul yawned and stretched his arms above his head. I stifled a yawn.

"You know," said Paul. "When we were bored doing the old stand duty gigs we used to take full advantage of the Doctors' Message Centre, create some fictitious names and messages…you up for that?"

"Bloody right I am," I said. I could feel my brain suddenly whirring back to life.

"The trick is not to write too many and keep them quite succinct," Paul said.

On the table where we were sitting there were some blank message cards and a pot of small pens. We sat and pondered for a while.

"Okay, here goes," I said. I wrote:

DR R SCLOUD, MEET ME UNDER THE BIG COCK AT 5PM TODAY. FROM:
DR BEN E FITZ,

"BRILLIANT! Love the misspelt 'CLOCK'. Look – I've got one," Paul said.

DR FRANKENFART, YOUR WIFE HAS BEEN ARRESTED FOR BREAKING THE WIND – PLEASE CALL THE HOUSE IN HAMBURG – THANK YOU. DR BUMRUSH.

There was a tray in the message centre where Paul was told to place message cards. He came and sat down next to me so he didn't have his back to the message board on the large LCD screen. We waited like two thirteen-year old boys who had just set up the biggest prank ever on their teacher. It was the most excited we'd been all week, which may go some way to explaining how mentally challenging exhibition stand duty can be.

Ten minutes went by, without a message being posted.

Then, PING!

The message board pinged and scrolled down to reveal Paul's message.

DR FRANKENFART...

We were trying not to laugh too hard so as not to draw attention to ourselves...the message centre staff had actually misspelt Dr Bumrush as Dr Bumbrush, which we thought was even funnier than the original message.

Another PING!

DR R SCLOUD...

The board pinged again, scrolled down and there was my message, from Dr R Scloud complete with a misspelt 'CLOCK'.

One idea that Paul's client had embraced was the free postcard, mailed to anywhere in the world. So, several months prior to the congress in Vienna, Paul briefed one of the graphic designers to develop some ideas for a post card that could be sent from the exhibition stand in Vienna. Development of this promotional item would often take up to four-five months from start to finish, because lots of people in the client's office wanted to be involved. Anyone would think that this was a major strategic element of the client's global marketing campaign, with the amount of time spent working on it, both on our side and at the client's office. It would include pictures of well-known landmarks in Vienna; on the reverse, there was a space for a message and to write the address to where you wanted to send it. At the end of the congress, Paul took the postcards back to the Promosign offices, where they were marked 'Postage Paid', and then mailed out around the world.

Now and then, Paul and I would go into the storeroom on the exhibition stand to check on how many postcards had been written and to check that the address had been completed with a country – those that had no country written had to be removed, unless the country could be ascertained from the senders written message.

On many occasions, we noticed that people sometimes left the message section blank. We thought that's a shame, it would be nice for the recipient to know what the sender was up to in Vienna. So, we would pick an occasional card with no message and pen a brief note to give the recipient a bit more information, along the lines of:

Dear Mother,
Freezing my nutz off in Vienna,
Love from your son

Dear Casper,
Just wiping my arse on the curtains in my hotel room. Adios!

We only did this for a handful of cards. It would have been a bit too risky to do it on too many postcards. We didn't want the client to go looking through the postcards only to come across our supplementary messages for the recipient.

They were just a bit cheeky; on some, we just drew a smiley face. All very juvenile behaviour for grown men, in positions of responsibility, who are supposed to be setting a good example, I wouldn't disagree. But you need a sense of humour with this kind of work and some mechanism for just getting through it. It was just another way of dealing with the long, tedious hours of exhibition stand management and it didn't cause anyone any harm.

Thirteen

It is not an easy task to estimate the amount of time that I spent 'living in denial' following my diagnosis. Going into and coming out of a frame of mind such as this doesn't happen overnight or by the flick of a switch. The boundaries between the period of initial shock following diagnosis, this period of 'living in denial' and the anger, the negative energy that followed are subject to much cross-over; so much so that it is difficult to give accurate estimates. These periods of time are likely to be individual to people with PD – just as everyone who has PD has experiences that are unique to them, periods of time of duration of these experiences will vary from person to person. I estimate that I spent around a year to eighteen months 'living in denial' about my condition, pretending, trying to convince myself that it would not have a detrimental effect on my life. Finally, I arrived at a place where I realised that nobody is answering the 'impossible to answer' questions that were continually running around in my head, such as:

- Why me? Why have I got PD?
- Why have I got this particular condition?
- What have I done to deserve getting this condition? It's so unfair.
- Why have I got PD while I am so young? I should be enjoying being in the prime of my life…

At this point, I was extremely frustrated with everything and everyone around me. I began to 'block out' people in my life: parents, friends, doctors, work colleagues simply because they were unable to provide answers to the unanswerable questions.

Anger takes over from denial in a pointless quest to try and uncover the answers. I would lose patience with close members of my family because I was frustrated that I could not answer the same questions that they were asking of me. I shunned attention from many of my friends; I felt vulnerable through being so angry with the way my life was going, so I shut down on many friends, making exceptions for the few that I knew I could trust and depend upon come hell or high water. At meetings with the Prof, in London, I would let my frustrations disperse to anger and on more than one occasion I stormed out of the meeting with the Prof, when he asked a simple question such as, "What meds are you currently taking?" Usually muttering, under my breath., "You should know for Christ's sake – you prescribed them…" As time went on, I had to take either my girlfriend of the time or a close friend to these meetings because I wasn't really paying attention to what he was saying. My exceptional friend Hils often went to these meetings with me, because I knew I could depend on her to pick up on anything important while I simmered away in the juices of my own anger and frustration.

Close family, friends, doctors – we are in each other's lives for mutual benefit. If I rant and rave, if I offend anybody in these groups, they have varying levels of awareness and understanding of my situation and are therefore likely to be more forgiving; I can depend on them not to take it personally. It's me – but I am just venting steam. Obviously, this is because they know me at an emotional level.

When it comes to work colleagues, things may be slightly different. Their awareness of my personal situation may be completely different from close family, friends and doctors; they may be inclined to be less forgiving in the event of an angry outburst or disagreement concerning a work-related matter.

At Promosign, my personality was often described as 'being similar to that of a smouldering volcano in the corner of the room, occasionally belching a puff of smoke or lava…' Loosely interpreted, this meant that I was perceived as being difficult or scary to approach, hot-headed and likely to bite your head off without a moment's notice. As time and my career progressed, I discovered I had a 'willingness' or 'a lack of fear' to challenge various individuals' point of view if I believed that there was a more effective way to get a message across. However, I think my passion for the work I was doing was often mistaken for anger, irritation and a general feeling that I would pursue what I wanted to pursue, on behalf of my clients. This was the 'recklessness' within my personality coming through in my work – a product of the anger I felt. If you are a challenge to work with in a close environment, such as on an exhibition stand installation, where you may be depending on various team members to support you with input from their own area of expertise, you need to have these guys on your side, ready, willing and able to work their collective butts off for you; otherwise, up go the metaphorical brick walls and there is a potential lack of co-operation. Of course, they are paid to do their job but I would rather they arrive motivated to work and feel like they are an instrumental part of the team.

---|---

Anger is exhausting. It is all negative energy. I found solace in offloading this negative energy by screaming into a bunch of pillows – a great way to clear all the negativity out but it takes up time. After half an hour of this 'therapy' I felt refreshed, renewed, almost cleansed; ready to go again.

For me, in order to get the upper hand on PD, it was critical that I was able to co-exist with the condition in some way. I needed to find a place where I could lay down the anger and frustration that I felt. I had to finally accept that PD was very much a part of me and the sooner I was able to come to terms with this, the better. But it wasn't easy to let the anger go – it helped keep the barriers of self-protection up; finally, when I did let the anger go, I felt better because of the feeling of calm that followed, which I felt was the beginning of 'Acceptance of PD'. I felt really in touch with my physical and mental beings – I was so aware of my body's mechanisms, I felt like I knew myself with a great deal more intimacy. Sound familiar?

For the first time in a long time, I started to feel something I hadn't felt since before my diagnosis – contentment and happiness – where once all I had felt was stress and pain. Motivation and some trepidation, but in general I could feel positive. Now was the time to stop fighting with PD; I knew I could achieve more by accommodating and accepting PD rather than battling with it.

---|---

Promosign was always a stressful company to work for; there seemed to be an undercurrent of low-level stress at all times. To my mind, this is what drove people to do well and put in a ridiculous number of hours in the name of multi-density fibreboard and off-white eggshell emulsion paint. It was almost like an invisible conveyor-belt; every morning you just latched on to the conveyor-belt and dealt with issues as they arose. There was no shortage of issues to deal with;

in a company the size of Promosign, there could be between ten to fifteen exhibition stands in various stages of development. The company employed so many people who smoked cigarettes and drank alcohol with gay abandon; at last…a place where I could belong.

How the exhibition stand designers loved to use off-white eggshell paint! In the UK, eggshell translates to a certain texture of finish, not as dull as matt, not as reflective as gloss…but somewhere in the middle, like a muted satin finish, with a slightly leather-like dry texture. Hong Kong was where I worked on one particularly fraught project for my main client MHP Health; eggshell finish literally meant eggshell texture. Before our arrival in South East Asia, the painters from the local exhibition build company added two hundred emptied eggshells to a fifty litre bucket of white emulsion and crushed the eggshells up with the paint with the help of an electric mixer. When the paint was applied to the exhibition stand, the eggshells became razor sharp particles adorning the entire surface of the exhibition stand. After it had dried, eggshell paint (Hong Kong style) was probably capable of removing skin just by dragging the back of your hand over a painted surface. When the exhibit designer and I arrived at the venue, I watched the blood drain from her face as she realised where her instructions had got 'lost in translation'.

It didn't help that shortly after we arrived, fresh from the airplane, a co-worker of my client in New York, appeared on the exhibition stand with his 'secretary' and began asking awkward questions, such as why was the wall so rough, to which I said, "Have you never painted a wall with primer and undercoat before?" knowing full well that he hadn't. I asked him and his 'secretary' to come off the stand, behind the tape barrier as it was still a live construction site, a request which they chose to ignore.

Then, while he was reading the product graphic panels on the stand, she managed to walk into a wet wall of white paint which showed up well on her red dress. When asked what I was going to do about it, I reminded him that I had asked him and his secretary to vacate the stand, as it was still a 'live' construction site, less than five minutes before she became at one with the freshly painted wall. I pointed out, with slightly more than a trace of sarcasm that I had forgotten to pack my emergency laundry kit, which went right over his head and didn't register. I suggested she kept the paint stain wet until she could get back to her hotel and let the hotel staff find a good cleaner, it was only emulsion after all.

After a heated discussion between Lynda, the Promosign exhibit designer and the boss of the local stand construction company ten men appeared on the stand with rotary sanders and proceeded to remove the surprisingly resilient eggshell finish of the exhibition stand (which by now I had re-named to Shark's Tooth finish). Following this, another ten men in white painter's overalls appeared with rollers, brushes and a new bucket of white emulsion paint devoid of eggshells. An hour later and the exhibition stand gleamed with a smooth all-over white finish.

Then one of the local construction crew managed to cut a finger clean off his hand, by getting too close to the business end of an electric rotating saw. Like we needed more drama on the exhibition stand. The entire crew disappeared in the direction of the hospital with the unfortunate victim. Why it took upwards of twenty-five men to help one man and one severed finger get to the hospital safely, I'll never know. I guess that is just the way things are done around here.

"That was a close call," I said to Lynda.

"I know," she replied. "He could have cut off more fingers if that saw had slipped any further."

I looked at her, a confused expression on my face. "No," I said, "I mean, if that had happened ten minutes earlier, we'd have been left with a half painted exhibition stand, with some walls still displaying your Shark's Tooth finish."

The entire crew were gone for the better part of two hours while their colleague's digit was re-attached in its original position. It was one of the more surreal examples of committed co-worker support I had ever witnessed.

---|---

People who claim they work at their best when under pressure and stressed out give me reason to laugh. I wonder if they truly understand what effect it has upon you to be in such a lonely, helpless place – stressed out and under pressure.

My client had booked the central exhibit space at an international chemotherapy congress in Lausanne. This was the first congress of the year for my client, the launch vehicle of a new product and we needed to create an exhibition stand that was 'all-singing, all-dancing, bells and whistles; turbo charged Disney'. An exhibition stand which positioned my client's company above and beyond that of any competition.

At the time, MHP Health was the second largest pharmaceutical company in the world. We called the exhibition stand The MHP Health Quiz Arena. Five contestants at a time sat at a screen and questions were fired at them. They could click on the screen to select their answer. Crowds gathered around the stand to watch the interactive robot, SICO who hosted the gameplay. The questions that were fired at contestants were shown upon the big screen, increasing the interactivity with the crowd. Housed within a contemporary exhibition design The MHP Health Quiz Arena was an instant success with long queues of people waiting for a turn.

What made the project such a big success was the cutting edge, futuristic materials used on the exhibition stand, coupled with extraordinary levels of interactivity. Graphic panels had multiple layers bolted together to give depth and created another dimension. The interactive robot SICO already had a long association with MHP Health and helped position the company as one to explore the future with.

This is what the client saw: their brand-new centrepiece for the exhibition, representing the company as a forward-thinking leader in healthcare.

In actual fact, the whole thing was held together on a wing and a prayer. While the exhibition stand itself was sound, the interactive multimedia was far from working as it should. At 9pm, with twelve hours to go before the official opening of the congress, we had to move rapidly to a hastily made plan B, because the computers which created this interactive wonder were still not communicating with each other correctly. For four days of the installation, I stood around on the exhibition floor watching the programmers and technical support staff struggle, trying to make the Quiz Arena work.

I sighed deeply. If there was going to be a problem on-site it seemed it was always the technology side of our business that caused so many sleepless nights. Plus, I never knew exactly what the problems were, just that it 'wasn't working properly yet'. The technician, Sara, would give me half an explanation, while I read her the full riot act.

"I'm telling you, Sara, if you haven't been shooting straight dice with me, and this multimedia fails to work how it should do, heads are going to roll," I said. "You guys have had three months to get this to work and yet here we are, the night before the congress opens and none of it is working." Steam and hot gases vented from the caldera of the volcano.

"It's a programming issue, Marco."

"It's always a bloody programming issue, Sara." I fired back at her.

I had been led to believe that this program would be flawless as it really wasn't that complicated. You have one large central screen, five remote screens. Contestants enter their name and country. Five product or disease related questions appear on the screens, one after the other; when everyone had answered question one, the computers would store the correct or incorrect answers and then move on to question two. At the end of the five rounds, the player with the highest score wins and this is flashed up on the big screen. The computers then reset to the name and country screen, so in theory, the system could run itself. MHP Health had some Swiss Army Penknives made up for each winner with the company logo printed on them, each in a presentation box. This was one of the reasons why the popularity of the MHP Health Quiz Arena was so high. The winner was selected from those who gave the correct answers in the shortest time.

However, as was the norm with Promosign multimedia, too much had been left until it was too late. It was bad time management on the part of the producers. Add to this the fact that various people had 'tinkered' with the programming and I began to understand why we had a dog's dinner on our hands. Over promising and under delivering.

Jules had been trying to sort it out for the past four days. He'd hardly left his room since arriving in Lausanne.

"The elements all work fine on their own but connect them together and they just don't want to play," he said. "We might have to resort to running it all manually, which is going to be very labour intensive."

"But to the client it would look like it was working correctly?" I asked.

"Yes – more or less."

"Okay, let's say we go for the full manual version – what would this involve?"

"Well, I'd be handling the master computer, getting it to pick questions at random, advancing the screens and making it look like it was automated. Sara would help to let me know when the contestants had all answered the questions, telling me who answered which questions. Sara and I will communicate with these headsets, so we can be discrete. Hank, the robot guy would need to be in on it, so he can whip the crowd up, keep them amused."

He paused. "I know it's far from ideal but it's our most convincing option, I think."

"Okay," I said. I turned to Sara. "Are you – and Sara – confident that you can pull this off?"

"No!" Jules laughed. "Oh, we'll give it our best shot. I'm sure we can handle it. It'll be an interesting few days!"

"Sara, are you up for this?" I asked.

She nodded her head. "Yes, no problem."

"By the way, Hank just showed up," I said. "He said he'd wait to see us down in the hotel lobby, he knows there are issues with the technology but I told him to keep a lid on it if he planned to run SICO around the lobby, interrogating hotel guests…"

In the dark is one of the worst places you can attempt to put me, especially when I am directly responsible to the client. I'm much more approachable and unlikely to spit brimstone and fire if I know everything I need to know. I was still quite annoyed that the multimedia guys had spent three months putting together a program that was not working and was beyond repair in the four installation days leading up to the congress.

"If I make it through the next four days and manage to hold it all together, it will be a miracle," I said to myself as I got ready for the opening morning of the congress.

---|---

Stress is one of the biggest issues that I have to deal with. Since PD is a condition that can be seen by people who are observing you, anything that exacerbates my PD is going to be seen by other people. This is something of a vicious cycle, whereby increasing stress increases the effect of PD on my body. It is related to the 'Fight or Flight' response in stressful situations; this occurs when the dopamine in your body turns to adrenaline, allowing you to get ready to 'escape'; the problem at this point is that there is no dopamine with which to make your muscles contract and take flight.

In this situation, I just go rigid, as I have done in Central Station, Sydney on more than a few occasions. I don't really get the shakes like a lot of people with PD – I guess that is one thing to be thankful for. Actually, that is not exactly true. I do tend to find that performing tasks which require flexible finger movement, such as doing up shoelaces, whether they are mine or someone else's often results in a mild tremor in the hands. Which is why I taught my daughter to tie her own shoelaces from a young age.

Fourteen

I often used to ponder the following question, mostly when I was learning to accept that I had PD:

- *If PD was a human being what or who would he or she be?*

To answer this question, I needed to evaluate what PD is to me, what lies at the very core of PD, how it exerts its effect, exactly what that effect is and what are you left with as a result of this. This is not an easy task to complete because it is easy to lose focus and end up wandering off along a particular train of thought; this may or may not help with the overall objective of identifying character traits of PD.

I think, in these words, in this book, this is the furthest I have got with this evaluation since my diagnosis. It certainly wouldn't have been something that I could attempt to complete rationally in those days of 'living in denial' or in the 'days of anger'. I was probably too scared to initiate any deep, meaningful thought processes for fear of unlocking more of the hidden strength that PD may have wished to express on myself and end up losing another few billion brain cells – just out of curiosity of trying to understand the nature of my condition. Hence, the need for an accepting and calm mind to work through this.

In many ways, I have done this type of exercise time after time with the brands I had helped create and deliver when I was working in advertising. In order to identify the core of the brand, the intrinsic reason for its existence, the brand team would undertake a workshop to evaluate *the brand essence*.

To start the process, we would identify the rational features of the brand and what rational benefits this brought to the end-user (bearing in mind that I was in healthcare advertising and for promoting prescription only medications the end-user was the patient, but *the decision-maker was the doctor*). This would then give way to identifying the emotional benefits that the brand can offer and, if you think about someone delivering these emotional benefits, what sort of character traits would this person have in order to fulfil these? In doing this, we have identified the brand character. The hardest part, as is often the case, is the most rewarding part of this process.

To arrive at the brand essence you simmer down, in your advertising saucepan, all these revelations into what is called the brand essence – this is the intrinsic core of the brand, the reason for its existence. The idea is that the brand essence aims to be between one and three words long; any longer than that and the creative teams working on ideas for representing this brand would not be focused enough on what the brands unique offering is. To reduce the chances of this happening, some people in the industry recommend that the brand essence needs to be 'one word'.

For me, if that happened as a natural outcome of the process, all well and good…but I would rather not have any 'must be' restrictions applied to such an important creative process. If someone suggested a six-word brand essence and felt very strongly about it, I would ask them to convince me and the team that this was the way to go. Finally, the brand essence should be something that runs for the duration of the brand's lifetime; we would say, "It's got to have legs…"

---|---

I feel that I have spent years evaluating all aspects of how PD has affected me, my life and the people who have been and those who still are close to me. Then I re-evaluated my original findings and re-evaluated my re-evaluations, and so on…you get the idea. However, the thoughts and feelings I have discovered over the years do *fit nicely* into my Brand Essence Workshop evaluation template. With a few adjustments it has helped me uncover what I feel are the character traits of PD and what the very essence of PD is, from my own perspective.

In the evaluation that follows, you may agree and/or disagree with some of the outcomes. This is fine; there are no wrong answers because everyone's experience of PD is totally unique to each individual. If everyone who reads this does this evaluation out of interest, I would be shocked if there were any evaluations which were 100% copies of each other!

Rational Features of PD

- Destroys dopamine producing cells in the brain
- Can lead to patient experiencing slowness of movement
- Slower to advance in the younger patient
- Cognitive function may suffer as a result of having PD

Rational Impact of PD Features on Patient

- Takes longer to perform tasks, such as showering, getting dressed etc.
- Lack of control of what is happening to your body, including changes to gait (walking pattern) and other 'involuntary physical activities'.
- Some people with PD may experience changes in cognitive ability.
- Gets tired sooner, both physically and mentally.

Emotional Impact of PD on Patient

- Frustration and anger because simple actions or tasks take so much longer to complete/may not be completed.
- Feelings of isolation from society, that you are different in a negative way, the shame and embarrassment you feel when people recognise that you have a medical condition.
- Eats away at your confidence, self-esteem and your self-worth; plays to your self-limitations, tries to limit your ability to aim for your goals in life.
- PD never lets you forget that it is always there, lurking in the recesses of your mind, you can never let it take control.
- PD takes time from your life that is not possible to get back, it is non-negotiable.

Character Traits of PD

- Unsympathetic, restrictive, laughing at you when your back is turned, stealing time from your life, relentless, destructive, mocking, ruthless, assassin-like, darkness.

Essence of PD

Time Thief

Central to the essence of PD is the fact that if you have this condition, it is going to slow you down; it is non-negotiable in this aspect. As a consequence, this means that performing tasks, whether it is simply pulling on your coat or trying to achieve one of your life goals by climbing a mountain, are just going to take more time than before you were diagnosed with PD. You tend to tire more readily when you have PD and this results in things being put off until later. So, extra time gets used up on tasks which before you were diagnosed with PD, you might not necessarily have needed to use before. Once it has been taken, you cannot get it back, that was never a part of the deal.

But it is more about 'how' PD steals time from people. It is sinister, menacing, a ruthless and covert thief that knows nothing about or has any respect for the preservation of human bodily functions. It does not care that by exerting its effect, slowly in some, quicker in others, but secretly in everyone, it is taking time from people without permission and against their will. It slips into victims lives unannounced and unwanted, like a thief at a large gathering of ordinary people, it uses its featherlike, probing fingers to effectively prise open our wallets and purses of life and take whatever time it wants to take.

It circulates around this gathering as if it were a bird of prey, hunting for its next victim, who is altogether unaware of the menace circling high above. PD does not select its victims based on certain factors, neither does it select its victims at random; it has traditionally been an older person's disease and still remains so – for the time being. Maybe it finds it easier to wreak havoc in a more elderly person's body. Perhaps this is why in the more elderly patient, the rate of progression of PD tends to be faster, stealing its victims' time at a higher, more savage rate. Without doubt, PD steals time from the elderly person with more ease of execution than it does with the younger person. The younger person, who wishes to Maintain Control of their Life is less willing to let PD in and take over, putting up whatever barriers to PD's advancing march they can, by some kind of physical intervention, psychological intervention, nutritional or medicinal intervention.

PD can get its claws into you deeply, unceremoniously and with little regard for your dignity. It chips away at time until it can chew off another chunk, literally stealing it from right under your nose; it doesn't ask permission, it just steams in and takes what it wants. There are no formalities with PD and it covers its trail by never attacking its victims in the same way twice. Every assault it carries out on its unsuspecting victims is different in its approach, meaning no two patients with PD experience exactly the same symptoms, at the same time, with the same intensity and with the same overall outcome. There are no protocols to follow; PD makes it difficult to define a pattern, where similarities can be seen between individual patients. It appears to follow a random plan of attack, relentlessly shutting down dopamine producing cells with a view to stealing time right out of your hands.

Fifteen

I knew I had to hire Swift the moment I met him.

At Promosign, we were just as proud of the team of project managers as we were of our commitment to providing excellence in design. Our most recent addition to the team was a short-ish guy with a mop of brown curly hair.

Swift.

What really stood out for me was the fact that during his interview, firstly with Deborah and then secondly with Paul and myself, was that he was chewing gum throughout the interview. While we were attempting to concoct outlandish questions to ask Swift, he would un-ashamedly be grinding the two halves of his jaw together. Initially I thought he was really nervous and he was grinding his teeth because of this, but then I caught sight of the gum in his mouth. He didn't seem to be the nervous type, quite the opposite in fact.

"Have you got a valid passport?" asked Paul.

"Yeah, where do you want me to go?" Swift replied. "Have passport – will travel…nowhere cold, though…I perform better at warm venues."

"Well, we can't really choose which congresses we go to based on the weather conditions at a given venue," I said, "but one of the projects I've got earmarked for the person who will fill this role is in Singapore. That warm enough for you? It's on the equator."

I was mildly amused by his whoops of joy for Singapore. "Yeah, that'd be ace," Swift said. "What's the gig, man, what's going down in Singapore?"

"For obvious reasons, I can't tell you but if you are fortunate to be offered this position, I'll tell you all about it then."

Such an unorthodox interview technique. However, you couldn't help but like him and his boundless enthusiasm for the role. Deborah offered Swift a position on my team, which he took without hesitation.

When he joined the company a couple of weeks later, he was so excited, like a puppy with a new toy.

"You know," I said to him, down at the pub one lunchtime. "We only hired you because we couldn't believe you had the balls to go through an interview with Deborah and Cynthia, then Paul and me – chewing gum throughout…I thought, I've got to have this guy on my team."

"Really?" he sounded genuinely shocked. "Sometimes, I don't realise when I'm chewing gum, it helps to keep me focussed if I am concentrating on something, like being in an interview, I tend to forget that I'm chewing. Did Deborah or Cynthia say anything about me?"

"Oh, the only thing that Deborah said was that she wasn't sure you'd make a good fit in the team," I said. "At which point, Paul interjected and said that he'd never met anyone who would fit more perfectly."

So, there it was. Swift was working on my team. I started him on the Singapore project as this was only six weeks away and there were a few logistical issues that needed to be actioned. The exhibition stand had an all over design that was essentially different fruits defining different product areas; the client had already signed off on the exhibition design, several weeks prior. It looked more like a fruit salad than an exhibition stand, but the client seemed to like it.

I kept an eye on the development of the project. Then it occurred to me that I hadn't heard Swift talking on the phone to the client, Mesa, who's office was in Philadelphia.

"How is Mesa, Swift?"

"Yeah, she's good…looking forward to Singapore."

"What did you talk about last time you spoke with her?"

"I've never spoken to her."

I looked round at Swift; he was pulling some chewing gum through the gap between his two front teeth, like extra thick dental floss, leaning back in his chair. "You've never spoken to her?"

"We talk by email," he said. "Look…" Swift waved his hand at his computer screen, listing messages from Mesa.

"So, you haven't just called her to say hi, I'm your new project manager…I'll be working with you in Singapore?"

"Nah," he said. "Thought you did that."

"I *did* call her, to say that you were working on her projects and you'd be in touch to say hello…"

"Ooops."

"Come on," I said. "She'll be in her office about now…let's just give her a quick call, just to prove you really do exist…"

---|---

"Hello, Marco speaking."

"Hello, whoops. Shit."

I rolled my eyes skywards. "Hello, Swift," I said. "How's it going in Singapore? You're on speakerphone so watch the swearing."

"Really? Why am I on speakerphone? I just spilt my drink."

"Just to prove you can hold a conversation without profanities," I said, winking at Paul and Cynthia who were stood in front of my desk. "How was the opening day of the congress? Everything go smoothly? I've got Paul and Cynthia here, so be careful what you say…Singapore is Cynthia's old stamping ground, in case you didn't know."

"Yeah, it's all going well, no major dramas, Mesa seems happy enough with everything."

"Hello, Swift," said Cynthia. "Let me know if you need to know where to go in Singapore, it's my hometown."

"There you go, Swift," I said. "Travel advice on the city's top nightspots…from someone who left Singapore twenty years ago and hasn't been back since…I'm sure nothing's changed in the last two decades, fast-moving city like Singapore."

"I'm actually out with Mesa and a few other people," Swift said excitedly. "We're in Charlie Chans, I was here on my own a couple of nights ago and these three girls asked if they could join me. Anyway, I ended up shagging one of them in the bogs…"

Most of the people in the office heard Swift's bragging and were laughing, just before I managed to lift the phone handpiece.

"Well done, Swift, good work, glad to hear you're taking the opportunity to soak up all that south-east Asian culture," I said. "Now, don't bring back any tropical diseases, will you, mate? And look after our client, there's a good chap."

Paul and Cynthia were talking to others in the office, they wandered back to my desk. "He seems happy enough," said Paul.

I smiled. "First time in Asia…I just hope he doesn't come home with the Singapore Clap."

"Ready for our meeting?" Cynthia asked.

---|---

I was in Paul's office.

"You won't believe what happened on the plane back from New York."

"Try me," said Paul, coming out from behind his desk to sit on the other sofa.

"Okay, you're going to love this…wait, Paul?" I looked around his office.

"What?"

"You've got way too much fucking space in this office it's huge…I mean, two sofas? Come on…"

"I know, it's embarrassing, it's bigger than any of the directors' offices. Even Geoffs. Some clients ask if I am running the company because they think the managing director should have the biggest office. Anyway, carry on…"

"So, we're at the client's office and you know their building on forty-second street? There's this new Vodka bar opened just down the road from Grand Central Station. It's like almost five o'clock and the client says, I'll just gather the troops and we'll go and have a few vodkas and some French fries before you guys head back to the airport."

"Jules, Swift and me are necking shots of the old Russian marching water, with the entire client team there which I think was a good sign for the proposal we had just presented to them. Anyway, with Swift being probably half my weight, and probably a third of Jules' weight, the Russians quickly went to his head, he was as pissed as a fart inside of half an hour. So was the client, now I think about it, but he's quite a big bloke."

"We got a cab back to Newark, after an hour in the bar. We're back at the airport and Swift is getting his second wind, he's saying let's have a few beers before we get on the plane…so we went to a little bar next to gate thirty, the gate our flight departs from."

"I know it well."

"So we got a round of beers in. I told him maybe he ought to take it easy, in the past I'd seen people half as shit-faced as he was right now getting bounced from the aeroplane. He didn't take a lot of notice of what I said and was trying to keep up with Jules, I don't know what he was trying to prove. But Jules can just pour a pint down his neck in under ten-seconds. I said to Swift, don't try and keep up with him, he's only half-human, I said. He's been programmed to drink like a madman and not get drunk, that's why he works in the multimedia department."

"Swift was hammered by now but, to his credit, he could still walk in a straight line and by keeping his words clipped, the only visual clues that he was drunk were the wavy lines coming from him as we shuffled down the jet way to the aircraft. Actually, he was doing incredibly well trying to keep up with Jules. He'd drunk almost four pints by the time they made the final calls to board the flight."

We had the three seats on the emergency exit row as they were great for stretching out on overnight flights back to London from New York; the air hostesses always ask if you are capable of operating an emergency exit to which Jules and I said yes; Swift just nodded. I doubt very much that Swift would be capable of focussing on one, let alone operating one. So, when we were settled in our seats, I tapped Swift on his arm and said, "That's the emergency exit, in case you were wondering where it is," I said, pointing to our immediate right. "See that door with the big handle and red arrows all over it?"

"Oh, yeah, ta," he replied. "I wasn't sure what she was going on about."

"It's nothing important, unless we have to crash land, by which time if you haven't been turned into paté, it'd be appreciated by your fellow passengers if you could open it…just to let a bit of fresh air in," I told him with a grin.

Swift turned his head to look at me, wide-eyed and ill at ease. "Paté? Shit, I need a drink…"

---|---

Paul laughed. "You have such a warped sense of humour, Marco."

"I know," I replied. "It's one of my finer traits. Anyway, Swift called after one of the air hostesses, 'Excuse me love, any chance of a drink?' His request was ignored, not even acknowledged."

---|---

"Jesus, Swift," said Jules. "We've had a skinful already. Do you really want any more alcohol before dinner?" Swift was sat between Jules and I.

"I'm a nervous flyer."

"Alright then," said Jules.

The aircraft began to taxi out to the runway. Within five minutes, it had left the ground and having stowed its landing gear the jet was flying smoothly up into the clear night time sky above New York city. The last ribbons of daylight became visible to the west as the cruising altitude of thirty-six thousand feet was reached and the aircraft levelled out.

The hostesses had already commenced their inflight service. One came over and apologised. "We can't offer a pre-flight drink in economy, sorry about that…what were you after?"

"I need a drink for medical reasons."

"I'll get you one immediately," she said. "What would you prefer? I have water, orange juice or coke?"

"Could I get a double gin and tonic, with a couple of extra gin top-up miniatures please?"

"Uhhh…ummm…" She smiled awkwardly. "That's not exactly…I'll see what I can do." She went away again.

"Christ, Swift, what medicine is that, what you're taking?" I asked. "Heroin, or something?"

"The alcohol is the medicine…I'm a nervous flyer," he replied.

Our hostess was back, with a glass half filled with clear liquid that had a pale blue tinge to it, unmistakeably gin and tonic.

"And here's some extra tonic water and an extra miniature of gin. Now gentlemen, what can I get for you?" she asked, looking at Jules and I.

"Just a water for me," I said. "Jules?"

"I'll have a beer," said Jules.

"Where's the toilet?" Swift blurted out.

"Just down at the next bulkhead," said our hostess, pointing towards the front of the aircraft.

Swift emptied the gin miniature into his glass and gave it a stir with the clear plastic spoon handle that doubled for a stirrer. Then he drained his glass in one go.

"You trying for the biggest hangover prize or something?" I asked.

"I get nervous when I fly, especially on these big jumbo jets," Swift replied. "I'd rather be comatose when the plane hits the surface of the ocean."

"Okay," I said. "You know you are probably more likely to die from alcohol poisoning based on what you've drank in the last four hours, than in a plane crash, statistically speaking," I said.

Swift undid his seat belt, staggered to his feet and stood there swaying gently for a few seconds. His eyelids were partially covering each eye, giving him a slightly dopey appearance.

"I'm going for a piss," he announced unceremoniously, then turned and staggered down the aisle towards the cockpit. "Don't let anyone take my seat," he said, looking back over his shoulder.

I looked at Jules. He looked back at me, eyebrows raised. "Who's going to take his seat…" he asked. "I wasn't aware that we might be picking up more passengers en route."

Five minutes passed, then ten minutes. Swift was still in the bathroom. A queue of three or four agitated passengers stood at the door.

A couple of air hostesses were knocking on the door, asking if everything was okay in there. Finally, after almost fifteen minutes one of the male stewards opened the door from the outside. Swift told me later that he'd fallen asleep sat on the toilet, trousers around his ankles. The noise of the steward breaking into the bathroom woke Swift with an unwelcome start; he just pulled his trousers up and staggered back to his seat. As he walked back along the aisle, one or two people in the seats he passed, started laughing as he stumbled by.

Swift made it back to his seat. I was dosing, I opened my eyes as he sat down. Then I noticed something was madly wrong with his trousers; I started to laugh.

"Swift," I began. "You do know your, uhhh…your manhood is on display, don't you?"

"WHAT?" he said, pulling his creased shirt up. "Shit – I didn't check just now when they unlocked the bog door, I just pulled my trousers up and got the hell out of there."

I was laughing properly now; Jules asked, "What's going on?"

"Swift just walked back from the bathroom with his meat and two veg out on display for all and sundry to see," I said, wiping the tears from my eyes. Swift discretely adjusted his clothing and sat back down.

"I must be drunk," said Swift wearily. "That's a first for me."

"I think it might have been a first for all the aisle passengers between here and First Class, judging by some of the looks you've been getting…"

Sixteen

"Leonard, it's nothing to do with work," I said. Then I thought, to hell with it, I've got to get this off my chest.

"Okay…three or four years ago, I started to get all these weird involuntary physical sensations and odd jerky movements."

I drained the last mouthful of beer from my glass.

"Anyway, after various tests and scans, it turns out that I have Parkinson's Disease."

A pause; I could see he was processing this information. He took a drunken step backwards, draining the glass.

I said, "Do you want another drink? What's up? Are you okay?"

Leonard looked like someone had just hit him in the face with a comedy rubber frying pan. Although he was mildly drunk, he looked shocked and disorientated as if someone had just pressed his 'sober up quickly' button.

Leonard and I had become good friends as well as productive work colleagues. We held a high degree of mutual respect for each other's role in the advertising agency that we worked for – JNA. He had been employed by JNA for five years and was now the Senior Copywriter of the agency; I had been with the company for just over two years as an Account Manager. The agency was so small, in fact, that Leonard did *all* the copywriting for the agency, from content for a shelf wobbler to go in a pharmacy campaign, to creating concepts for a new business advertising pitch. We both shared the same, dark sense of humour and regularly enjoyed a few beers (and cigarettes, in the early days) after work, which on many occasions began as a swift pint on the way to catch the train home, only to descend into several beers and some food 'on the hoof'.

We had several favourite watering holes around Covent Garden that we frequented, but for some reason we often found ourselves gravitating towards the Princess of Wales pub on Villiers Street. Perhaps it was that it was on the way home for Leonard (and one day, in September 2006, became a pub on my way home as well, when I moved into Central London, just half a mile from Leonard's flat) and was next to Charing Cross train station, which was also useful to me for getting home to Walthamstow in East London.

It was a very plain pub; there wasn't really enough substance to the pub to even label it as 'rustic' – more threadbare. It was basically the bar, some seats and some tables. We rarely sat inside the bar; one of the reasons we liked to drink at the Princess of Wales was that there was a constant stream of good-looking women walking towards us and then away from us, on Villiers Street, momentarily entering and leaving our lives and then walking straight past us, instantly forgetting our lustful stares and carrying on with their lives, as if we never existed.

"Shit, Marco," said Leonard. "Talk about dropping a bombshell. How long have you known about this, when were you diagnosed?"

There were a couple of other reasons Leonard and I were good mates. Firstly, he had lived in Walthamstow Village, a British Heritage listed Conservation Area, moving out of the area shortly before I moved into it in late 2000. So, we had a lot of conversations about 'the Stow', what it was to live there, which was the best pub and which restaurants we favoured. Secondly, shortly after admitting to Leonard that I had Parkinson's we realised that he had worked at the National Hospital for Neurology a few years prior to my diagnosis and had been part of the team that my consultant (who I have always referred to as 'the Prof') was part of.

"A while, two and a half years or thereabouts," I said. "I'll just get us another drink."

"Yeah, cheers," he said. "That was quite a shock."

"Was it?" I said, laughing. "Imagine being told that you've actually got the condition…then you'll know what a shock feels like."

I went to the bar and was back with another couple of pints in minutes. That was another thing we liked about the Princess of Wales; it was never busy. I had never had to wait at a crowded bar in the Princess, with four other people in front of me, like so many bars in the area. It was an old man's pub, but we didn't care – it was just a place to admire women while we drank beer.

"Have you told Noddy? Or Malcolm?" Leonard asked.

I shook my head. "Of course not," I said, shaking beer off my hand, where the glass had been overfilled and spilled over the rim of the glass.

Noddy was the boss; the JN part of JNA. We called him Noddy behind his back, never to his face, although I'm sure he knows we used to refer to him as Noddy. Noddy had built the business up from nothing into a creative advertising agency, servicing the health care advertising sector; it was a creative 'hothouse' of ideas, thriving on the development of truly unique brands that helped get medicines into the hands of doctors and their patients. Kind of ironic, in a way, that I chose to carve out a career in this sector.

Noddy was an advertising man from start to finish but he clashed regularly with Malcolm the Creative Director and Leonard. He knew the power of strong brands and he was inspiring to work with and learn from. However, he could be equally frustrating to work with. Sometimes he would start an argument with the creative department because he knew it would encourage the creative teams, of which there were two pairs (art director and copywriter) to think even harder about what they were developing.

I've been in so many meetings that started in the middle of the afternoon and continued as a heated discussion well into the evening. Noddy could be something of a 'loose cannon' at times, when the mood took him, which is why I had been reticent about telling him that I had PD. I was concerned that he would view it as a weakness and hold it against me or use it to gain an advantage against me at some point in the future. Although I'd worked alongside him for a couple of years, I still didn't know him *that* well and I was concerned about appearing vulnerable in front of my employer. The last thing I needed was for him to have any concerns about my ability to do my job.

"I am really concerned about telling Noddy," I said. "I'm worried he might use it against me."

Leonard shook his head. "Aw…I don't think he is that malicious, I think you might be surprised by his reaction. He'd probably just want to make things easier for you, if and where possible."

"I don't need any special treatment," I said defensively.

"I meant more like if your chair provides enough support, that sort of thing. I'd never have guessed that you had Parkinson's anyway but now I know, I can understand that it must get you down…but just looking at you, nobody would be able to tell…"

"Thanks, Leonard, I appreciate that; it's one of the things that I worry about the most…well, that and how I'm going to support myself financially in the years to come…"

135

"Yeah, I can imagine you have loads of things on your mind…"

He paused to take a mouthful of beer and then continued.

"Do you mind if I tell Malcolm? He's been asking if you are okay recently, with us having lost those two pitches a couple of weeks ago, he thought you were at a bit of a low ebb?"

I thought for a second. Normally, *I* preferred to deliver this information to people who were unaware of my PD. But I knew I could trust Lee to relay accurate information to our mutual colleague – after all, that's what he does for a living, being a copywriter.

"Yeah, I guess so, it's just that I'm really private about this kind of thing…I was pissed off about those pitches but that's the business we're in…you can't win them all…but there's no harm in trying, right?" I took a gulp of my beer.

"You really need to tell Noddy," Leonard said emphatically.

"I know, I know…I don't really have a choice now, especially if you tell Malcolm," I replied. "It's just about finding the right moment…I just don't know what he's going to say…or do."

"Sooner, the better, mate."

Then, almost immediately, he said, "Holy shit, look at that…she's alright, tidy look…"

In a way, it was reassuring that Leonard's attention could be diverted back to the good things in life so quickly by a passing beautiful girl.

Once again, the Universe was in equilibrium with itself.

---|---

I learned some days later that Leonard had phoned Malcolm after our drink at the Princess of Wales as he walked back to his flat on the south side of the river and told him my 'news'. Malcolm told me that he was not surprised that I had been diagnosed with a medical condition; he said he 'hoped' that maybe I was suffering with something more transient, less serious, like depression; he said he was genuinely surprised to hear that I had been diagnosed with Parkinson's. He was also quietly emphatic that I should tell Noddy as soon as possible. I told Malcolm and Leonard that I would try to tell Noddy about it that day if the opportunity arose.

I wasn't concerned that Leonard and Malcolm would tell Noddy directly about my diagnosis, but if I left it 'hanging' either one or the other might have been tempted to feed him some clues about me having some 'issues' that needed to be addressed. Noddy had all the subtlety of a lead brick and would have wasted precious little time in picking up the phone, asking if I could come into his office for a minute before commencing his interrogation. This is entirely the wrong approach to take with Noddy, as he would be in 'protect and defend the company mode' whereas I didn't want to go into this with him thinking I had issues with the company.

I wanted to tell Noddy when I was ready; after all, it was going to be stressful whichever way I approached telling him. I didn't want to have Noddy trying to extract information from me; he would be stressed out, I would be stressed out and I would probably just clam up and not divulge any information at all.

---|---

Noddy was hardly ever at the office before 10:30am. I could probably count on one hand the number of times I'd seen Noddy in the office before this time, during the six and a half years I worked at JNA. If he ever arrived before 10:00am, he would normally receive a few well-aimed sarcastic comments from Malcolm and Leonard about 'not realising he had started working full-time at JNA instead of just part-time' or 'we didn't know the Inland Revenue were visiting today…'

It was obvious that he enjoyed the office banter because he would go back at them with as much tenacity as he could muster. Inevitably other people, including myself would get involved in this harmless jibing and poking fun at the boss. Eventually, he would exercise his 'mock' authority over us all, threatening to cut our pay if we didn't get back to work immediately; I won the final laugh one morning from my colleagues when I cheekily retorted how could Noddy cut back on salaries, 'that were barely making minimum wage, anyway'?

Noddy said his morning start time was justifiable as a reflection of the effort and time he had invested in the company to get it up and running in the early days of JNA; it was amusing to see him get a bit up-tight about this; usually I got an 'order', something like: "Marco, get the fuck back to whatever it was you were wasting your time and my money on…" Add to this the fact that he wasn't the most patient of people; he could not abide driving into the city in the morning rush hour traffic. In order to avoid the evening rush hour, he would often work to 7pm or later.

So, much like any other day, shortly after 10:30am Noddy strolled into the office, a large skinny latté in one hand and laptop bag in the other. I felt that it would be best to approach Noddy in the late afternoon, provided that no crises were occurring with any of our clients' business. The afternoon seemed to be passing quietly. Leonard appeared in the doorway of the Account Handler's Office, and gestured towards Noddy's office, meaning had I spoken to Noddy yet? I shook my head and mouthed the words 'No, not yet'.

The late afternoon approached so I thought, *I'll try to talk with him now.* I picked up the phone and dialled his extension. He picked up the phone.

"Marco?"

"Hi, are you busy?"

"Marco, I'm always busy…chasing around after you lot…" My eyes rolled skywards.

"Okay, I need to talk about something with you."

"Oh. Okay. Well of course…come into my office."

The agency was made up of six rooms, taking up half the third floor of a building positioned on The Strand. It was either late Georgian or early Victorian and was quite palatial on the inside, with massive spiral staircases. The agency overlooked the entire length of The Strand. Leonard and I would often throw the sash windows up and climb out to have a cigarette on the veranda as the view was spectacular. Noddy wasn't really happy about us going out there, I don't think he was concerned for our safety; he was probably more concerned that we were stealing his money if we weren't working.

The Account Handler's office, where I worked with my two female colleagues, was positioned between Noddy's office and the creative department; the other rooms were a boardroom, the production/artwork/traffic department and a reception room. The building was without air conditioning; in the humid London summers, we would have rotary fans on at full blast, trying to move the moist, uncomfortable air around in an effort to make working there a bit more bearable.

I walked around to Noddy's office; he was standing behind his desk looking uneasy. I closed the door behind me.

"Don't worry, I'm not resigning," I said with a smile. "Just have a slightly more personal matter that I think you need to know about."

"Oh, right. Sounds a bit mysterious. What's the problem?"

"Well, there's no problem. First of all, you need to know that I'm a very private person and I don't like to burden people with stuff that's going on in my life. But this is significant and important enough for me to feel that you should at least be aware of it."

I paused for breath. "Okay, alright," said Noddy, fidgeting with his pen.

"Around five years ago, I started to get these really sudden depressive episodes, out of nowhere, and these were followed by really terrible headaches that would last for a few days. As time went on, I began to notice physical things: my foot would curl in on itself when I was out running, my arm would position itself as if I was wearing an imaginary sling and my finger started to move, flicking around out of control."

I had his full attention now, I could see his mind was whirring, trying to interpret my symptoms into a diagnosis. I decided to put him out of his misery.

"Anyway," I continued. "Long story short, after some fairly substantial investigations, it turns out that I have Parkinson's Disease…"

I watched as his jaw fell, he blinked and looked up at me in astonishment. Clearly, he wasn't expecting that. He put his pen down on the desk.

"Parkinson's Disease?" he said, quietly. "Are you joking with me?"

I sat back in my seat. "Do you honestly expect me to answer that?"

"How long have you known? I mean, when were you diagnosed?" He took his spectacles off and began polishing the lenses with his tie.

"Remember my first interview with you, in March 2001, you made me do that campaign exercise and I had to present it to you, Malcolm and Leonard? It was around that time, two and a half years ago." He nodded his head and breathed on each lens before picking up his tie again to continue polishing.

"Are you taking any medication?"

"Yes, I take an anticholinergic called benzhexol and a dopamine receptor antagonist called cabergoline, so it's pretty well controlled…I don't have the shakes, I get more symptoms of rigidity down the left and right sides of my body, shame it's not down the centre of my body!" It took him a second or two before he realised what I was referring to but eventually, the penny dropped.

"I'm glad that you are able to laugh about it, Marco, I think for a lot of people who get Parkinson's, it's a life sentence!" He squinted both eyes to check the lenses and placed his spectacles back on his nose, hooking the arms over his ears.

"I have my moments, but I need to continue to work, so…well, my choices are limited. I'm trying to maintain a positive outlook."

"Well, I want you to feel comfortable at work, so if you need anything, like a new chair or bookshelves or a footrest, just let me know."

"Thanks, I really appreciate that."

"Are you sure you are okay?"

"Yes, I'm fine."

"You know that we've done some work on that Parkinson's drug, Symmetryl, I was thinking you might want to handle it…"

"Yeah, I thought you might ask me that, I think I've got enough on my plate concerning PD and because of that I'm just so close to the condition…I don't know if I could be objective about the whole thing."

I deliberately avoided the opportunity to be the Symmetryl account handler, simply because I felt enough of my life had been given to PD already. The last thing I needed was to be working in the therapy area in addition to living in it.

At this stage in my relationship with PD, I hadn't got around to feeling that I had reached a point where I could feel 'acceptance' of my condition. I was still somewhere in between 'living in denial' and 'acceptance'; I was still angry about the fact that I had PD. I know this is the case because I was so keen to keep my condition under wraps from people like Noddy for fear of how they might react. It annoyed me intensely that telling my employer 'was the right thing to do'. Noddy was fairly quick to jump to the wrong conclusion, so in retrospect, it was the right thing to do. He needed to know about anything that might have an impact on his agency, its employees, clients and brands.

I resisted the opportunity to take on the Symmetryl account because it made me feel annoyed to think that just because I had PD, people would assume that I would do a better job than someone who didn't have PD. It wasn't Noddy's fault; that was just the way his mind worked, making connections, seeing opportunities. With the passage of time and the maturing of my mind, I might have felt different about taking on such a role at some point in the future. Co-incidentally, I started using Symmetryl for my condition around three years ago, to replace the use of an aging anticholinergic medication that I had taken for many years.

---|---

Several years later, when I was thriving as an account director at another advertising agency in London, I was asked to oversee the work being implemented on an anti-Parkinson's product for what was the biggest pharmaceutical company in the world at the time. I was told that this would be a temporary responsibility while they looked for an appropriate account director to take on the position. My employer knew that I had PD; I only told the CEO and my direct line manager after I signed the contract. I didn't feel the need to divulge the fact that I had PD at the interviews because it wasn't visible at this time and it really did not interfere with my day-to-day life. Strangely, the CEO said, "I wish you had told me this before your interview." I wasn't really sure what he meant by this: did it mean he wouldn't have employed me, or did he mean it would be good for the culture of the company? I never got to the bottom of this. Maybe I will email him to find out what he meant by this!

Overseeing the activity on this account meant that I would be accompanying the senior account manager to client meetings to discuss the current campaign materials. My line manager advised the client of this, so it wasn't a surprise for the client when I turned up to the meetings; I asked my manager if he had told the client I had PD, prior to my first client meeting but he said it wasn't necessary – he said he would only divulge such sensitive information if it were to affect business adversely. He reckoned that my experience with PD could only enhance the business relationship with the client and it was up to me if I wanted to tell the client.

I chose not to tell the client. I was curious; I wanted to know how visible my PD was. Where better to test this than at the world's biggest pharmaceutical company, in a room full of marketing, sales and medical Parkinson's Disease Specialists, while we ploughed through the Sales Detailing Brochure discussing each and every point in intricate detail. My colleague Belinda, the senior account manager marked up changes on a copy of the brochure; thank God that task wasn't left to me, the intricacy of updating information required a level of familiarity with the brochure that only Belinda possessed, having worked on the account for at least the past eighteen months. My experience, in advertising and in PD was clearly beneficial during these discussions.

However, I was surprised that not one person from either the marketing/sales or medical teams appeared to have picked up on the fact that I had PD. I guess it is possible that somebody *may* have picked up on it and either decided to keep it to themselves or maybe they could have discussed it with colleagues and decided not to raise it with me. Had this been the case I felt that I would have spotted more people 'observing' my movements, gestures, how I held myself and so on, but this didn't happen.

So, I assumed I had 'slipped through the net'…*what an achievement*, I thought. Belinda and I found it highly amusing to chat over the reasons for this as we drove back to our office in Central London.

The truth is that even seven or eight years post diagnosis, my PD was still pretty well managed with oral medication and there were relatively few visual clues which might have given the game away. I had clearly reached a point where my level of acceptance of PD being a part of my life was enough that I felt comfortable enough to apply my skills in advertising to the therapeutic area of PD. The only 'mismatch' was perhaps in my perception of how visible my PD was at this stage and the fact that there were fewer people taking an interest in my bodily movements than I actually thought there were.

I probably went to three or four of these meetings before my manager hired another account director to replace me and develop the account.

---|---

"So, who in the office knows about your condition – anyone or everyone?" Noddy asked.

"After you, just Leonard and Malcolm," I replied. "I just told Leonard at the pub last night and he spoke to Malcolm…I hadn't intended to – it just sort of 'popped up' in conversation."

"Also, it just occurred to me; do you have any insurance policies that offer critical illness cover?" said Noddy. "I think you would probably qualify for a full payout irrespective of your employment status."

"That would be awesome, wouldn't it?" I said gleefully. "Then, I could come and work for you for free!"

"Very funny," he said. "Seriously, it's worth looking into."

I had already checked this, some time ago. I did have critical illness cover for a short period of time when I was probably in the best shape I would ever be, but I didn't renew the policy. When you are in your early to mid-twenties, you think you are indestructible and critical illness cover seems like a waste of money; money that could be put to better use 'here and now' in whatever pub I was in. I don't regret not having critical illness cover, over twenty years on from my diagnosis I would probably still be wrangling with the insurance company, trying to convince them that I did indeed have PD and was diagnosed two decades ago.

"I've looked into it, I don't have cover with any of my policies," I told him. "I know it's probably quite irresponsible of me, I suppose, but I haven't got any dependants."

"Yeah, I know," he said. "It just takes the pressure off if you find it difficult to keep going at work."

"With hindsight, I might have done some things differently," I replied. "Or a lot of things."

---|---

After telling Noddy about my medical condition, he recommended that we tell my colleagues at the agency. He took Leonard and Malcolm into his office to discuss the most appropriate way to do this.

Being such a small agency had its advantages, one of these being that you could quickly email individual members of staff about sensitive information. This was the recommended method that was suggested by Malcolm and Leonard; it was straight to the point, lacking in emotion…everything that Noddy wanted it to be. I attempted to sabotage the email before it was sent to my colleagues, claiming I wanted to include a quote from the 'Sound of Music' – something like, "Remember! The hills are alive, with the sound of music…" I don't know why I found this so amusing? Some things are better left uninterpreted.

Upon receiving the email, my colleagues were very gracious and showed genuine concern for me and asked a few questions, which of course I was happy to answer. Then, it quietened down to the same level of background noise that had resided prior to my conversation with Noddy. Everyone was doing what they were required to do, moving on with business and their lives.

Seventeen

I actually worked at JNA over two separate periods of time. The first time was for three and a half years, the second time for just over three years. In between these two stints, I made the gravest of errors and accepted the role of Account Director with an advertising agency that had been bought out by a network agency. I only found out that this had happened after I had signed a contract there. So, I went from being part of a sharp, creative hot house to a floundering, soul-less, conglomerate of biblical proportions.

It proved to be a disastrous move. The agency that I was working for lost all its character and became one of three or four genericised advertising agencies within the newly formed Healthworld Group, all vying for work in the healthcare advertising sector. The idea was that clients could work with us and we could provide a 'one stop shop' for all their branding, advertising, sales materials, PR, medical communications, medical education, clinical trials management, Government lobbying, etc. My manager was a salesman, definitely not an advertising man; there is nothing wrong with being a salesman. If you can sell creative advertising concepts, you can sell pretty much anything! My manager had only a fleeting interest in creativity; he was more interested in the bottom line. Creativity would always take second place in his mind. I struggled with this because I knew that compromising the quality of the creative impacted the bottom line.

The CEO of our agency (my manager's manager) *was* an advertising man. He understood the power of brands as he had run his own agency for a number of years before it folded; co-incidentally, years before Noddy put JNA together, he used to work at this agency as one of the partners, before being ousted by the now CEO of our newly formed Healthworld agency. Legend has it that a disagreement occurred which turned physical and Noddy was head-butted by our agency's CEO.

I didn't find this hard to believe; the CEO had an interesting approach to work and respect for his employees. Every time a woman walked by, he would letch and leer at her; he would often make a comment. I totally lost respect for him in a very short space of time. This wasn't an occasional, isolated incident; this happened all the time.

I refused to play along and reciprocate, if I was showing him something and he passed comment on a woman, I would just smile. I was counting the days until I could get the hell out of the toxic environment of this agency. I still wasn't sure how to turn this dream into reality.

Then, opportunity knocked. Essentially the management were looking for someone to pin the blame on for the loss of a recent pitch. It was disappointing that we didn't win this pitch; I blame the creative director for producing twenty-plus concepts that he presented to the client, misguided into believing that it showcased the breadth and depth of our thinking. What it clearly showed was that we couldn't narrow our concepts down to the two or three really strong ideas. Instead, it just showed that if you threw enough shit at a wall, some of it will stick; I believe this was his pitch strategy.

I had been *trained* to work a different way: show the client our top three or four concepts, then agree ahead of the pitch which one we would recommend as our number one 'most effective' concept. This showed the client that these guys were all committed to the same idea. We were then all seen to be 'singing from the same song sheet'.

When the client contacted the CEO to advise him that our agency had been unsuccessful on this occasion, I threw myself under the wheels of the bus, by admitting to the CEO that I wasn't sure that this role was right for me in this agency. The CEO jumped at the chance to pin the blame on me for the loss of this pitch, it was all total nonsense, a complete farce. Even in my exit interview, the CEO was pulling faces behind the HR Director's back. It was more like a kids' playground than a global leader in advertising. I had no doubt that getting out of this hellish agency environment was the right thing to do.

---|---

Some weeks after the dust had settled, I found myself back at JNA as a freelance account handler. I handled a pitch which we won and this allowed me to stay on as a freelancer. Noddy really wanted me to go full-time permanent, but I resisted this. I felt like I wasn't in the best psychological state of health, I was a little messed up. I never felt the need to undergo a full psychological evaluation. I needed to take care of myself for a bit and putting pressure on myself in the form of full-time employment was not exactly what I wanted to do.

---|---

Why was it that I felt like I wasn't in the best psychological state of health? In the past six or seven months, I had been through a variety of experiences. I had been caught up in the Boxing Day Indian Ocean tsunami in Thailand, been stung by a stingray in my left foot the day before the tsunami in Thailand, on Christmas Day 2004. I had been through a turbulent break up with Liz who, six months post break-up, I was still in love with and I didn't know why or how to move on. I had also been through a toxic job experience and termination at the Healthworld Group and almost got blown up in the London Underground terrorist bomb attacks on the very day that the toxic job ended. It was purely by luck that I was on the train in front of the train that was blown up at Edgware Road in London; on any normal day, I would probably have been on the train that was bombed. On the day of the terrorist attacks I took a slightly earlier train to make sure I wasn't late for my 'exit interview' which was scheduled for a 9:00am start at my office.

From my perspective, that's quite a lot of life-defining events to take part in, over such a short period of time, with three near-death experiences and two more that nearly drove me insane. Now that my career had entered a more 'laid back' phase, I wanted to give myself some time off, reset the counters, re-charge my batteries and re-centre my life, find some balance. I hadn't intended for my career to take a 'nose-dive' but I felt with some time and patience, I could get things back on track again.

Nine months after coming home from Thailand after Liz and the tsunami, I flew back to try and lay some ghosts to rest; however, I did not go to Koh Lhanta where my previous girlfriend and I had been caught up in the tsunami. I went to Koh Phi Phi, the next island over, which was where Liz and I had made a booking for two days after Boxing Day 2004, as the Phi Phi Princess Resort was full over Christmas 2004 and despite our efforts to adjust the booking to allow us to go to Phi Phi for Christmas, the fact that there were no spare rooms probably saved our lives. When I arrived in Phi Phi nine months after the tsunami, I asked a local guy where the Phi Phi Princess Resort was; he showed me the Welcoming Gazebo and the swimming pool pump. That was all that remained of the resort.

I had also just started dating an Australian girl, Jayne who was to be my future wife and I was enjoying getting to know her. We flew down to Australia for a couple of weeks where she introduced me to family and friends.

The effect of such traumatic events didn't make the management of my PD any easier. The most significant event was without any doubt, the tsunami. Being involved in such a major international disaster and the aftermath, with the amount of death and destruction that it delivered, effectively elevating my stress levels to the point where I was experiencing side effects from one of my PD medications (cabergoline). These side effects were audio and visual hallucinations, a well-documented side effect of cabergoline. Add to this the stress of the incredible physical pain I experienced as a result of my altercation with a sting ray on Christmas Day 2004 and the emotional pain of my relationship with Liz ending in Thailand – it is not difficult to see that I was a physical and emotional wreck when I arrived back in London, totally unfit for work and life in general.

My GP thought that the cocktail of medications I had been taking for the stingray attack (anti-biotics, anti-inflammatories, strong pain killers) may have interacted with my PD medications in some way, rendering them less effective. He stopped me taking the cabergoline and started me on leva-dopa (synthetic dopamine for the treatment of PD symptoms) and referred me for a deep vein thrombosis (DVT) scan, as both my legs were showing characteristic effects of DVT. I tried to explain that I felt it was the poison from the stingray that had got into my lymphatic system. The DVT scan came back negative to all the doctors' surprise. It took another three months for my body to rid itself of the sting ray's poison. On one Saturday morning in March 2005, I felt distinctly odd; it wasn't long before I was arse-glued to the toilet with explosive diarrhoea, while I somehow managed to manoeuvre my head to face the sink so I could successfully vomit into it.

With the amount of fluid exiting my orifices, I was seriously concerned that I might induce a vacuum in my intestines. There had to be a limit to the amount of fluid that I could expel, wasn't there? It felt like my body had just said to itself, "Enough is enough! Let's get rid of this poison once and for all!"

So, I spent the weekend on the sofa watching movies and the television, occasionally running to the bathroom. Over the coming days, the swollen skin on my lower legs gradually disappeared and I found it slightly less uncomfortable to walk. The stingray had stung me on the fourth toe of my left foot; to this day, I have hardly any feeling in that toe. It is numb from the middle to the end. I learnt some time later that a sting ray injects a concoction of different chemicals into unsuspecting victims; in addition to strains of nasty marine streptococcal bacteria, they also inject digestive enzymes, which are the main cause of the pain at the sting site and the subsequent 'numbness' after the tissues have healed.

When I arrived back in London I tried to focus on getting myself back to work at the Healthworld group as quickly as possible. I felt this was the best way to deal with the stress of the stingray attack, the tsunami and my relationship break up.

I was due to go back to work the day after I arrived back in London but I was barely able to walk in a straight line because I was so drained. I called the Healthworld Group office and told them that I was something akin to a car wreck and in no fit state to work. I was still relatively new to the company so they were sympathetic to my situation – they knew where I had been on vacation.

My body clock had taken a beating, I was sleeping when I felt like it and could be awake very late, well into the following day; it took me a couple of weeks to get my body clock back on track. In an effort to get my sleep pattern back to normal, my doctor gave me a script of quetiapine, which is an anti-psychotic medication. I understand why I was given it; it knocked me out cold (I guess that's what makes it a good medication to give to psychotic patients). I was due to go back to work the following day, but when I woke up the following day, I was still under the influence of this medication. I could not shake it off as it was so powerful. It made me just want to sleep. My office had arranged for a car to pick me up at 8:00am; at 8:30am, I was asleep in the shower! By the time I managed to get myself together, it was well after 10:00am and when I arrived at the office, I was promptly sent back home in the car.

It was past mid-January in 2005 by the time I was in the right frame of mind to go back to work. Even so, if I got overly stressed out in the weeks after venturing back to work, I found myself having a 'white out' – this would happen if multiple issues were piled one on top of each other and I could not resolve them. My vision would just white out completely. It was momentary and resolved itself within seconds – it just meant I had too much on my plate and I was having trouble dealing with work issues.

My body's response to leva-dopa was positive, but it took about a month to get the dosage and timing of administration right. However, I didn't experience any audio or visual hallucinations after I had got rid of the cabergoline, which was a massive relief.

Eighteen

Promosign was an agency with an eclectic mix of people from all walks of life. What made them interesting and often hilariously funny were the experiences that came back to the office from the various client projects that we developed and implemented around the world. Most of the projects turned out to be very successful. We were committed professional people and revelled in our client's pleasure at their project's success. With this success, there was often a great deal of alcohol consumption, which very often would pave the way to anecdotes that you could recite over dinner for years to come – we had a very strong 'Work Hard, Play Hard' work ethic.

Of the many favourites, one anecdote involving another account handling colleague, Rose, who was maybe six or seven years my senior and had been with Promosign for three or four years, is particularly memorable, mostly because it seemed unlikely that something like this would happen to her – which is what made it all the more funny.

Rose was quieter than most, was considerate and careful with what she said to the management and colleagues. She was professional to the extreme and rarely had any problems to contend with. Any challenges that came her way were resolved in a timely manner, in the absence of any drama. Clients liked her quietly confident, re-assuring demeanour along with her dark sense of humour and shrieking, contagious laughter. Tall and slim, with dark brown short hair and flashing hazel eyes, I respected and admired her. She made an excellent role model for new members of the Projects team.

One morning, Rose was back in the office following another successful exhibition stand project in Brussels; she was telling me about a dinner she had organised with her client at the end of the congress.

"So I took them to Al Piccolo Mondo, where we had lunch before with your client, Glenda, remember?" she said. Glenda was my New York client and Rose had been babysitting the account until I was employed by Promosign. We'd made plans to meet Glenda in Brussels for a congress site inspection several months earlier in March.

"Oh…yes, I love that place, I always try to go there for dinner every time I'm in Brussels," I said, which seemed to be every few months now, what with it becoming such a popular congress venue.

"Anyway, it was the final day of the congress, so we probably had a little more wine than we would normally have." She laughed. "Then the client ordered a bottle of bubbles to the table…"

She rolled her eyes skywards with a smile and continued. "Champagne always goes straight to my head, so by the time I got back to my hotel room, I was feeling really quite sozzled, you know…"

"I might've been there…once or twice," I said with a knowing grin.

Rose continued. "I wasn't flying back until the following early afternoon and I was so tired…I just crashed on the bed, I think I was asleep before my head hit the pillow."

I nodded and she adjusted her seating position so she was a little closer to me, across the other side of her desk. She lowered her voice a fraction.

"So, I wake up, open my eyes and I can see my watch, it's just gone seven in the morning and my head is hurting," she said, trying her utmost not to laugh. "I can feel something sticky on my ear and on the side of my face so I lift my head, that's when I noticed half of the pillow is covered in what looks like blood!"

Rose paused for a second. "Next thing, I'm sitting bolt upright and I can feel blood in my ear, in my hair and on my fingers…so I start to panic, thinking I'm having a brain haemorrhage!"

"Shit, seriously?" I was genuinely shocked.

She nodded and continued. "I was just about to call the front desk to request an ambulance, when I noticed on my fingers mixed in with my 'blood'…were pieces of tin foil wrapping paper and some brown substance which looked remarkably like chocolate…not only that, my 'blood' smelt of strawberries…"

She started to laugh. "I was so knackered the night before that when I crashed out on the bed, I didn't notice the 'Goodnight' strawberry syrup filled chocolate placed on my pillow by the hotel's bed turn-down service…my head probably just landed straight on it and flattened it."

"Awww…no way, that's too funny," I said laughing.

"I was so embarrassed I wrote a note to Housekeeping and put it on the pillow trying to explain what had happened." She laughed. "I had to wash my hair about four times before I was sure I'd got all the foil, syrup and chocolate out…!"

Nineteen

It took a great deal of courage to admit to my employers like Noddy that I had PD. I wasn't altogether comfortable bearing my soul to my employer. It was so far out of my comfort zone, discussing my PD with him. I had always thought it would be safer to play my cards close to my chest and keep sensitive information about my health away from my employer – particularly if I thought they were the type of person who could manipulate a situation and use it to their advantage. I was concerned that they would put me 'under the microscope' and watch every step that I took at work, using any mistakes to their own advantage. I don't think I could work in an environment where I was constantly being observed. On the flip side, I wouldn't want an employer to waive the fact that I have PD off to one side and completely ignore the fact – it's about finding an appropriate balance.

If I thought that my PD might have compromised my safety and welfare, or a co-worker's safety and welfare, I would waste no time at all in talking to my employer. This is where you have to be realistic about these things. Clearly, it would be a major problem if my condition could put others – or myself – at a heightened level of danger. I feel I have a moral responsibility to uphold and that is to make sure that nobody is compromised because of my medical condition. It is the same with driving – my GP completes an on-line form once a year which confirms I am fit to drive. If I ever get to a stage where I am unsafe to myself or others, I will quit driving and get around another way. It just isn't worth taking the risk.

Most of my employers have been very considerate when it comes to my PD. They are usually very sympathetic and considerate about my plight. I have never asked for anything to make my job easier or to compromise my job in any way. By this, I mean I have never asked for any extra time away from work; I would never use my condition as an excuse for not getting to work. I would take hospital appointments as early as possible or after work, so that it did not impinge on my work hours. I worked so closely with my colleagues that any time that was compromised would usually be doubled in terms of time taken to complete a task. This means, if I was out for an hour at a medical appointment, the true impact of that one hour means that two hours were lost. As the saying goes 'time is money', you don't need to be a mathematician to work out that time spent out of the agency not 'working' is very expensive indeed!

The worst treatment I have experienced by an employer is my experience at Healthworld. Even though I told the CEO that I didn't feel I was right for this role, he gave me no chance to consider what *would* make it right for me. It was patently obvious that he just wanted me out of the agency and despite all things considered, I was happy to go.

Not all of my experiences with large network agencies were negative experiences; I joined EURO in 2008, after leaving JNA along with Malcolm and Leonard. On one occasion I was in Berlin for business with my line manager at EURO, we were at the airport wandering around the airport shops. We walked into a shop which had polished tiles and for some reason my legs locked up and I froze on the spot. It was the first time my PD had been on display to a manager of mine. I do find polished surfaces more difficult to walk over; maybe my feet feel more secure on rough surfaces?

We were in Germany, chasing a global 'pipedream' project which had the potential to add a significant number of zeros to our agency's bottom line. I had made two visits to try and charm this client; my manager had made at least four – including some overnighters. The client was very gracious, but we never seemed to make any progress in terms of work. The fact that she only knew two more words of English than my line manager's and my total combined German vocabulary did not help. *That might have something to do with it*, I thought.

She did seem to enjoy our 'discussions', particularly because my manager would insist on buying her an expensive lunch after each fruitless meeting. Okay, so it was all starting to make sense. This was my manager's 'slow burn' project, which in his words "…might not add much to the bottom line this year but we may be in a position to show a profit next financial year…" It meant that he could occupy himself, spending some time and a little of the New Business budget, lapping at the coat tails of his buxom, blonde 'client,' entertaining her to his heart's content.

"Are you sleeping with her?" I enquired, on our way back to Hamburg airport. It would not have surprised me in the least if he was. The question was delivered in a very direct, almost accusatory tone but I would know from his reaction whether he was telling me the truth or not.

"What? Who, with Anna-Christine?" he replied, with a nervous laugh and a mocking surprise tone of voice. "What gave you that idea, Marco..?"

I continued to stare out of the window on my side of the taxi. Raindrops continued to spread themselves across the tinted glass.

"Oh, I don't know," I said, feeling slightly jaded. It had been a long day. "It's just that between us, we've made half a dozen trips over here and we're still no closer to getting any work...plus, I'm not actually sure she *knows* that we want her to hire the services of our agency."

"And you think I'm sleeping with her because..."

"Well," I replied, shifting my gaze to the windscreen. "The fact that we haven't got any work out of her tells me one of two things...either she has no work for us to do, or...she doesn't think you are any good in bed."

He sat staring out through the windscreen as the wipers cleared exploding droplets of water from the reinforced glass.

He didn't answer me. Nobody likes to admit to being no good in bed, even if they know it is the truth.

We made it back to the airport in time for a quick stroll around the shops before my PD decided my legs were tired enough for my shoes to become apparently superglued to the polished floor tiles I was walking over.

---|---

Maybe I shouldn't joke about it?

Perhaps you think that I should take it more seriously?

After all, that actually did happen in front of my manager – and yes...it really did feel like my feet had wandered into a superglue trap!

Could it be retribution, from the gods of Superglue themselves? Was this payback for all the times I'd superglued a bunch of one Euro coins to the detailing desks on whatever exhibition stand I was working on, then, watching the increasing frustration of passing 'coin collecting' congress goers as they realised the coins were, to all intents and purposes, spot-welded to the surface of each desk. Without the aid of a wallpaper scraper, there was no way to lift those coins – which must have been the exact same thoughts of one enterprising congress goer at a meeting in Belgium who returned the following day after his first, tool-less attempt, wielding a scraper like it was King Arthur's sword, 'Excalibur'. Imagine his dismay at finding nothing on the flat surface of each desk but a vase of fresh flowers, the coins having made their one and only appearance (for that congress at least). It was just another way of amusing ourselves on the long, long days of exhibition stand management, as our feet began to ache and our brains became more and more idle.

Twenty

Having PD is no laughing matter. Nobody ever woke up and said, "Awww, bloody 'ell, I've been up all night with that terrible Parkinson's Disease again…" Believe me, when you have a condition that drives you to the edge of your sanity and erases the road markings back, you tend to take it very seriously.

I'll be mindful of how I say this; I don't wish to come across as being too cavalier, or too dismissive or just downright insulting. But I feel now is the point at which I should say that one of the most effective instruments I have in my arsenal for managing PD is my sense of humour.

Just think about this for a second: if I had a dollar for every time I'd heard someone tell me 'laughter is the best form of medicine', I would be significantly more wealthy than I am at present.

But there is some sense in this overused saying. How good do you feel when you have one of those unavoidable fits of laughter, that start at your feet and well up through your body, to finally erupt and explode out of our faces? Remember them? When did you last laugh like that, when did you last feel like you were going to pass out because you were unable to catch your breath? Remember the time when you were at the theatre to see some amateur dramatics performance and the lead actor, strode up to the front of the stage and promptly forgot his opening line. I was there when that happened, because a friend of mine asked me to come and watch her act in this musical amateur production. I cried real tears of pain mixed with laughter disguised as a cough, I came very close to losing what composure I had left in the theatre, as the other friend I was watching the play with was experiencing the same uncontrollable urge to laugh her arse off, too.

People tell us we should be laughing more, just because it feels good, it makes you feel happier. How many times do you think that young children laugh on a daily basis? The answer is a staggering 300–400 times a day. Adults – 20 laughs per day – and that's a maximum. Imagine how good you would feel, if you could genuinely laugh 300 times a day? With two billion humans under the age of fourteen, that is a lot of laughing going on. Laughter relaxes us, it puts us in a positive, receptive mood. Ever noticed how relaxed and supple a child's limbs are? Compare their softness and flexibility with your own sore and tense limbs.

You could argue that children have no responsibilities and have nothing like the 'pressure of modern life' to contend with. But we cannot hide behind this; the simple truth of the matter is that children are watching our every move, observing the stress that we experience and learning from us, as parents and guardians, what they think is the best way to handle all kinds of situations. So, children are exposed to stressful situations that adults need to resolve. Yet they still manage to spend a significant amount of the day engaging in laughter. It's no wonder really when you think that one of the first responses we try to encourage from a new born baby is 'the first smile'. We interpret this as the infant recognising its parents' faces and feeling secure and happy; it is something we encourage by offering new born babies all manner of toys designed to encourage a pleasurable experience for the infant child.

So, we should ask ourselves: When and for what reason did our laughter grind to a halt? By this, I mean what changed to make us go from 300 laughs per day to around 20 laughs per day. There could be a number of reasons, for instance, you could be unhappy with aspects of your life. Or you could find that you are under extreme pressure in your working life. Everybody will have their own personal reasons.

In these situations, it feels like *we have forgotten how good it feels to laugh*; how exhilarating, therapeutic, refreshing and relaxing a damn good hard laugh can make us feel. I would challenge any adult to enjoy a heartfelt session of genuine laughter even 20 times a day. I would love to challenge adults to aim to laugh a huge 50 times during the waking hours of the day. Can you imagine how fantastic that would make you feel? You would have to spend a portion of your day looking for opportunities to laugh but given the amount of our free time that goes to waste each day, I doubt you would feel that you are compromising any 'block of time' that has been reserved for other purposes.

I feel that this is a valuable lesson that we can learn from children.

---|---

The science of this makes sense. Endorphins are molecules that the brain releases during physical activity, as well as activities such as eating chocolate…and laughing. So, laughter brings about the release of endorphins, in response to pleasurable experiences, which makes us happy.

It's little wonder that all our kids want to do is laugh.

---|---

Without wishing to sound blasé about having PD for over twenty years, I am so used to its effect on my body that I might appear not to take it as seriously as when I was first diagnosed with the condition. This is not true; I have the greatest respect for the condition. I have been through so much with PD, from suffering with terrifying hallucinations as a side effect of one of the medications I used to take for relief of the actual symptoms of PD, to undergoing the Deep Brain Stimulation (DBS) procedure which involved the insertion of two titanium electrodes into my brain – under local anaesthetic – which act on a specific collection of brain cells. When electrically stimulated they are able to knock out the distonic effects of PD that arise due to a lack of dopamine. Essentially, DBS stops the 'bad movement' signals getting through and exerting a negative effect and lets only the 'good movement' signals through to exert a positive effect.

It has, to date, been an emotionally charged journey, who knows what PD has in store for me in the next twenty years? The thought of this may be too much for the average person to get their head around. For me, I think that taking it day-by-day allows me to cope more than successfully with the emotional burden that this condition puts on my shoulders, so thankfully I am able to laugh about it more than I cry.

Yet it is true, the Time Thief has done his work well but, on measure, with all the pharmacological and surgical interventions that I have experienced, it no longer feels like PD has the upper hand. For sure in the early days, it was quite a shock when I realised that I was no longer in complete control of my body and the various limbs and appendages hanging off of it – of course, I was absolutely devastated when I was diagnosed; just to think that PD was going to have the overriding decision on how my body moved itself, that it would be responsible for dictating how effective my movement was and would leave me emotionally unstable for quite a few years post diagnosis. Thankfully, with myself back in control of my body's movements (or, at least, at no disadvantage against PD), I have found myself to be far more emotionally stable as well. I put this down to the years of experience of playing this game of Cat and Mouse with PD.

Through my own, unique acquaintance with PD it gradually became clear to me that I would need to have complete 'Acceptance' of having PD in my place of work, if my career was to flourish. By this I don't mean that I rammed it down each new employee's neck in their first hour of employment, I took a far more measured approach with every employer since I was at JNA. As per this experience, with future employers, I would tell the Directors initially, moving on to Senior Managers and then junior staff. I used to tell colleagues down at the pub, which kept the conversation nice and light. It is a somewhat cathartic process to go through.

However, I knew I had complete acceptance of my PD when I was able to use my condition to create humour during an agency meeting when I was at JNA. Included in the meeting were Malcolm and Leonard. At some point in the meeting the conversation between Malcolm and myself was getting somewhat heated, which wasn't anything unusual. On this occasion, I put down my pen, placed my hands on the table and said, "Malcolm, are you saying this just because I have Parkinson's Disease?" There was half a second of uncomfortable silence, after which he winced in mock pain and Leonard exploded into laughter. Perfect timing and a dead pan facial expression were key to the successful delivery of my joke. Of course, it had taken me several years to get to the stage where I could use PD as a source of humour. To be honest it is not something I would do regularly; the mood was right on this occasion and I was confident that it would work and have the desired effect, which it did. Otherwise, you run the risk of being labelled as not taking it seriously as you should which might not be a good image to portray in the workplace, where ultimately, you do want your colleagues and peers to take you seriously.

Twenty-one

In 2008, Jayne from Australia and I were married in London. Within a year we had decided to go and live in Australia – it was too cold for too much of the year in the UK. Our decision was based on the idea that Jayne would secure a PR job down under, which she did and I would get work over there in advertising, sometime after arriving and settling in Sydney. We needed to have guaranteed work for at least one of us. Sydney is where we planned to base ourselves, as a large percentage of the pharmaceutical industry was there along with the associated specialist agencies such as advertising and PR. Originally, I was keen to live in Perth – I had fallen in love with the city and Western Australia in general on previous trips. Also, it was 10% British! However, there being no pharmaceutical industry in Perth made the decision for us.

So, with two and a half months to go until we flew out to Sydney, we looked forward to our last British winter.

In early December 2009, we were delighted to find out that we were going to have a baby, who would be joining us in Sydney in early August 2010. By the time Ellie Victoria arrived, I was doing contract work in an advertising agency in North Sydney. Jayne had settled into her new role, probably more quickly than originally planned, but she had enjoyed a successful first five months.

Whilst Australia claimed not to have been affected by the Global Financial Crisis (GFC) of 2008, by 2010 most industries were hit by the sting in its tail. It was crazy to have assumed that because of its geographical location the GFC would circumvent Australia and New Zealand. A surprising number of people took the attitude, "Mate, the GFC didn't affect us down here…our contribution to the global economy is nothing compared to that of the United States or Europe…"

It took me four months to find an agency that would offer me a contract; this agency was part of the dreaded Healthworld Group who had paid me off back in 2005. I couldn't believe how poor my luck was!

In a more buoyant job market, I probably would have taken a different opportunity (had one presented itself to me) as I wasn't overwhelmingly joyful about re-joining the Healthworld network after the way in which we parted company four or five years before. The problem was, as I quickly discovered from conversations with a few recruitment specialists that there were simply not enough jobs to go around. My CV was not in question; it was strong and relevant, there were associations with many blue-chip pharmaceutical client companies, proof of leadership qualities as well as several diverse, integrated advertising campaigns under my belt.

One of the big reasons for the lack of jobs on both agency and client-side, was the fact that the industry in Australia was a fraction the size of the pharma industry in Europe and the USA. In 2010, Australia's population was approximately twenty-two million; compare that with sixty-two million in the UK and it is not difficult to understand the reasons for such a difference in the relative levels of marketing activity.

Another 'limiting factor' in my pursuit of work in the Australian healthcare advertising industry was an anomaly to do with the TGA, the Therapeutic Goods Administration, which I still don't understand, I am fairly sure I haven't misinterpreted this anomaly. Essentially, one of the main responsibilities of the TGA is to say *'yea'* or *'nah'* to whether or not a particular medicine/therapeutic goods can be marketed in Australia. My understanding of how this occurred in 2010 was that as soon as a product was ready to receive a marketing authorisation, the TGA had a number of months in which to give the final approval. So, the 'approved for marketing' product could be placed in a 'holding pattern'. Consequently, teams of marketing specialists would have to be set up, in a matter of hours if a product suddenly descended from high above and required marketing; the product managers and the marketing specialists would literally need to 'hit the ground running' in order to make the most of the product launch and all the peripheral activity that takes place at a new product launch.

Therefore, you needed to be lucky to a certain extent; you had to be in 'the right place at the right time'. If I was in an agency at the moment a new brand/new client walked through the door and I'd just taken part in a sublime, faultless interview, where the interviewer mentioned they may need to pull a team together at a moment's notice and was I interested in being part of the team…this may have improved my chances of getting a job.

But this is all fantasy; there are too many planets to align at once in a situation of this kind.

--- | ---

I found it quite unnerving, surrounded by a lack of opportunities in 'Australia…the lucky country'. I found myself perpetually wandering through a kind of 'no man's land', isolated in my personal quest for work. I was in a country that was becoming a bigger challenge than London had been for my career, on my way to the next meeting with a recruitment specialist or to have another agency interview. I guess that this was the Australian way. I had Jayne and our soon to be born baby on my mind all the time. All I wanted to do was provide for them, for as long as my PD allowed me to.

Another 'smaller' factor that could have played a part in my lack of employment was my shortfall of sporting enthusiasm. This was definitely 'the Australian way' of doing things. I like rugby, or 'footy' (played in the National Rugby League or NRL) as it is known here in Australia, not to be confused with football, or soccer…or rugby union. Then, there is the AFL, the Australian Football League, which I used to watch with my mates after coming home from the pub on Friday nights in the UK, all those years ago when it used to be called Australian Rules Football and was a lot rougher than the game is today.

However, I wasn't a keen enough sportsman to warrant joining a club to make social connections, which may or may not turn into professional opportunities. In weighing up the pros and cons of this approach, I didn't feel it would yield enough fruit for my labours.

My contract with Healthworld reached its natural end and I was glad to be free of the network again. Over the following few months, I managed to secure a couple of shorter contracts with other advertising agencies in Sydney.

Then, towards the end of 2010, like water draining from a sink, all of a sudden there was…nothing. The whiplash from the Global Financial Crisis had finally reached Australia.

Jayne went back to work in early November of 2010, having spent the first three months being an at home Mum. Now I had taken up the role of a stay at home Dad, I had time to develop my relationship with our new-born baby, Ellie. But stress, rising out of anxiety brought about by the job situation, meant that my PD was not as well controlled with the oral medication I was prescribed;

consequently, trying to secure further work began to play against my PD, with all opportunities somewhat just out of reach despite doing my very best to secure a position. As I was aware that my PD was becoming more visible to potential employers, each interview became a dilemma before the event – do I tell the interviewer that I have PD, or do I hope the interviewer doesn't notice?

---|---

It is disappointing that I was unable to find a position in the advertising agency world as I had a great deal of relevant experience, knowledge and enthusiasm to give to the right agency. Maybe I just never managed to find the 'right agency'? I had accrued some excellent experience in the roles of account manager and account director over several years in the advertising business in London, which was a harsh proving ground but nonetheless, remains the high-point of my career – I felt I had finally 'arrived', when employed by the agencies that I spent years working in. These were the places I felt I truly belonged. In the London advertising business, I had no choice but to swim…or sink…or be sunk. There were many eyes watching your every decision, every move. It was impossible to hide behind colleagues; I was accountable for every outcome of my accounts. I proved that I was capable of managing and leading accounts that developed and placed advertising that made a difference.

In London, I learnt and experienced working practices that in terms of complexity superseded any work that I did in Sydney. In London, the level of expectation and sophistication was far greater than down under in Australia.

In Sydney, I often see mistakes in consumer advertising which make me wince, or errors and inaccuracies which are just careless and frustrating, because it cheapens the brand. For instance, I recently watched a TV commercial for a Sydney based furniture retailer, and their on-going Easter Sale – Easter had been and gone almost three weeks ago! With a bit of foresight, extra voice over could have been recorded when the full advertisement voice over track was being recorded and patched in to say, "Our on-going autumn sale." Some people might say I am splitting hairs but clients pay a great deal of money to have a little 'ad magic' sprinkled over their brand; the *least* that should be expected is flawless accuracy.

According to some, I was a very good account handler. This was due to having excellent Client handling skills, excellent Project Management skills, good Team Management skills and strong financial skills. I know where my strengths and weaknesses lie; I could have strived to be better at managing a team. I just wasn't as interested in appraising people's performance or dealing with their petty individual issues. My view was that each member of the team had an area of responsibility and while they were at work they were being paid for their expertise in a particular area. My opinion was '…leave your personal issues at the door, this is work…'

I never worked on an account which was straightforward – there was always at least one underlying issue; by this I mean the accounts I was assigned to work on often had extra challenges, which were normally client and/or brand oriented. For instance, we may have just started to work on a brand that was passed on to us and with its current campaign underperforming, the client was likely to be a little 'sensitive'. I spent many hours talking with clients, feeling my way through their thoughts to try and ascertain what the best course of action was for this particular client and/or their brand.

I had an eye for a good idea and well-designed solutions to our clients' problems. It wasn't difficult for me to get passionate about a winning idea; creativity coursed through my arteries and veins then, as it still does today. The fact that I could appreciate and was interested in a good idea that was clearly on brief, helped to develop productive working relationships with the creative teams in the agencies I worked at.

However, with the effects of the GFC on businesses it seemed that this element of my career was rapidly coming to a standstill. With the contract work suddenly evaporating it became very clear very quickly that I could end up 'flogging a dead horse' for a very long time if I tried to defy the odds and continue trying to secure a position in advertising. Something needed to change and that change needed to occur fast.

Twenty-two

The situation got to the point where I needed to consider what my options were and where could I go from here. Having spent much of 2011 trying to pull out all the stops and secure a new role with no success and my PD becoming ever more visible to potential employers, it was my wife Jayne who suggested if it hadn't happened by the end of 2011, it might not happen at all.

It was time to look at other options for earning a living. Jayne was very supportive of my passion for photography and was very supportive in my transition from 'photography as an artistic endeavour' to 'photography as gainful employment'. So, by the end of 2011, I had become at one with the fact that I might never work in advertising again, at least, as an account handler and I was now a 'professional photographer' even though I had never actually made any money as a photographer. That said, I had a fairly strong portfolio of work at friends' weddings, where I had 'ghosted' as a second photographer to capture another perspective of the event, all with the blessing of the brides and grooms, but occasionally resulting in a disgruntled 'paid for' wedding photographer when my work turned out to be more effective at capturing moments from the event, illustrating the atmosphere and emotion of each wedding.

In those early days, I was working really hard to develop a style of photography which gave a big nod towards the 'reportage' style, giving my work more spontaneity, '...did that really just happen?' with less of a staged, 'everyone say *cheese*!' approach. I tried to strike a happy median, with 50% reportage and 50% staged, to ensure that I didn't pigeon-hole myself into just one style. I didn't want to be taken as a 'one-trick pony', I wanted to maintain a broad appeal, to create as many opportunities as possible.

I joined the AIPP (Australian Institute of Professional Photographers) to get affiliation with a professional body, to add gravitas to my work and show that I took my work very seriously, to provide reassurance to clients that they were getting a quality service from me.

My first paid-for contract as a photographer came completely out of the blue…late one afternoon, I received a call from a guy who ran an on-line newsletter magazine and needed help with a party.

"Yeah, 'ello Marco, my name's Frank…sorry for the direct approach… somebody passed your details on to me…you're a photographer right? Are you free to work this evening at a launch party?"

Frank was clearly from London; his cockney accent was strong, immediate and strangely comforting. Like John Thaw apologising to a call girl in the gritty TV show from the 1970s Police show set in London 'The Sweeney': "Sorry love, it's just in this job you meet a lot of tarts…"

I was excited. "Yes, I'm free and I can make it. Where's the party at?"

"It's on Oxford Street near Riley Street, in a downstairs bar called The Art Works."

"What's the party for?"

"We're publishing a book of paintings, drawings of a local, fledgling artist, so the party is to promote the launch of the book," he replied.

Frank continued, "The artist makes his art in an unusual way; he places a block of paper in public places, with a dozen or so lead pencils and lets members of the public 'make' his art for him."

"What, he just lets them draw and write whatever they want? Genius…"

"Yes, he likes to think his work is something of a social-statement, rather than art," replied Frank. "Nothing is off limits."

"Okay," I said, "sounds interesting…what time do you want me there?"

"Probably from seven…seven-thirty to around ten, I can pay you a hundred and fifty dollars…how does that sound?"

"Sounds good…thanks."

"At the party venue, we have rigged up a large block of paper and a bunch of pens for party goers to 'make their mark'…this is what we'd like you to focus your attention on, capturing photos of people doodling, writing messages."

"I take it that you'll want shots of all party goers, too?"

"Oh yes…let's make sure of that, they are mostly creative ad agency people, so they will definitely have stuff to draw and create art about."

"Okay, well, I don't have any more questions," I said. "If that's all okay with you, I'll see you around seven to seven-thirty…"

"Be lucky…ta da," said Frank, before he hanged up.

The party was good fun and I had fifty or sixty decent shots for Frank to use in his on-line newsletter magazine. I loaded them to disc and he picked them up the following day. I shot and edited the work in the reportage style wherever possible, keeping staged shots to a minimum. The party was quite raucous and was just perfect for a reportage style photographic account.

I particularly like to take photographs of a subject while they are unaware that the camera is on them. Their natural humanity then seeps out of every pore and the footage is enthralling. Sometimes I like to offset the subject in the photograph, to illustrate the environment they are in, or perhaps to focus on a secondary subject. I enjoy editing the subject to the left or right of frame; sometimes, if the shot is right, I like to crop it so that only a segment of the subject remains in frame i.e. I would crop the main subject in half through the either the horizontal or vertical plane. I find this only works if the main subject is doing something extraordinary or has an extraordinary appearance. It is all about playing in the margins, seeing how far you can stretch a piece of work, yet still preserving its meaning and the emotion. I just enjoy looking for different ways of expressing the energy in a particular scenario.

---|---

It was around this time that we noticed that Ellie was not putting on as much weight as she should be in her first eighteen months or so. Jayne and Ellie regularly attended the baby clinics where they weighed and measured the children. The measurements that were recorded on charts, which showed the 'healthy growth' curves for weight, then the waist girth and head girth. She should have been at least following the general direction of healthy weight, waist and head girth, which was upwards on the charts. In these measurements, she was heading in a downward direction off the bottom of the charts, or at best somewhere way off to the right of where her measurements should be. We could see that if left without intervention this was going to become a serious problem in a very short space of time. We met with Ellie's GP who immediately referred her to a paediatrician at the Prince of Wales Hospital in Randwick, Sydney. The doctor quickly established what Jayne and I did for a living – Jayne worked full-time in PR for a firm in Sydney, I worked 'unusual hours' as a photographer which was interpreted as part-time. Ellie was going to a long day care centre in the city, close to where Jayne worked, four days a week. The doctor told us that

Ellie needed to spend more time at home, basically eating to put on enough weight to be heading up the charts as opposed to down and off the bottom.

"She can spend time on socialising when her weight is up and her charts are headed in the right direction," the doctor said, waving her hand dismissively. "She doesn't need to be burning off calories tearing around at day care at the moment – she needs to be loading them up."

She paused to take a breath and continued. "Dad – since you have more time on your hands, I want you to become Chef du Maison and start giving Ellie eight smaller meals a day, instead of the three meals currently. Do this on the four days you're at home and at the weekends. It is really important that you give her enough food spread out across the day because at the moment she is missing out on healthy amounts of the key nutrients – she cannot get enough from the three meals a day that you both have. It may take a little while to get her to adjust to eating more times during the day – this is probably the biggest challenge here, but once she has settled into the routine, you should see her putting on weight hand over fist."

Initially, I felt this was not going to be an easy job. Ellie had always been quite selective about what she wanted to eat. The doctor re-iterated the importance of being assertive and sticking to eight small meals each day without compromise.

We decided that the best way to introduce additional meals was to increase the number by one each week. This we felt would give Ellie a chance to get used to a slowly increasing number of daily mealtimes. So, week one started on a Saturday morning, with four meals per day spread out across the day; each Saturday the number of mealtimes increased by one, until we reached eight. It was easy to chop some fruit and call this 'one meal,' as we could put it in an air-tight box and take it with us if we were going out. She would happily chomp through pieces of roast chicken breast…this turned out to be one of her favourite foods.

The key to the success of this strategy was to give Ellie enough food at each mealtime to ensure that her appetite was satisfied but knowing that within an hour to an hour and a half, she would *start* to feel hungry again; it was all about correctly timing the mealtimes and quantity of food. This was something that developed as our awareness of the variables involved improved; it became easier to get timings correct after a week or two of implementing the strategy.

Another important consideration in the first month or so was at what point should we increase the number of meals per day. We decided that it was best to do this when we were all at home, so Saturday seemed like the best day because if any day was going to be more stressful than other days it would be the day that changes to the strategy were implemented. So, to minimise any potential stress we felt it would be fairer on everyone involved if changes were implemented when we were all at home.

I was determined to turn this around and bring about the required positive changes, as was Jayne. I made my photography work fit around the needs of our daughter; obviously, my work took second place to Ellie's health. After nine months of hard work, we had Ellie's weight, waist and head girth growth curves back on track. Additionally, we had saved a small fortune in day care costs, but the main reward was that Ellie was a good deal healthier than before our mealtime intervention plan of action was implemented.

---|---

Fortunately, I stumbled upon some corporate photography work through an old contact who I knew from London. Millie said, "I will get you on board with anything which is a bit left-field or way out there, because you think differently to others."

I replied telling her that 'my ability to think literally was laterally just a liberated state of elaboration I escape to, where I can pretend to be dyslexic'.

She just shook her head. "What?"

This went right over her head and she just gave me her bemused 'I'm not sure what you mean' expression.

I started working with Millie on some projects with The Red Cross. Some support projects at one particular centre were sponsored by Millie's company; it was a shelter for abused mothers and children. I was creating a photographic record of events that took place at the centre, such as painting various built structures in the gardens of the centre. The company sponsored a huge planting program to cheer up the gardens of the solid, brick-built building. I guess buildings that offer 'protection' are more functional in appearance; the aesthetics of the structure will always take second place. Volunteers from Millie's company came to the centre to help out with the painting and planting.

The work involved taking photographs of the mums with their kids; it was very delicate work, I could see that some of the women were nervous about having their picture taken because it confirmed their presence at this address. I reassured the mums that the photography would not be re-produced in public; it was to be used internally at Millie's company to illustrate how the company interacted with the local community. No names of either the children or their mothers would be attached to any photographs. Nonetheless, I always asked permission to photograph the children, either with their mums or on their own. Some of the mums asked me to take photos of the children so that their faces could not be seen and they could therefore remain anonymous.

You didn't have to look hard to see the barriers these women had built up around themselves and their children in a bid to protect these kids and themselves. It made me feel quite ashamed that men could do this to women and children. I also asked if I could address the children by their name; otherwise, as I explained, it would be very difficult to get the children's attention without using their name. I gently tried to encourage a sense of 'celebration of the children' in a bid to try and get both the mothers and children in a positive frame of mind. It worked with some but not with others. I could easily see those who were suffering more than others; for this reason, I was discrete and careful not to raise any concerns. It was tricky when some of the children would not come anywhere near me – clearly, whatever had occurred in their young lives had left them with wounds which had scarred their minds, wounds which without some help, might never heal properly. Without doubt, it would take an awful lot of very sensitive, caring work to put these wrongs right again.

Millie, true to her word, offered me involvement in some other 'non-run of the mill' projects that required photographic support. I was asked to cover a couple of 'meet and greet' evenings with famous sports personalities who were signed up by the company to be brand ambassadors. The audience at such evenings comprised mostly of current and future clients of Millie's company; I ran around taking photographs of the sporting royalty in whose presence I was. Of course, I was very gathered and professional at all times, pretending to be totally unphased by it all. Starstruck members of the audience were invited to have their photographs taken with the brand ambassador.

On another occasion, I found myself down on Balmoral beach in Sydney, at five-thirty in the morning, waiting for a former Iron Man to kayak his way into the beach with a bunch of support people 'in his wake'. However, by 7am, he still hadn't materialised; I suggested to the increasingly frantic PR team maybe since he was a man of iron, perhaps he had sunk én route? It turned out that before the team made it into Balmoral Bay, one member started having undisclosed health issues which obviously needed to be dealt with before the remaining team could progress (I am certain that if I found myself in a souped-up canoe, in the middle of the ocean, at a time many would call 'still the God damned middle of the night'…I would be having significant health issues too). We found out about this shortly after he made it into the beach, landing like a hero on the golden-white sand. Being the outdoor type of rufty-tufty man that he was I was disappointed to see that he was the brand ambassador for a range of sun-protection products. Surely, this man with his rippling biceps, six pack, his snow-white teeth and all over tan exterior did not need sun protection?

Apparently, he did.

With the brand logo adorning every space available on the PR people's tent, the beach flags and sails, I made sure I had plenty of footage to work with. However, when I viewed the footage later that day, I realised that while I had plenty of shots of both the former iron man and the product branding…but not one shot of the brand logo *together* with the Iron Man.

How could I have missed this?

Thank God for Photoshop…two-hours later and I had several shots with logo covered surf boards attached to the muscular arms of the Iron Man. Sorry about that, Millie!

---|---

The other side to my photography work was Wedding Photography. This was where my passion lay; I could stamp my photographic style all over each wedding that I shot. Each event was an opportunity to become increasingly more creative, capturing moments in time. The atmosphere at a good wedding is second to none; it should be a feast for all the senses.

I had got to know a couple of marriage celebrants in Sydney and we had an unsigned agreement to recommend each other to potential clients. So, if I was contacted in the first instance, I would recommend they talk to these two celebrants as a means of progressing with making their wedding arrangements. Likewise, if a client asked the celebrants for details for a photographer, they would usually recommend me.

This seemed to be working out, when all of a sudden one celebrant decided to pull out of all activities on the grounds of ill health. Then, within a week, the other celebrant decided to cut the number of weddings she worked back to one or two per month. It was frustrating – I felt like I was always taking two steps forward and three back.

Photography is not perhaps the first career that springs to mind for someone with Parkinson's Disease. In the past, you had to worry about camera shake that would occur 'naturally'; this would be the 'background' shake. You can pay a small fortune for a camera lens which will auto-correct for any shaky hands which I did on more than one occasion, even though I do not generally have the shakes.

I started to take photographs of kindergarten aged children, which turned out so well that a group of parents asked if I could do a bespoke package of their children. My photography was much more appealing than the formal photographs taken annually – I called my work 'Active Portraits', because they were shots of the children playing and interacting with the environment. These photo sessions were taken at early childhood education centres, starting at the centre my daughter attended, and then to other centres within the group's other early childhood education centres in and around the city.

However, as time progressed, I found that the work was starting to get quite thin on the ground. I spent a lot more of my time chasing work, the actual photography seemed to be less and less a part of the whole process.

I came to the conclusion that it was costing me more to try and find work, than I was actually making from photography itself. This was a problem; everyone would be undercut by the next person in line. There was no loyalty; the clients would look for the cheapest price and run with it. Little did they know but they were killing a slice of the creative industries and it was not sustainable as most photographers were taking work at a financial loss.

Twenty-three

I was almost a year into a relationship with Helena from Nitteroi, which was the city across the bridge from Rio de Janeiro in Brazil. Nitteroi has a very futuristic modern art gallery perched up on a cliff as you drive into the town centre; it resembles the Starship Enterprise of Star Trek fame. I have seen several great shows at the gallery which has an outstanding permanent exhibition. One exhibition I found really interesting was a collection of portrait drawings by Picasso and other contemporaries. The portraits were small scale, each one a matter of three to four centimetres in dimension.

What I found particularly mesmerising about these drawings was the incredible detail and the regularity of each drawing. These images would draw me in until my nose was resting on the glass. By regularity, I mean the pencil marks on the paper were consistently the same shade of grey; whether it was the detail in her eyes or the curls in her hair, the artist showed immense skill in drawing with consistent pressure from the graphite of his pencil.

Unfortunately, Helena's father had passed away during a routine medical procedure which obviously sent shockwaves through the family. Helena called me in London shortly after she had received the bad news.

"Hello, darlin'," I said, smiling into the phone, "how are you?"

It was sometime between two and three in the morning in London, or somewhere close to midnight in Rio. I could tell Helena was upset for some reason.

"Not…not so good, Mark…my dad just died."

"What the fu…" I sat bolt upright in bed. "I mean when, how?"

"We don't know yet. He was having a minor operation, he died in theatre…"

She was crying while talking. I told her I would bring my trip to Brazil forward by a week; I was actually travelling for work, én route to manage an exhibition stand for one of Paul's clients. Now, getting to Brazil had become my priority – I wanted to be there to support my girlfriend.

Paul had put me on a crazy trip around Central and South America, which was nothing new. I needed to go via Rio to pick up some graphic panel artwork from one of our exhibition stand building contractors, Certamé. Upon arrival at the exhibition and congress venue in El Salvador I needed to mount the panel artwork to foam board ready to display on the client's exhibition stand. As it happened, there was a 'small' problem with the panel artwork.

After ten subdued days in Niteroi, Helena and I went shopping for foamboard, scalpels with spare blades, stainless-steel rulers and the largest cutting mat I could find. I had worked out that each panel needed to be 1188mm by 840mm (or the same area as sixteen A4 pages in a 4 x 4 portrait-oriented array). There were a total of twelve panels to make up. *That's a full day's work*, I thought, as the shop assistants wrapped the foamboard. Now I just needed to go to Certamé, pick up the printed panel artwork, go back to Helena's house to pick up my case and then head to the airport. Easy…

Jose, the owner, met me at the gate entrance to Certamé. It was quite an establishment but then Jose and his team worked all over Latin America.

"Marco…tudos bien…welcome, welcome…"

We shook hands. He took me to a meeting room upstairs.

"You look busy, Jose," I said. From our elevated position, I could see that the factory was a hive of activity.

"This is always a busy time of the year," he replied. "Marco, so we received the artwork from your London office, here it is…" I sat down at the meeting table and popped my eye glasses on; Jose sat opposite me.

Jose pushed an A3 sized envelope towards me. I looked at it for a second, looked up at Jose and looked back at the envelope. I reached for the envelope, smiling to myself. "Okay, let's see what we've got here…"

Inside the envelope were twelve A3 sized pieces of paper, each with a different graphic panel printed on them.

"I really like the design of these panels," Jose said.

"Oh yes, I grant you that, they're very nice, but they're a bit small, you need a magnifying glass to read these…where's the full-size versions, the big ones?"

Jose looked at me blankly.

"What do you mean, are they meant to be bigger?"

"Well, yes, Jose… in a word. You didn't think the panels were meant to be this small, did you Jose? Sue's email clearly says re-size all panels to 1188mm by 840mm before printing."

Jose muttered something under his breath, which I assume was Portuguese for 'Oh shit'. He picked up and read Sue's e-mail before picking up the desk phone, dialling a number and shouting at whoever was on the receiving end in angry Portuguese. He ended the call and turned to face me, his face a storm. Then, his face brightened into a smile, he laughed lightly and gestured to the black, leather sofas.

"Don't worry," he said. "It got lost in translation. I will get these printed to the correct size. You want a coffee, beer… Please, Marco, make yourself comfortable, make yourself at home."

I got the distinct feeling I was going to be there for some time. High resolution colour printing at those dimensions was not a five-minute job.

"Coffee's fine," I replied. "Look, Jose…I'm flying out to Miami tonight, and I've got to go back over to Niteroi to get my stuff. These panels need to be rolled gently and put in a wide cardboard tube. With a handle."

I paused for breath. "So, I guess what I'm asking is how long is it going to be before I can take the panels?"

"I don't think it will be more than an hour from now," Jose said looking at his watch. The receptionist brought me a cup of coffee and some pastries.

Two and a half hours later, I had left Certamé and was in a cab heading back over the bridge to Niteroi, from Rio. It had been a very hectic afternoon and I was fast running out of time.

Helena usually drove me back to the airport, but I didn't want her walking back to her car in the airport car park late at night on her own. So, instead we took a cab and charged it to Paul's client. Helena's mother and brother also came along on this occasion. I hated leaving Helena, it never got any easier, the long-distance relationship thing; it would be at least another six weeks until I would see her again whether I flew out to Rio or if I flew her over to London.

---|---

Paul asked Anita-O to book the flights for me on this trip. Initially I flew from London to Rio, via Sao Paulo in Brazil which was about an hour from Rio. When I left Helena, I flew business class to Miami ; this meant I could get to use the arrivals lounge in Miami Airport – complete with hot showers. Then I flew to New Orleans, and then on to San Salvador in El Salvador.

There wasn't much of an airport arrivals hall in San Salvador where I had picked up my luggage. I noticed a number of *very* dodgy looking characters wandering around. Fortunately, I noticed a guy holding a card with what looked vaguely like my name scrawled on it. I went over to him and said, "Hello, I'm Marco Preshevski…" He took my luggage trolley and motioned for me to follow him.

I hoped it was my name that was on the driver's card as I followed him to the small car park in front of the arrival's hall. Otherwise, I didn't fancy my chances if I was kidnapped and held for ransom by a Mexican drugs cartel. I doubted that Promosign would pay my ransom; it would be too difficult to disguise that cost as an on-site business expense.

The driver led me to a black Ford sedan; the boot door popped up and he placed my suitcase, my package of foam board and my cardboard tube carefully in the car before pulling the boot door back down.

As I got into the backseat of the car, in the distance I could hear the unmistakable sound of gunfire from an automatic weapon. Even though it was extremely warm in the car I left the windows wound up, hoping that the glass was bulletproof.

Unlikely…

After half an hour or so, we arrived at the hotel. It was huge, as it incorporated the congress and exhibition facility. There were several armed guards milling about in front of the entrance to the hotel. I dumped my gear in my room and went in search of a bar. The hotel boasted a vast roof top terrace with a bar and a shop. I bought a cigar and a large gin and tonic. I sat in the early evening sun, puffing away on the cigar, trying to remember lines from 'Scarface'. Somewhere down at street level, I heard more bullets being fired from what sounded like a handgun, but who was I to know? I'd never even held a gun much less compared the audio profiles of different types of firearm.

"That's fucking it, then," I said to myself. "This hotel is big enough for me to hole up in for a week." I didn't leave the hotel until my driver showed up again the following Saturday. By the end of the week I had learned to ignore the gunfire; it was just part of the background noise.

One thing I was amazed by was the sheer dramatic beauty of El Salvador; a row of volcanoes extending maybe one hundred miles to the east created a stunning backdrop to the hotel. Rainforest extended to the lower slopes of the volcanoes, before the slopes became too steep to support any type of vegetation.

The following day, I checked the exhibition stand had been correctly and successfully installed, before I spent a very long day making up the twelve graphic panels for the exhibition stand. They all needed to be precision cut to size and with me being a perfectionist, it was an arduous task. My hotel room boasted a large bathroom with smooth vinyl flooring so after I had mounted the panels to the foamboard I trimmed them to size, using the cutting mat on the bathroom floor. I was glad to get that back-breaking task over with. In the evening, there was a congress opening ceremony in the exhibition hall. The client was running a symposium and they had a guy from their medical education agency in the UK on-site to manage the symposium for our mutual client.

Now, I'm not anti-social (well, not intentionally) but when I am working at a congress, I prefer to restrict my socialising to the people I need to talk to – my clients, my team, my employer and congress officials. I find it really tiresome when someone forces themself onto me, invading my personal space by standing too close in front of me or to one side because they feel they must be friends with me – especially when that someone is a total clown.

It's like, 'do I have a sign above my head which says: Please be my Friend'. I usually take a step back or a step to the left or right (I can't stand smelling another person's exhaled breath or feeling their arm knocking against mine).

I tend to get brutally sarcastic, hoping that I'll offend them subconsciously, but just enough to get them to vacate my personal space. This guy, from the medical education agency, was clearly a total clown and he was attempting to latch himself onto me, like a leech; I had to take evasive action – it was now essential.

"What are you doing this evening?" asked The Clown.

"Oh, I don't know, I was thinking I might order everything off the room service menu, and charge it to your account," I replied with mocking laughter. "Tell you what, go and grab me a couple of beers from that free bar down there, then we can make some plans that exclude one or the other of us…how does that sound?"

"Uh…great…yeah," said The Clown.

Then I left the exhibition stand before he reached the free bar.

The evenings were warm so I would get out of my work clothes as soon as possible and make the most of the roof terrace bar and cigar shop. I was reading 'Post Office' by Charles Bukowski.

The exhibition and the congress on the whole remained fairly quiet throughout the whole week. Traffic to the exhibition stand remained steady but not crazily heavy. I had to suffer the attentions of the annoyingly friendly Clown, while I was on exhibition stand duty. Maybe I am too cynical; perhaps my attitude explains why I have been not just single but 'alone' for a significant portion of my adult life? There is a difference, I would rather be 'alone' and not surrounded by Clowns who *need* friends. They depend on others to make decisions for them. The problem with making decisions for these people is that you become accountable for their actions and that is a position I don't want to find myself in. Send them back to the office, I say, that's where they're needed.

My journey back to the UK was uneventful, if somewhat indirect, flying from San Salvador to Houston, Houston to Washington DC, then DC to London. But by now, I was used to the madness of the Promosign lifestyle.

On my journey back to London, I was expecting some awkward questions at either the United States or United Kingdom customs, enquiring into my movements around central and south America over the past two or three weeks. I half expected them to cart me off to a private room in Houston or London and start pawing their way through my belongings, looking for suspicious white powders or vacuum wrapped packs of cannabis stashed away in false linings of my luggage. Of which there were none of course, but the prospect of being wrongly singled out as a 'narcotics mule' was quite fascinating, especially when I started to think about the times I had used cannabis, cocaine and ecstasy when I should not have. It is possible I suppose, that somebody had 'muled' these substances successfully across borders, for my future procurement.

This was in the days before random drug tests were performed on drivers in roadside tests or on the street. On one crazy Sunday, I was so stoned by 11am that I had to telephone one of my mates Nigel, to tell him I was going to be late for our planned boozy afternoon unless he came round and helped me tie my shoelaces. He was smoking a spliff, several of which had been given to him by his boss for his birthday. Nigel had given me a couple of these long, tightly wrapped spliffs. I tried to remain serious about my predicament.

"I don't know what's in this spliff, but it's making me feel extraordinarily high," I said, "and I need help with my shoes, I can't remember how to do up my laces…"

Nigel started to giggle.

"I'm serious," I implored. "I can't walk with my laces undone, I need help…by the way, do you know what day it is?"

"It's Sunday today," said Nigel.

"Are you sure?" I asked.

"I'm positive."

"Have you checked? I thought it was Saturday, how sure are you that it is Sunday?"

"I'm very sure, absolutely sure."

"I think someone has doctored the calendar, it just doesn't look right."

"Doctored?"

"I was sure it was Saturday, can you just double check for me?"

"Marco, I'm one hundred per cent sure that it is Sunday."

"It can't be Sunday, I can't remember anything I did yesterday, it must be Sunday tomorrow?"

"No, tomorrow's Monday. You're just stoned…that's why you can't remember yesterday."

"Hold on, I can't move… any of my muscles. Oh Lord…I think I'm having a seizure!"

"Marco…calm down."

"Shit…I think I sat on a tube of superglue… My arse is stuck to the stairs…"

"I'm coming over to yours, to help with your shoelaces."

"Can you bring a calendar? I think it was a tube of toothpaste…not superglue."

"A colander? Why do you want a colander?"

"I need a calendar, you know, one with days and months on. I'm not convinced that it's Sunday."

"It's Sunday, not Saturday…wait a moment – what's the difference between a colander and a strainer?"

"What are you talking about?"

"I'm just not sure why you need two things which perform the same basic function."

"I imagine a strainer is something which covers all utensils which allow you to separate a liquid from a solid…"

"Is a colander a specialised strainer then?"

"I suppose so, you could strain vegetables using a colander, but you wouldn't want to use a colander with rice, no…because the rice will slip through the holes, they're too big…look…are you coming over to sort my laces out?"

It took Nigel an hour and three-quarters to undertake the thirty-five minute journey between our flats. He arrived with a colander and a sieve.

"I got confused. I couldn't remember if you wanted me to bring one or the other, or both?"

"Or neither," I replied. "I don't suppose you bought a calendar…no…yeah, I thought that would be asking too much."

"I got some really weird looks from people on the Tube."

"Did it not occur to you to put your kitchen utensils in a carrier bag before you left the flat?"

"I thought about that when the colander kept falling off my head."

"Why, were you using it as a hat?"

"The forecast said rain today."

"On the Tube, though?"

"Better to be prepared than to not be, as the saying goes."

"Ah yes, the benefits of being prepared for indoor rain…never mind about that…what are we going to do about my shoelaces?"

We were going into London to a big weekly party in Kings Cross in London. The whole area was covered in train tracks, crossing and weaving like cooked spaghetti. It was in Bagley's studios or one of the other big warehouses in that area. The weekly party was more of an institution than a party organised by and for the benefit of London-based Australians and Kiwi backpackers, held on a weekly basis between midday and four pm. It was four hours of Stella Artois slinging drunken debauchery where several hundred beer-soaked antipodean revellers came to cut loose and celebrate the fact that they were…well…alive!

There was also a strong UK presence of which Nigel, myself and our other mate Kevin, who we picked up en route, were part of. The bar was more of a bottle shop than a traditional bar type of arrangement.

"What can I get yer, mate?" asked the green and gold decorated bar keep.

"Can I get six cans of Stella, please," I replied, trying not to look or sound stoned.

The bar keep swooped and in one well-practised move, scooped up a six-pack of 'Fight Fuel' (otherwise known as the French beer Stella Artois) into a plastic bag, which had no handles; it was more like a small sack. With our refreshments in hand, we wasted our first can shaking it up and spraying perfectly decent beer over each other to the tune of raucous laughter, making sure we were doused in alcohol and in full party mode.

Interesting activity was occurring in the rooms of the venue. A naked woman was dancing on the stage in one room. A DJ was spinning records on a record player; it seemed perfectly normal to have a naked woman dancing on the stage. There were many drunken Aussies and Kiwis strewn about the place. In the main room, a performer known as Mr Methane farted well-known, popular songs into a microphone. It was kind of like karaoke for the weird and bizarre. I found it quite confronting when we entered this room as the door was right next to the stage; Mr Methane was on the stage, lying on his back legs spread, merely five feet away from me wearing a lime green, skin-tight, all-in-one leotard; apart from his hands and his partially covered face, the only skin of his that you could see was where a circle of his suit had been snipped out, revealing his highly vocal anus. I forget the song that he was 'singing' (it might have been Queen's *'Bohemian Rhapsody'*) into the microphone that was pressed close to his sphincter but it was clear he was having a minor wardrobe problem; one of his clean shaven testicles had put in an appearance where the missing circle of material of his suit once was. Mr Methane struggled with the errant bollock, he tried to tuck it under the green material, but that was not enough. A few seconds later, it would pop back out into the spotlight, as if it were trying to steal the show. Each time this happened, an Australian guy behind us shouted 'Bollock!' like some kind of testicular alarm clock that made me half jump out of my skin each time he bellowed in my right ear.

Drinking races were occurring in another room, with teams representing the New Zealand, the UK and Australia. We continued to drink our way back to Nigel's flat; as long as our legs would carry us, there was no need to stop. We'd forgotten the fact that our employers paid us from eight-thirty every weekday morning to implement wonderful things; this included the following day – Monday. I was still slightly intoxicated when I pulled up outside the office; with that came a banging headache. Something told me that this was not going to be one of my most productive days.

Twenty-four

One of the most disarming factors about having PD is its effect on sleep and sleeping patterns. This in turn has an effect on your ability to function properly, to be able to think clearly and to lead a safe, productive existence at work.

Unfortunately, there is evidence that PD causes enough disruption to sleep to the point where it can lead to depression. People who may have once enjoyed eight hours of unbroken sleep before being diagnosed with PD may find that this is reduced significantly as their PD progresses. The fact that they wake up in the middle of the night, apparently for no reason whatsoever and find it next to impossible to fall back to sleep like they could before they had PD becomes a source of significant frustration night after night for some people with PD...myself included.

Even before my diagnosis, I always considered myself to be a 'light sleeper' because I thought that I would be woken from sleeping by the smallest of disturbances. I rarely feel like I had a 'really good, deep sleep' – I always felt that I was sleeping just below the level of consciousness where you are technically asleep, but it wouldn't take much effort to wake me up. I can understand and appreciate why this leads to depression in some people with PD; your body tells you that you need a few more hours sleep, so you shut your eyes, too tightly and you start to feel your limb muscles tense. You try to relax your eye lids, your limbs and you start debating internally whether or not to try and roll your eyes back manually – will this work, you wonder? Suddenly you realise that you are more awake now than when you woke up earlier...and now you need to use the bathroom. Great...You are reaching out with your left arm to the bedside cabinet. Where is my mobile phone? That's it, there it is...shit – it's only 2:16am.

Within five years of my diagnosis of PD, I had moved onto Westminster Bridge Road, one of the busiest streets in central London. It probably didn't help that living in Central London meant that you could be disturbed by the sound of emergency vehicles at any time of the day or night. Moreover, my wife and I chose to buy a flat which looked out onto a street with an emergency ambulance station located on it. Every so often – day or night – the wails of a departing ambulance would find its way up to our flat on the top floor of our building, venturing out into the city in search of its next patient. We also discovered that we were living more or less under the approach flight path for aeroplanes landing at Heathrow Airport, west of London. Heathrow operates a curfew period between midnight and six o'clock in the morning; outside of these hours aircraft lined up in an orderly fashion outside our window, from the east if the prevailing westerlies dictated so. After a while, these 'disturbances' just become part of the background noise of life in a big city – you still hear them, but they are blended together in a cocktail of varying decibels.

I don't think I ever got to the point where I became depressed about having PD curtailing my daily sleep; instead of seeing it as a problem, I saw it as an advantage. It meant that I would have more time to do the things I needed or wanted to do, late into the night – painting portraits, for example, which I had been doing for several years since my days in London.

---|---

In my darkest moments on this journey with PD, I found myself reacting to one particular medicine called cabergoline (or Cabaser – this is its brand name). When I use the words 'reacting to', I do not mean 'stimulated in a positive way'; cabergoline is a very effective medicine for treating the symptoms of PD but in my experience, it disrupts sleep patterns to the point where I would be lucky to get two or three hours of sleep per night, for several consecutive nights. Cabergoline made me feel like I didn't *need* to sleep. I would prowl around our flat in complete darkness until the small hours. Eventually I would make it to bed and would wake up a few hours later, exhausted through lack of sleep. Although I wasn't really aware of it, I was not in any fit state to undertake gainful employment. The fact of the matter was that I was 'existing' in a hazy nocturnal world, as well as the daytime world.

My experience with cabergoline is one where I experienced hallucinations that were so real, I could not distinguish between what was real life and what was being conjured up by the chemicals in my brain. I've taken a few hallucinogenic substances recreationally in the dim and distant past –

184

cabergoline beats them hands down in terms of its propensity to incite extremely life like, disturbing audio and visual hallucinations. The only difference is that the hallucinations experienced with cabergoline seemed to take a number of months of usage before they started to happen.

People ask:

Q. How can you be so certain that it was cabergoline that caused these hallucinations?

A. *I know this is the case because there have been two occasions in my life, two periods of time when I took cabergoline for PD. Both periods ended with cabergoline needing to be removed from my regimen because the medication caused significant hallucinations on both occasions.*

Q. Why did you try this medication more than once, if the outcomes were so undesirable?

A. *When I arrived in Australia in 2010, I was using a 'patch' medication, called rotigotine, that was available in the UK but not available in Australia. Cabergoline was the closest medicinal alternative to rotigotine on the Australian market licenced for the treatment of symptoms of PD. Having had previous experience of cabergoline and its propensity to develop hallucinations I reluctantly agreed to using cabergoline in place of the rotigotine patch medication with closer monitoring to watch for unwanted side effects.*

There is no way of predicting when or where I would have hallucinations brought on by cabergoline. One regular occurrence I would observe was seeing people take form out of leaves on trees. Shapes formed as the wind blew through the leaves, giving rise to legs, arms, and other parts of the body. Bodies would come together, dancing, drinking or just talking with one another. Closer monitoring of side effects didn't really work; the hallucinations I had appeared so be so life-like that I accepted them to be real. Why wouldn't I? The only times I have started to doubt their authenticity is when I felt my welfare was at risk and I had no alternative but to seek the assistance of the Police. This happened on one occasion, when I had a severe and scary episode of hallucinations. When the Police arrived at the flat, the hallucinations disappeared, but the officers were reluctant to come into the flat; I'm sure they thought I was having a bad trip on methamphetamine. Obviously, I was not, but I can understand why they might think this and take caution in their approach.

Having less time for sleep didn't mean I was becoming an insomniac, I just convinced myself that I did not need a full night's sleep. I was taking just a few hours each night, but I would pay for it the following day – I was perpetually drained of energy.

On two separate occasions, I was so exhausted because of my nocturnal activities that I fell asleep at the wheel whilst I was driving our car. The first incident was the most dramatic; I drove our car into three stationary vehicles with, I'm ashamed to say, my wife and child in the car. This is what I mean when I say with excessive tiredness your ability to function properly becomes impaired, leaving you unable to think clearly. I was literally too tired to recognise that I should not have been behind the wheel of the car.

The second was far less dramatic; almost a year after the first accident, I was alone in the car and I had just dropped my wife and child into the city one Friday morning. I was driving back to our flat through New Town, totally exhausted, feeling really sleepy. I woke myself up by unintentionally pulling down hard on the right side of the steering wheel. The car lurched to the right – I drove across the white markings into the side of a hire car leaving a sizable dent in the driver's door. I exchanged details with the other driver but I never heard from the hire car company.

I was lucky; I could have been killed or I might have mowed down an innocent party. How could I live with myself if I killed someone because cabergoline had driven me into this state of perpetual exhaustion?

---|---

In addition to believing that I was a 'light sleeper', as far back as I can recall I was never a *long* sleeper, unlike my parents who used to love their weekend sleep-ins. It is rare for me to have eight hours of undisturbed sleep. An optimal amount of sleep for me is seven to seven and a half hours. Any more than that and I feel quite groggy and sleepy during the day that follows; my theory behind this is that I have slept into my 'next sleep' i.e. the following evening's sleep.

Quite often, I wake after sleeping for between six to six and a half hours. From a work point of view, I do not like to have less than this amount of sleep before a work day otherwise I feel slightly under power at work; it is more arduous to get through the day and therefore it is less of an enjoyable day than usual. I consider this to be the lower boundary of a normal length of sleep for me.

However, I have found that I can cope with work and activities such as safe driving without compromise if I have two or three consecutive nights of six and a half hours sleep each night. If this were to drop to anything less than six hours for more than two or three nights, this is when it could become a problem. My response time could be compromised and I might feel I was possibly putting myself (and/or others) in a less than 100% safe environment.

After more than one night of less than six hours sleep, I am reluctant to drive. I will not drive if I do not feel '100% safe', especially because my daughter is usually my principal passenger. This is one of the main advantages of having a shift-based job that quite often has many afternoon shifts on offer – so if my sleep pattern has been compromised for some reason, by selecting afternoon shifts, I can continue to sleep for an hour or so longer to bring my sleep closer to the optimal seven hours for that night.

It may sound trivial but getting the right amount of sleep when you have PD is incredibly important. Your symptoms of PD will magnify by some degree, depending on how effectively or ineffectively your 'optimal' sleep pattern is followed. For me, that pattern is an optimal seven hours each night up to a maximum of seven and a half to eight hours per night. It begins to make sense when you consider these numbers across a one or two-week period of time. If you were to plot your 14-night 'Hours of Sleep' the smoother the line on the graph, the more effective your sleep will have been for those nights – and this will be reflected in your output at work. So, for instance, if you had four consecutive 7.5-hour sleeps, retiring and waking at approximately the same time each day, by day three or four you could be performing with more energy, drive and commitment than you ever thought possible!

Of course, these are routines and regimens that I have formulated over two decades of experience with PD, that I have found work for me and are based on a few broadly accepted ideas:

- It is dangerous to drive when you are tired*
- 7 to 7.5 hours of sleep per night is the recommended minimum for adults*

- It is recommended that you go to sleep (at night) and wake up (in the morning) at similar times on consecutive days*

*sourced from the internet

These outcomes have not been tested under laboratory conditions. They are merely routines that I have found work in my own personal surroundings.

---|---

This book has never been a planned manual of techniques for coping with the wraths of PD. I am not arrogant enough to suggest that I have (any of) the answers to coping with the challenges that PD brings into one's life. I just feel compelled to share with the world the strategies I used for handling various aspects of PD. The outcomes for other people with PD may be different, as PD is an individual medical condition and therefore it follows that routines may show different outcomes with different people. Some of the strategies that I use may be relevant and effective to me alone, whilst being completely in-effective in others.

---|---

I take one Sinemet 200/50mg prolonged release tablet before I go to sleep. The prolonged release feature gives me approximately eight hours of cover from PD symptoms. If I know in advance that I need to have an optimal night's sleep, my GP prescribed 10mg tablets of temazepam that I can use. However, I prefer to take just a fraction of this – I break the tablet into roughly 3mg portions and take one of these. It just takes the edge off the need to go to sleep and I do not feel compromised in the morning.

---|---

Paul called me into his office the morning after he returned from a meeting in Basle.

"Are you free for a bit, I just have to tell you what happened yesterday in Switzerland?"

"Give me two minutes and I'll be there," I replied.

Paul was representing Promosign at a client meeting with a large, global pharmaceutical company who had their international headquarters in Basle, Switzerland. He was there principally to be a voice for the agency and to make sure that nothing compromised Promosign's interests in the forthcoming schedule of medical congresses, and moreover, the exhibition stand designs that the agency would be putting together in accordance with a detailed time schedule for the year. The lead client, Kieran, who was the head of International Congress Services for the company took control of the meeting early on in the proceedings.

"We have two representatives from our symposium production agency here, David and Elaine," the client said in his rich Swiss accent, gesturing towards the couple sat opposite from him. "And Paul is here from Promosign, our exhibition design agency, he'll be taking us through the exhibition stand design for the Geneva congress a bit later this morning."

As Kieran said those words, Paul felt a lightning bolt go through his body, but instead of being fried, it felt like he'd been frozen solid. When Paul had met with Kieran briefly just prior to the meeting, Paul had made it clear to Kieran that he did not have a full design proposal to go through at today's meeting. The site-visit for the congress and exhibition stand had just been carried out earlier that week so it would be at least a couple, maybe three weeks before the exhibition stand design would be prepared for discussion. So why had Kieran announced to the group that the exhibition stand would be discussed later in the morning, effectively throwing Paul under the wheels of the bus?

There could be any number of reasons, but to Paul it smelled like somebody had fucked up somewhere and that somebody needed to deflect the 'blame' onto somebody else. In this case it sounded like Paul was being set up to 'carry the can' for one of Kieran's mistakes. *This is going to be rough,* Paul thought as he half listened to David from the symposium production agency.

"Thank you, David, sounds like the symposium is coming along well," said Kieran, turning in his seat and nodding towards Paul. "Okay, well, before we break for coffee, Paul…could you please take us through the exhibition stand design."

"Yes – well no, actually, I don't have the stand design with me, per se. Just this week we carried out the sight inspection and I have…"

Kieran cut in, talking over Paul. There was a note of frustration in his voice. "Wait a moment, please Paul," Kieran said impatiently. "I thought you told me that we would see the design for the exhibition stand for Geneva, at this meeting."

"Nnnn…I think there has been a mix-up in communication, probably our fault," Paul spoke quietly. "But I do have copies of the site inspection report, which has tempered our thoughts about how the exhibition stand should be oriented…"

"Paul, this is simply not good enough," Kieran went on. "It's very embarrassing for me as Phillip, our company chief executive is here today at our meeting and was specifically here to see the new exhibition stand design."

"I'm…I'm…" Paul felt backed into a corner. Suddenly, his mobile phone, which he had placed on the table lit up. The ringtone couldn't have been more appropriate for the way the meeting was going – downhill, rapidly – it was the Laurel and Hardy theme tune, from the haphazard comedy duo's 1920s and 1930s shows. If Kieran had jumped up, ran over to Paul and stuck a pasting brush on his chin then punched a hole through a bowler hat before placing it on Paul's head, this would have been entirely acceptable given the current circumstances.

It seemed appropriate, given the atmosphere in the room, to let the ringtone play itself out. A couple of people in the client's team and the executives from the symposium management agency were smiling, trying not to laugh, but clearly appreciating the comedy parallel of the moment. Paul just stood at the meeting room table, eyebrows raised up on his forehead.

The phone stopped ringing abruptly and there was a mildly uncomfortable silence in the room.

"Right then, shall we go through the site inspection report?" said Paul, forever the professional, acting as if nothing at all had happened.

---|---

Kieran took Paul to one side during the coffee break.

"Kieran, what the hell?" Paul asked emphatically. "What was that all about?"

"Okay, I'm sorry, man, I know…I apologise for throwing you to the dogs, it's just…it was either you or me…and that's what agencies are for… occasionally."

"For what? You could have given me a heads up when we were talking before the meeting, earlier."

"I forgot that Philip was coming to the meeting today, and I'd told him that the exhibition stand design was being presented. If I'd said that I'd forgotten that there was no stand design, it would look bad and make me look like I don't know my arse from my elbow. Which I don't, of course, but you do – that is why I pay to have you on my account."

"You could have told me in advance so I knew what was going on."

"If you'd known about it in advance, it might not have seemed so authentic, I couldn't take a chance, it was too risky. Philip isn't stupid and he is going to be who I report to soon. Besides, you're a big boy, you can take it…a bit unfortunate that your phone went off when it did and with *that* ringtone…but you handled it and we don't have to worry about it anymore."

Twenty-five

I have never considered having my PD labelled a 'disability' – I have consistently referred to it as a medical condition. This is why, after driving around London and Sydney for the past twenty years or more, I have never applied for a disabled parking permit. If I was awarded one, I would be tempted to abuse the privilege, in supermarket or hardware store car parks for example. That is about as far as my rebellious nature extends to now: to cheat a bona-fide 'disabled' driver out of a disabled parking space in the supermarket multi-storey car park. But I wouldn't consider doing this as I am not disabled. My PD is well-managed and I have a very full, unrestricted life.

On the odd occasion, in my late teens when my clubbing friends wanted to drive to a night club, we would go via my grandparents flat and into their residential carpark. My grandfather's little white Morris Minor was never locked so I could easily remove the disabled sticker off the inside of the windscreen and pop it in our car for the evening. Gone are the days when we would consider pulling up outside a tub-thumping night club and park in the restricted traffic zone, making sure that the disabled parking permit was clearly visible on the dashboard but this is what we called 'fun'. The security guys couldn't deny us access to the club, especially when Chris the driver appeared, dragging his left leg behind him. At the end of the evening we would return the hi-visibility sticker to its rightful car.

In all seriousness, I don't *need* a disabled parking permit and I am the sort of person who likes to think that I put the needs of others before my own; there is someone out there who needs that parking permit far more than I do. Besides, I would probably run into that person in the supermarket car park, as I walk back to the disabled parking space where I have parked. I would feel like I had imposed on their rights, almost as if I had stolen from them. The pangs of guilt run deep…even though I might have saved several hundreds of pounds or dollars in parking tickets, if I had one.

It's like, my body is made this way, yours is made in a slightly different way. Not necessarily the wrong way or a way that can be misconstrued as being *disabled*...just different.

If somebody asked me to define what a disability is, I would be cautious in this politically correct world for fear of inadvertently offending someone. It would probably look something like this:

'A disability is any condition of the body or mind (impairment) that makes it more difficult for the person with the condition to do certain activities (activity limitation) and interact with the world around them (participation restrictions).'

(Taken from the internet)

This begs the question: can a disability be reversed? We know that PD could theoretically be reversed, if research was able to identify how the dopamine producing cells 'switch off' and stop producing dopamine. Could this perceived disability be reversed if one day, we made this important discovery?

With all the interventions I have explored over the previous two decades, I could argue that my PD has been at the very least, 'partially' reversed (although I would have to be in a particularly argumentative frame of mind to prove this beyond reasonable doubt). I would probably have more chance of winning the argument surrounding the evidence that my PD has slowed considerably or has perhaps even been 'arrested' in terms of its progression. After all, my PD Specialist in London, many years ago commented that my PD was extremely slow in terms of its rate of progression. Whilst in my case, the condition may still be 'progressing' the impact of symptoms may have been highly suppressed.

I would love to be able to say that my PD has been reversed, but this rests on discovering exactly what happens to dopamine producing cells in the brain, making them stop producing dopamine and switch off. Once the key to this amazing treasure trove of answers has been found, we can expect a flurry of international activity and research, which could lead to new strategies for managing PD. We will be another step closer to finding a means of reversing this medical condition and will be able to move it another step away from being labelled a disability.

I guess it is just a question of perspectives. I would never consider my condition a disability – to me it is just a part of me, which acts up on the odd occasion like a petulant school child and needs to be put back in its rightful place.

PD doesn't control me; whilst it may have some 'influence' in how quickly I can perform a certain task, by no means has it ever stopped me from doing what I want to.

However, I can understand that if your PD affects you to the point that you find it difficult to walk safely and therefore the use of a wheelchair is warranted. It follows that people requiring assistance in moving around could be labelled as being disabled. This does not sit comfortably with me – they are just people with PD.

Thankfully, my PD is not severe enough to warrant the use of a wheelchair. Every time I have been offered a wheelchair I have respectfully declined. The only time I have accepted an offer of a wheelchair is in the Emergency Room when I broke a bone in my toe, in two places at once. I'm not sure how I managed to break the toe bone in two places, but it began to hurt like hell; towards the end of the Sydney Bridge walk that I walked with Jayne and Ellie in September 2012 in the Sydney Running Festival. By the end of the event, I was in significant pain. I managed to exacerbate the pain by thinking there was a step down outside the entrance door of the pub where I'd just bought two beers for Jayne and I. This meant that I landed heavily on the offending toe. I could barely stand because the pain was that intense. However, I managed to keep hold of the two schooners I was holding, without spilling a drop of beer. Thank God for that…

I wasn't ready to waste good beer in the name of pain. When I put any weight on the toe, it would drop me to the floor in agony. I managed to drive the thirty or so kilometres back to our local hospital before giving the car keys to Jayne outside the Emergency Room.

I crawled into the Emergency Room on all fours – I had no option. Sometimes dignity is forced to take second place. I crawled to the desk. Then some kind soul scooped me up and helped me into a wheelchair. I think it was a hospital porter but it could have been a benevolent passer-by.

"Good afternoon, I think I may have broken a bone in a toe or in my foot," I told the nurse behind the desk.

She just raised her eyebrows. "Really?" she said. "By the way you dragged yourself in here, we thought you must have broken both your legs…"

---|---

I was referred to a government agency, who specialise in finding work for people with disabilities. This surprised me somewhat, for the reasons I have given above – I guess their definition of disability was more inclusive than I had originally thought. I had long conversations with people there, who tried to give me reasons why I should be working through them. I told them I had no desire to become a government disabled statistic.

That said, I did have a desire to work, as I needed a diversion from what was happening at home. My marriage was coming apart, furiously unravelling itself at the seams and it was all I could cope with, left alone at home. Everybody had a 'reason for existing' – something which gave them time off from thinking about the demonic shambles that the marriage was in. Jayne had her job and Ellie had day care. I was desperate to have a diversion of some sort, preferably in the form of a wage paying job otherwise I was certain my sanity would take flight and make for the hills.

Through the government agency, an opportunity was forming which eventually became a part-time sales and marketing role for a privately owned business in Cronulla; the business was built around hiring out their four 'luxury' coaches for whatever reason could be found. They took groups of people to the airport, to cruise ship wharves, to sporting fixtures, race days, Christmas parties and weddings amongst others. I could see that the force behind the business was the director Les and to him, to take a marketing approach to help develop the business, meant increasing sales. Exponentially, as it turned out, were his 'expectations'. My background in Brand Building was somewhat at odds with Les' 'sales, sales, sales' approach. I tried to get the director and his wife, who basically stressed herself out answering the phones morning, noon and night taking bookings and cancellations, to see that we needed to position the business clearly in the minds of potential customers, so that they could see what offerings were unique to the business and how that differentiated 'us' from our competition.

When I put this to Les and his wife, it fell pretty much on deaf ears. Les was very much 'old school' and believed that just canvassing local businesses for sales opportunities would bring in the bucks. Les seemed to think that money grew on trees and all you had to do was find the right orchard. I was tempted to ask what species of tree it was where the money grew from; however, I could see that it would expose the sarcastic 'I don't really believe in this nonsense' side of me and I couldn't let this opportunity slip away. Well, not for a little while longer at least. At least not before my separation was complete.

It was very frustrating trying to sell the services of a company without having a really well worked out understanding of our position in the local market. Les was keen to get a slice of the school transportation market. But that's where his idea started to fall down and crumble because this work is all on contract. Some schools have a long standing contract with transportation providers for many years. Nevertheless, Les felt that it was there for the taking should he feel he wanted it.

It was a challenge to make him see that the fleet of vehicles that he owned would not be able to handle the volume of children that needed transport to school; being medium-sized vehicles, there simply were not enough seats across the fleet. If a contract came up for renewal, it would be because the current provider had messed up in some way. I wanted to ensure that the business would be able to fulfil all the needs of the customer and be able to meet their needs.

I suggested to Les that, where schools are concerned we should position ourselves as the provider of transport services, that could provide support for excursions, sporting carnivals. This type of service could be required at short notice.

"If we could leverage our way into schools in this way, starting off with one-off projects, maybe we build trust with the school," I said to Les, as he pretended to read whatever was on his computer screen.

"Or we could suggest that they purchase ten projects from us," said Les. "That's where we want to be with them, not doing just one project, but doing multiple projects." He picked up a jam-filled doughnut from the plate on his desk, bit one-third of it clean-off. Jam oozed out of the hole on the side of the doughnut.

"Yes," I replied. "And no…"

I paused for a second. "It would be a lot more realistic if we could focus our efforts on doing one project well with a school, rather than get schools, who the vast majority of which don't actually know us, to sign up to ten projects…don't you think Les?"

"I guess Rome wasn't built in a day," Les said.

It was clear that Les could not see the benefit of doing a little self-evaluation of the company in order to fully understand our offering. Unfortunately, he was more enthusiastic about going door-to-door, in a kind of scattergun approach to increase sales. It perplexed me that he could not see that this was the opportunity to build a relationship with a given school and the stronger our chance of being asked to tender a proposal for the main contracts.

I was getting nowhere with Les. A leopard never changes its spots, as they say. It was clear that I wasn't going to break any marketing records working for Les, so I just shut my mouth and did what he wanted me to do. Unfortunately, this was as ineffective as predicted.

However, working for eight months for Les had served its purpose and given me something else to think about while I was navigating my way through the breakdown of my marriage. Sad times…

---|---

Several years ago, I was given the opportunity to try a new, non-pharmaceutical technology known as the duodenum leva dopa 'pump' which can be used as an alternative to oral leva dopa. The Duodopa pump deposits a gel version of leva dopa, directly into the duodenum (the small intestine) over a period of up to 16 hours continuously. The advantage of by-passing the stomach means that you can effectively avoid the consequences of reduced gut motility caused by PD – whereby oral leva dopa may be delayed in being absorbed, possibly leading to more 'off' time (that is, time spent experiencing the classic 'off' PD symptoms of tremor, rigidity and generally being unable to move, as opposed to the 'on' periods of time, when you have enough leva dopa in your system to decrease the effect of PD symptoms).

This is fantastic new technology and it will be appropriate for a certain group of people with PD, who may have issues with gut motility.

I declined the opportunity to try the new technology, for a number of reasons. Firstly, I think that the oral form of leva dopa works effectively enough for me. It's not perfect by any stretch of the imagination but it's a great deal better than some of the other medications available. Secondly, I understand the benefits of utilising a pump system to bring about a consistent delivery of the active compound but I cannot think of a more invasive or more uncomfortable method of delivering medication. To have a tube going from outside your body into your intestines makes me feel particularly squeamish. I really do not think that it is a viable option if you are of working age.

The operation of the pump unit appears to be cumbersome and awkward. The pump unit itself has a cartridge which needs to be attached to the pump unit and locked with a coin (which I rarely have on me!). For someone with PD, I think that this and the management of the delivery tubes could be quite confusing, at least in the short term. The instructions that are given on the digital screen are not what you would call 'user friendly'. In particular, I think that the elderly patient may have issues about setting up the Duodopa pump – it appears to be quite fiddly, with different tubes to lock in place and instructions to follow.

---|---

Oh crap. For about the millionth time in my working life, I was once again without a rewarding, fulfilling job to go to on a regular basis. Let me be perfectly honest – I was happy enough to drop the 'rewarding' and 'fulfilling' prerequisites – I just wanted a job. Somewhere to go where I could make a contribution to the business of a company that valued the input I could make. 'Frustration' doesn't really do justice to how I was feeling; it was like I was running out of steam, like I was a train that was still burning coal but was running out of water the boil up into superheated steam. The wheels were getting more and more difficult to spin and I wasn't sure if I could gather enough torque to keep them turning once they had developed enough traction. I was past caring if my future employer was in another sector of industry – I was not loyal to the pharmaceutical sector. Yet I still went for the occasional interview, mostly with recruitment agencies, who always 'had a really amazing opportunity for me if I was interested' which of course was no longer available by the time the interview came around.

An interesting job became available at the Sydney office of a production company who had their head office in London; they developed, produced and directed short films for organisations such as the United Nations, specialised agencies of the UN such as UNESCO and also the World Health Organisation. Some of their work involved filming in difficult or dangerous parts of the world. They were looking for an Account Director to manage some of their clients and drive their projects forward. It sounded exciting so I arranged an interview at their Sydney office. Unfortunately, the interview had to be cancelled because the director needed to be in London on the day my interview was scheduled. It just so happened that I was going to London for a family visit the same time as the director so we made arrangements to meet in London. Unfortunately (and yes, you guessed correctly) the director had to cancel our meeting. There was no time left in the director's schedule to meet in London apart from a tight coffee slot one Friday morning; I made myself available for the morning, as the director said she would call on the morning of the planned meeting. At 10:45am my cell phone took a call from the director but went straight to voice mail without notifying me that I had received a call. I didn't realise this until roughly 11:00am. Cursing the God of mobile phones, I phoned the director immediately, only to find out that they had decided to offer the role to another Account Director – who was based in Sydney. It materialised that she had got confused and mistakenly thought I was based in London and had been visiting Sydney recently, instead of the other way around.

I seriously considered asking her if this was the best excuse she could think of but instead I was polite, disappointed and non-challenging. I could not afford to burn any bridges.

Twenty-six

Something was bubbling away inside me, something which would one day spill out of my head and fulfil this creative urge that was locked somewhere within the dark recesses of my mind. I did not know what this entity was but it felt significant. I knew that it would present itself when the time was right; it was an exciting feeling, so I was happy just to go along with it.

In the early part of 2016, I founded a company called Marco Preshevski's Professional PowerPoint Services (such a snappy company name, just trips off the tongue, doesn't it?) The idea behind the business was to provide excellence in PowerPoint slide presentations. I had a stack of PowerPoint experience, acquired during my years at Promosign and this continued when I made the move into advertising. Nonetheless, I took myself off to some advanced level training in PowerPoint, so that I could claim the position of in-house expert.

The work presented to me in many ways but the predominant brief was to 'make this PowerPoint presentation come-to-life'. There are myriad techniques for implementing a brief but where a client often comes unstuck is where slides become overloaded with various information.

The most effective PowerPoint presentations *support* what is being discussed – they are not a script for the presentation. The presentation should confirm the key points being discussed – some people suggest that the maximum number of words on a slide should not exceed four and that the visual should provide the key message being made. It's very simple: one message per slide.

I utilised my contacts within the pharmaceutical industry to get some projects going to get the company ticking over. The work was steady for the first six months or thereabouts; I had clients in the UK and Australia. I came close to securing a fantastic contract with an agency in New York. I would have been the 'go to guy' for anything to do with PowerPoint. Unfortunately, I was unable to take the contract because one of the stipulations of working with this agency was that I needed a USA social security number. Which threw a spanner in the works, making an enormous noise; unfortunately, nothing ever came of it.

I began working with a medium sized pharmaceutical company who had developed a treatment for PD with a novel delivery method and were now ready to launch in Australia. Predominantly, it was my personal experience of managing my condition that the client was interested in. They had developed a number of patient materials to help patients with PD and wanted me to go through the materials one-by-one in order to check that the patient was guided along the correct pathway. By virtue of this program, they would get the most benefit from the medication. Also, I had experience using this product for my PD when it came to market in the UK, seven or eight years before the product was launched in Australia.

The medication was delivered through a trans-dermal adhesive skin patch and it was complicated by the fact that the patch should not be applied to the same area of skin more than once every two weeks. The reason for this is to avoid unwanted side effects on the patient's skin which may occur if too much of the product is absorbed into the skin through multiple use of the same delivery point. This had been 'brushed over' by the client but I pointed out that any communication with patients needed to address this issue as it was a very important aspect of the treatment. This means the entire patient program had to be revised accordingly. Believe it or not, it is not easy to find fourteen suitable adhesion sites on your body. You have to consider where it is positioned with respect to clothing (which could rub against the patch and pull it off of your skin without your knowledge which would be a disaster), how much bodily hair the patch has to contend with (I'm reasonably hairy, which is a problem for getting strong skin adhesion of the patch) and how much you are likely to sweat in a given area (the patch loses its adhesive qualities and can easily come off if the skin below starts to get wet).

By brushing over this issue, I felt that the client was missing a trick. It was an opportunity to turn a potential negative issue into a positive marketing opportunity. Instead of 'sweeping it under the carpet', I recommended to the client that the patient program should identify fourteen areas of skin where the patch could be applied to maximise the chances of successfully delivering a therapeutic dose of the medication. This should have been the key issue that the patient program dealt with: "…Let's make it so easy for patients to use, it is impossible for them to get it wrong…"

It was difficult to know whether or not the product manager I was working with agreed with my recommendations. After all, I had effectively carved up his patient program and shredded it before his eyes. But I was in the unique position of having used the product as a patient, so the issues were patently clear. I figured that I'd be doing my client a disservice if I didn't suggest a new strategy for addressing these issues. Patients would be far less forgiving than me, if they were asked what their views were, at some point in the future.

I didn't hear back from the client after I received initial feedback (which was mostly an acknowledgement that the work had been received and it would be reviewed in due course). Looking back, I wonder if my 'brutal honesty' approach had been too scathing? For this reason, I might have come across as being 'too proactive'?

These questions will probably never be answered.

---|---

Towards the end of 2016, a client asked me to prepare a one-hour presentation for delivery at the company's Shanghai office about how to launch a successful start-up company. It took me a week to prepare and the client flew me over to Shanghai to give the presentation. I flew into Shanghai two nights before the presentation as I was interested in getting to know the city. I checked into the hotel along with my client and decided to go exploring as it was only about ten o'clock in the evening. I strolled around the more or less deserted streets and went to a bar for a beer before going back to the hotel. Jet lag had got the better of me.

The hotel was on the main street that led to the Bund, the river that snakes through Shanghai. This street was one of the main tourist areas, with many restaurants, bars and huge shopping malls, geared up to take as many tourist dollars as possible.

The following day, in the early evening, I was standing in the street, just wondering where to go for something to eat when I suddenly became aware of an attractive Asian girl standing behind me.

"Hello," the girl said.

I looked around, thinking she was talking to someone else. Then I realised she was talking to me. "Oh…hi," I said.

She laughed; she was very good looking. "My name is Michelle…what's yours?"

I looked around us, expecting to see a producer from a comedy show moving towards us. Beautiful women don't normally approach me out of the blue.

"I'm…my name's Marco."

"Hello, Marco," she said as she swung her long dark brown hair over her left shoulder, looking up at me with her stunning brown eyes. "This is my friend, Bella."

Bella was as tall as Michelle, slim and equally as attractive. I turned as she walked up behind me; I was sure I was being set up.

"This is Marco," Michelle said.

Bella kissed me, gently on the cheek. "Hi, Marco," she whispered in my ear.

I pulled away slightly, checking my wallet was still in my jacket pocket – this was almost a 'reflex', an involuntary reaction; I didn't have to think about it for it to happen.

"Whoa, ladies," I said, relieved that I still had my wallet. "What's going on? I mean, do you approach every stranger you meet in this way?"

"What do you mean?" Bella asked, trying to sound innocent. "We just thought you might like to take us for dinner, that's all…don't you like us?"

I laughed. This was madness, things like this *never* happened to me. I was certain I was being set up; I looked all around, convinced that I would see a film crew in the vicinity. But I couldn't see anyone with a camera filming me. Maybe there was a God after all, one that created beautiful creatures such as the two women standing in front of me? What had I done to deserve this, I wondered? Or was I faced with an opportunity where I could be getting myself involved in a Shanghai underworld, the scale of which has only ever been seen on the '80s TV show Miami Vice'? Was I about to be kidnapped and held for ransom? Suddenly, I had a vision of myself, sedated, lying in an ice bath, a cell phone taped to my left hand with a horrible wound that started below my ribs, finishing at my hip bone. I envisaged a life with only one kidney. I was praying for the 'I just discovered there is a God after all' scenario to be true. However, things that seemed too good to be true usually turned out to be exactly that, in my experience.

"Of course I like you," I replied with a nervous laugh. "How could I not like you?"

"Well, do you want to have dinner with us?" asked Michelle. "My friend owns a restaurant a short walk from here."

"I was just going to go to McDonalds or something."

"We'll take you to a *nice* restaurant," said Bella, taking my right hand. "Then afterwards, you can do whatever you want with us, go for a drink, dance, have some fun, yes?" Michelle was by now holding my other hand and together they steered me down the bustling main street, and then off to a side street and towards a very ordinary looking Chinese restaurant. Then Bella disappeared into the restaurant.

"People who know where to go for good food, they come here," said Michelle. "It is very much a local's restaurant."

I was still suspicious. "Okay…"

Michelle stood in front of me. "Hey, are you okay? You seem to be tense…"

"No, I'm fine, thanks. I'm just a bit spooked by all of this…it has happened so quickly."

Bella returned, standing in the doorway of the restaurant. "I have a table, for three," she said with a grin.

Michelle put her arms around my waist and pulled me close. I could feel her breasts crushed up to my stomach. Her eyes found mine. "It's just dinner. Come on…"

She released her grip on me and took my hand.

We entered the restaurant; the décor was traditionally Chinese with scenes from life on the wallpaper. Lanterns hanging from the ceiling everywhere. A couple of the larger rooms were full of people of a wide range of ages, probably having family meals, I thought.

"You need to give the waiter your credit card," Michelle said. "We'll give ours too…now, what do you want to drink?"

"I'll have a beer, thank you," I said as I gave her my credit card. "Where's the menu?"

"Don't worry about that," said Bella. "We've ordered for you, we've ordered some of the house specials for you to try."

Our drinks arrived, and the girls ordered another round. This time I had a vodka tonic, followed by two or three more. The food was good, although I couldn't get used to eating prawns with the shells still in place. Baby prawns I hasten to add…Crunchy, is how I would describe it.

I was quite drunk by now, the vodka tonics were going down a treat…I had completely lost track of time and had forgotten that I was giving my presentation the following day. Bella and Michelle were flirting outrageously with me. I was trapped between the two of them on a semi-circular padded seat, behind a semi-circular table as they sidled up to me and pressed their bodies up against mine. I don't normally eat Chinese food while being sexually aroused but I think if that had happened somewhere private I could have railed the two girls on the table right there and then, with or without the food.

With the food over with, the waiter bought the bill for me to sign. I guess I assumed everything was in Yuan, so I just signed the visa receipt, trying to work out the conversion rate from US dollars into Australian dollars. In the end I gave up; Michelle gave me my credit card, as she pocketed her own. I had convinced myself that the meal had cost me in the region of AU$300, which I thought was a bit expensive, but, hell, just take a look at the state of my dinner guests, with perfect breasts, butts and legs as far as the eye could see.

"Where shall we go now?" said Michelle.

"Why don't we just head back to my hotel room?" I suggested. "It's like a five-minute walk from here…"

"No, let's go get some more drinks and watch some movies," said Bella. "I know a place."

Before I could even attempt to try and swing interest in my spacious, warm hotel room my hands were being pulled in the direction of the Bund, while the rest of my body followed, a little reluctantly. It was freezing; to be honest I didn't care where we went, anywhere that was warm would do. I was a little pre-occupied at the thought of getting my hands on my two gorgeous local tourist guides.

A few minutes walking and we were at a place called VideoBar. The door was opened for us as if the proprietor was expecting us. Downstairs, the bar was empty; there wasn't a single person in this part of the bar. I thought, *that's a bit weird.* We were ushered up a flight of stairs by a middle-aged woman to a small box shaped room with a large plasma screen on the wall. There was also a large leather sofa in the room, which the three of us fell onto, laughing. I could hear people talking and laughing in other rooms.

The middle-aged woman was back with a tray of drinks; there was probably five or six tumblers filled with ice and alcohol on the tray. The woman spoke to Bella; she turned to me.

"We need to put our cards in," she said.

The woman disappeared out of the room again with our credit cards, and re-appeared a few minutes later with another tray of drinks. Michelle, Bella and I were getting to know each other quite intimately by now. The vodka tonics were deceptively strong and it seemed that I was the only person drinking them. We couldn't agree on which video material we wanted to watch so we didn't bother. Our host didn't seem to mind either. Several minutes later she re-appeared with yet another tray of drinks and someone asked me to sign four receipts. I signed three of them, but I couldn't understand why they were for different amounts: one said 450, another 575, the third said 500 and the fourth was for 495. Also, we had only 'ordered' three rounds of drinks.

"These are all in Yuan, right?" I said. The woman looked confused, muttered something in mandarin and shuffled out of the room. I sat back down on the sofa and took the three receipt copies out of my pocket. I looked closely at the currency. Fuck, no way, these were in US dollars! Suddenly, I felt very sick – in a matter of seconds I had realised that I was being ripped off, these bastards and the two girls were racking up massive, inflated bills on my credit card. I had been set up, from the moment they lured me into their web out in the street, for dinner, all the way to the fucking VideoBar, where I was signing for individual trays of drinks, each drink costing around US$50. I was livid; I had been tricked into paying almost US$2,000 on dinner and drinks, the girls had even handed over their credit cards to make it look like we would split the costs three ways. It was clear that they had an 'arrangement' with the VideoBar and the restaurant from earlier in the evening.

"What's wrong, Marco?" Michelle asked, cleverly feigning concern in her voice.

"Like you don't fucking know," I replied, grabbing my coat. "Fuck you – and you." I nodded towards Bella. I was too angry to look at either of them, now their game had been uncovered. I was also angry with myself, for being stupid enough to allow this to happen.

"Let's just call it a night," I said. All I wanted was to get back to my hotel room and cancel my credit card. "You know what you are doing…" The woman was back with another tray of drinks, and a visa slip for me to sign.

"I DIDN'T ORDER THESE BLOODY DRINKS!" I was losing my temper. "I'm not paying for any more…get one of these two to pay for them." I gestured towards the two girls.

"Where's my credit card?" I said to the woman. She fished around in the pocket of her apron and held it out for me. I snatched it from her fingers and put it in the pocket of my jeans, keeping my hand on it just in case these people were world class pickpockets in addition to being hardened rip-off merchants. Nothing would have surprised me.

"Right, how do I get out of this shithole?" I questioned the woman; she showed me to the stairs. I was quite drunk now and I slipped down a couple of the wooden steps that led the way back down to the empty bar. I grabbed the handrail; I figured if I injured myself in some way in this place, I would be proper fucked.

"Marco, wait a minute," Bella called out.

I chose not to reply; I had nothing to say to my two witch-like ex-companions. I made it to the ground floor sustaining no injuries and walked straight to the door we had entered the VideoBar by less than an hour ago.

"Marco?" I heard Bella calling my name as I left the VideoBar. I didn't want to talk to either of the girls; I glanced over my shoulder just to check that I wasn't being followed by anyone. I was surprised that I hadn't encountered any resistance in leaving the bar. Fortunately, in going to the VideoBar we hadn't strayed too far from the main tourist street that led down to the Bund. The hotel was a fifteen-minute walk from here, in the opposite direction to the river. Although I was still intoxicated, I was still angry and amazed at how stupid I'd been to let my guard down and 'allow' myself to get into such a desperate situation. I was walking quickly, aiming for the warmth of the hotel, a refuge in a city I had started to hate. Every girl who looked at me as they walked past me, was given the best look of sheer disgust I could muster. I was suspicious of everyone and I trusted no one. I kept my hand on my wallet the whole walk back to the hotel; I didn't hear the footsteps running up behind me…

"Marco, slow down." It was Bella.

"Jesus Christ…what do you want now? You and your pal have just fleeced me of almost two thousand dollars, haven't you had enough? Where's your shame? Just fuck off and leave me alone!"

"I think you are confused, Marco."

"No, I don't think I am, Bella."

"I thought you were familiar with how bars work in China. You rent a private room, you have to pay for the room, it is split over several drink bills. You weren't being ripped off, honest."

"Bella, I've lost nearly two thousand dollars this evening. Two thousand. I had no idea what was going on, what you and Michelle were up to. If I had, I would never have allowed this to happen. I can't afford to lose that kind of money on food and booze."

"Do you want to go somewhere else for a drink?" she asked.

"No," I said. "I don't want anything more to drink…but if you want to come back to my room you can raid the minibar, just to keep the theme of the evening going."

"Back to your room? I would need to let Michelle know."

"Why? Is she your pimp? You can text her or something, if you have a phone," I said. "Come on – chop chop – it's not getting any warmer out here…make your mind up."

"I just need to think," she said.

I was starting to get frustrated. "Right. Well, you can do that out here, if you feel you need to…see that big tall building there, that's my hotel…"

What the hell am I doing? I asked myself. *Why am I inviting this woman, who has been complicit in stealing almost two-thousand dollars from one of my bank accounts, back to my hotel? She could pull a knife on me at any moment up in my room and take my passport, wallet, laptop, phone; I don't think I would stand in her way. If she has the nerve to come to my room, she might be some kick-ass, martial arts, black belt killing machine and would put me on my back before I knew what was going on. Or worse, if she had a blade on her, she could slice me up like cooked ham. Ruthless to a fault.*

I decided that enough was enough.

"You know what, you are so damn lucky I am not going to the Police about this," I said. "Forget about coming to my hotel…you're no longer invited…you've taken enough from me for one night."

With that, I turned towards my hotel and walked as quickly as I could. I didn't stop until I was back in the warm, air-conditioned main lobby. Nobody followed me.

---|---

Back in the safety of my room, I sat on the edge of the bed, my head in my hands. Did that really just happen? I berated myself continually for being such an idiot. As a general rule, I consider myself as someone who *doesn't* drink alcohol, yet tonight, I was drinking for England. I needed to cancel my card immediately, so I called the emergency number on the reverse side of the card.

"Hello, card services, how can I help you?"

"Oh hello…I think I have had my card stolen," I said, trying to sound humble and despairing at the same time. "I'm in Shanghai; I think I was pick-pocketed earlier this evening."

"Oh dear, let's see what we can do…you say you have one card registered with us…I just need to ask a few security questions to ascertain that I am talking with the account holder…"

That's the explanation I gave, I was too embarrassed to divulge the actual truth. When asked why did I not report the incident shortly after it happened instead of three hours later, I said I didn't realise that it had happened until I couldn't find my card. I said that's when I remembered somebody bumping into me in the street, earlier in the evening. That was the only physical contact I'd had with another person, until I met Bella and Michelle. Lies, lies, lies…just to save me from ridicule.

The evening had cost me a cool one thousand, nine hundred and seventy-five US dollars. That didn't even include having sex with anyone, which just added to the misery.

---|---

The following morning, I woke up suddenly, like something bad had happened. I sat up in the bed. That's when I realised I was still intoxicated from the night before.

Great, I thought. *I'm still pissed…that's just what I need for the presentation.*

What had I been drinking? I didn't want to think about it. It was probably not even worth trying to vomit it out of my system.

I collected my belongings after spending half an hour under a hot shower, reflecting on and re-living the events of the previous evening. It felt like a distant bad dream.

I still felt like my brain was spinning on the top end of my spinal cord and my eyes were spinning in the opposite direction. I made contact with my client and explained how I had 'lost my credit card'. He suggested that I get a police report in order to file an insurance claim. I said the people I spoke to at card services in Australia needed to have been notified within an hour of the incident for the insurance to be valid and I hadn't reported it until a period of three hours had lapsed.

I changed the subject to try to remove the look of confusion on his face; what was the schedule for the presentations, I enquired? He told me I was due to give my presentation between 11.00–12.00.

At least the presentation ran flawlessly. After it had finished, my client came to me with a troubled look on his face. He said he would be willing to put in an insurance claim through the company. Moreover, he felt really bad that I'd had such a bad experience whilst working for his company.

I told him that the insurance process was in motion, so he needn't worry. Nonetheless, I was racked with guilt but what could I do? Should I have told him the truth about how I got ripped off for two-thousand dollars by a couple of street girls?

I was now counting the minutes until I could get the hell out of what had turned into a horrific city. Sadly, my experience in Shanghai has resulted in me having an intense dislike for the city, like no other place on earth. Hopefully, I will never have reason to visit the city again. I would find it very difficult to be comfortable there for any length of time. I would be uneasy, suspicious of anybody that talked to me. Currently, I can't think of a single reason why I might need to visit the city again. I hope it stays that way.

This disastrous trip set the tone for the business for the next six months, whereby after less than a year in operation, I was starting to consider if it was worth keeping the company running. It had become a full-time job trying to find people who needed a PowerPoint expert to integrate into their work. I was spending 95% of the time looking for work, and 5% of the time actually doing anything like creative work. After all this was the reason I founded the company, to do something that was creative and needed by clients.

Sadly, I lost my main UK client, they could no longer afford to farm work out to specialist suppliers like myself. It was more cost effective for them to take these skills in house. My clients had their own clients and they put pressure on everything, from the top down, so we had our share of the pain. Two/thirds of the business evaporated almost overnight.

I made some in-roads into the pharmaceutical industry on my own steam. A chance meeting and conversation at an industry function occurred between myself and a senior marketing manager, which led to a small number of PowerPoint projects before he left to go on sabbatical leave. By coincidence, I knew a lot of the same people he knew back in the UK, having worked for his current company in the UK in a previous client-advertising agency relationship.

I closed the company in 2018 after almost a year and a half in operation.

---|---

At this point, I decided to have a good look at my life, my employment and myself. Things were coming to a head, I felt like I didn't have much room left for many more career changes. At the age of 47, I felt I probably had one more major change of direction left in me. I wanted less change and more stability in my life. I was willing to re-train in order to have an income-producing career of sorts.

As well as consideration of my illustrious 'career', I still felt like there was a great creative upsurge brewing inside me. It was like trapped wind without the pain developing in my intestines but not quite ready to put in an appearance just yet. I was allowing my creative wind to develop at its own pace. You just cannot rush these things. But I knew that when it came, it would come quickly. I still did not know how this was going to manifest itself my initial thoughts were that I had a major painting project developing in my sub-conscious mind. Whatever the medium was, I knew my PD was the central theme of it. I'm pretty sure I could paint Parkinson's disease quite well by now.

One thing I was sure of was that I had sailed pretty close to the edge of my sanity these past couple of years. I felt I had come reasonably close to attempting suicide, too close for comfort in fact. I had really lost my reason for existing. What use was I to anyone, what useful contribution could I make or what difference could I make? I got really spooked when I found out that just thinking about suicide energised and excited me. This is not unusual – by the time you get to the state my mind was in, suicide seems to be a logical next step. The excitement, or feelings of elation, are felt in response to the realisation that you can actually make this happen. It felt like it was a 'positive step' after a number of failed attempts to deal with and solve the problems that dogged my existence.

I just couldn't see through the trees to find a way out of the forest I was lost in. Every 'way out' looked the same – a black tunnel with no light at the end of each tunnel. I still felt like I had major obstacles to overcome and I was sick to the back teeth of having issues in my life that were beyond my control. But I knew that suicide wasn't the answer to my problems, I knew that the impact of taking my own life would be felt deeper. It would impact more lives than I could count; many lives would be damaged to varying degrees and I could not bring myself to put my daughter, family and friends through that. I wasn't going to let PD play its joker card on me and win, absolutely no way.

Besides, I had realised that my life did have a role to play in. That role was in the life of my daughter. She needed guidance from two parents, not one. Collaborative parenting by Jayne and I would give Ellie the opportunity to reach her full potential, whatever that was going to be. So, I made a commitment to be there for Ellie, no matter what life throws in my path; it is the least I can do for her, after all the reason and value she has given to my life. She is the most important person in my sphere of existence.

Twenty-seven

So, what now?

Well, I did re-train, as an Early Childhood Educator (ECE), so now I can work with kids aged 0-6. At the time when I was going through the enrolment process, male ECEs accounted for around 14% of the total educators in Australia. For me, becoming an ECE ticked a few boxes:

- I wanted to work with children.
- I wanted to do something that required me to re-train for the role.
- It had no connection to my previous, illustrious career in advertising.

The course was twelve months long and was pretty much a full-time endeavour. I was one of two guys in a class of twenty-five. During training, I was able to get a few days' work here and there. This helped financially, but with the amount of course work and practical 'placement' work involved, there wasn't a great deal of time for extra-curricular employment.

Since we were to be working closely with children we were obliged to become Mandatory Reporters for child abuse if we suspected or indeed, were witness to the abuse of a child. Our suspicions would be raised if a child volunteered to us that they were being abused at home, or other places. There is a detailed protocol that we need to follow which would determine if we needed to take it as far as the Police.

Some people might look at this job choice and might consider that it is just time spent playing with the children; what could you possibly be teaching children aged between six weeks old and six years old, that is going to have any lasting value? The work we do is based more on creating appropriate learning experiences for children at different stages in their development. Sure, the child just sees this as another 'play opportunity' but it's a rare occurrence that a learning experience has had little or no thought put into it. Every single experience must have a learning outcome attached to it, otherwise it is redundant before it gets going. Obviously as the child progresses from zero to six years old, the challenges of a learning experience get bigger. This is because we are responsible for preparing the children for the transition from pre-school to primary school, which is possibly one of the most 'traumatic' of transitions that children make throughout their schooling career.

There is a great deal of repetition-based learning at this level in order to cement the ideas in place. Repetition is important to have the greatest chance of embedding knowledge in their young brains, particularly as their attention span is so short at this age. It also allows the child's brain to make connections. The sort of topics that are appropriate for learning include recycling, sustainability and the water cycle to name but a few. The more visual, the better.

I took the decision to become a 'casual' early childhood educator because it suits my lifestyle better than a permanent full-time or even part-time role. It also pays a lot better than full-time or part-time roles. I can work around Ellie and her school activities on the days that she is with me, so I can get a variety of shift lengths in different centres.

Another element of this job which I am proud to be a part of is the role that we, as early childhood educators have played in the Covid-19 pandemic. I have successfully managed to avoid discussing the pandemic simply because I have nothing to add that hasn't already been said by people far more qualified to comment. The most important contribution I have made is to get myself vaccinated with two Pfizer shots and a booster even though at the time, people in my age bracket were still not routinely being given this vaccine; the Astra Zeneca vaccine was recommended at the time for my age group. That lasted for another two weeks after my second shot, when the Pfizer vaccine became the recommended shot for people in my age bracket. On the booking form for the vaccination, which my GP completed for me he included the fact that I had PD. The vaccination centre just asked me to complete a disclaimer, to note that I was being given the Pfizer vaccine and that I acknowledged this. The difference was that I had PD; this made all the difference.

So, being optimally vaccinated against Covid-19 means that I have confidence in continuing to work as a casual educator, now that ECEs have been officially recognised as 'essential workers'.

It works like this: we take care of the very young children (0–6 years) of other essential workers. I don't think in the early months of the pandemic that people realised just how vital it was that ECEs were protected and kept in working roles. I was actually unable to get shifts between 19 March 2020 to 19 June 2020 because children's centres were closing down like they were going out of fashion. If we didn't undertake this responsibility, thousands of health care professionals, emergency response professionals, teachers, Australian post workers, supermarket workers, waste management workers and many other professionals would not be able to get to work because they would be taking care of their own children instead of fulfilling *their* own essential roles while the pandemic was in full swing.

As I tap away at my keyboard, we are in the grips of the New South Wales Covid-19 'Delta Variant' outbreak and lockdown that started in June 2021. Who knows when it will end? Whilst I am extremely cautious about going into areas that are known Covid-19 hotspots, I am still going into these areas in the Sydney and Greater Sydney areas to work. I take all necessary precautions to make sure I am as well protected as I can be. Life has to go on and until our country reaches appropriate, significant levels of vaccination, this is the new norm. However, I am looking forward to a return to the days when we can move freely about the world, like in the world before Covid-19. I miss being able to see my family in Europe when I choose to; I do not like to be dictated to by a micro-organism. Covid-19 free days are a luxury that I am looking forward to…and, I promise, I *will not* take them for granted!

---|---

The creative urge that had been building up inside me for a couple of years finally revealed itself. It was just after Christmas 2019, that I felt an overwhelming, almost uncontrollable urge to get the story of how I managed having PD over the previous two decades committed to paper. Although the journey so far has been full of emotion, with many ups and downs, along with plenty of challenges I was not going to write an 'Oh, woe is me…' account of my experience with PD. I don't really know how I have got this far but I am not in a position to pen a 'how to' manual, claiming I have all the answers to the challenges that people with PD face on a day-to-day basis. I am kind of making it up as I go; the experiences I have written about, in my first and second books are purely handled as they arose.

I am not following somebody else's experiences and making them my own. Neither am I a multi-millionaire celebrity with a team of movement specialists at my beck and call. I have no special privileges with more access to see my specialist doctor than anyone else on his list; if I need to see my specialist, I have to make an appointment and get in line – just like everyone else. None of this would have helped in developing the communication objectives for my book; I wanted readers to take positive messages from the book, not to dwell on the negative aspects of the experiences I had.

I simply wanted to write about the experience from the point of view of the average man-on-the-street. I discovered that there was very little printed matter available to buy in retail outlets. I found only two titles in the flagship store of a major bookstore chain in Sydney. For one of the most common neurological conditions, this is appalling and it added to the motivation to write the book, it spurred me on. One of the two books on this shelf was a 'Living with Parkinson's Disease' type of self-help book, which is obviously needed, but I wasn't going to write another book for this genre; the other title was what I call the 'Magical Cure' type of book, making hollow promises about how you can 'reverse' your PD just through exercise and/or changing your diet, which I find insulting to the thousands of highly qualified medical research doctors who have invested many hours searching for ways of improving the quality of life for people with PD. In addition, this type of book brings nothing but false hope to the reader. PD is harsh enough without having to add ridiculous, unachievable goals to the equation.

Is this all that patients with PD deserve when it comes to finding out what was going on in their bodies? I wondered.

No. This simply was not good enough. People with PD deserved more. It was time to set the bar at a higher level and write an account, which needed a great deal of courage on my part to delve into the memories of the challenges I had faced, yet at the same time was full of inspiration and brutal honesty. The book, which goes by the title *'Drivin' Daughters and Parkinson's'* is a no-holds-barred, just 'say it just like it is', often hilarious story of my time both with and before PD, in which the characters are played by my friends, family and many acquaintances. Throughout the story, I endeavour to impart that I am an ordinary guy, with an ordinary life that was made more entertaining and exciting by finding myself occasionally in the wrong place at the wrong time. This made for some unforgettable life experiences in addition to experiences for which PD was inherently responsible.

So, the book – my first – was written for anyone who has been touched by this condition; whether you have PD, or your husband does…maybe your brother has PD and you want to understand how it might be making him feel? Or perhaps you are a second-year house officer working in neurology in a regional hospital and you want to understand in plain language, what it means to live *and* function with PD? Maybe you are a nursing professional considering a career change and you are considering working with PD patients? I wish to exclude nobody from reading '*Drivin' Daughters and Parkinson's*' as it was written with a view to having broad appeal, meaning that it would make sense to and could be read by just about anyone. I would be thrilled if the book helped raise awareness and improved understanding of the condition.

Ultimately, I wanted readers to be able to connect with the book and the personal experiences I talk about; even though everybody who has PD has their own set of unique experiences given the nature of the condition. I wanted people to read the book and feel like there is an understanding between the reader and the author. Essentially, I wanted the reader to understand that there are people out there who may have gone through *similar* types of experiences over the years; so you are not the only person going through these alone, even though at times you might feel this way.

---|---

Writing had become my 'new career' and was the perfect vocation to undertake. I found that I was better at writing in the mornings, rather than later in the day. I had no manager looking over my shoulder watching what I was doing. I actively sought afternoon shifts in my Early Childhood Educator role so that I could write when I felt more creative. Come the evening, all I wanted to do was to chill out and relax.

'*Drivin' Daughters and Parkinson's*' took almost six months to write. It literally poured out of my brain onto my laptop screen, with minimal effort. It is as if it had been somewhere in the recesses of my mind, waiting to receive confirmation to proceed. I think that says a lot about the intensity of my experiences and how deeply ingrained in my memory they are.

People often say, "I'm going to write a book about that…" in an off-hand way, about all manner of subjects. I ask them, what does the first page talk about and what is it about the subject that is going to make it a book that is so compelling to read the reader cannot put down? Writing a book is not easy, especially when the subject is so personal, as is mine.

However, putting pen to paper was exciting, intense and a relief. I finally felt I had turned a corner and was furiously enjoying making sure that what I was writing made sense, fitted with what I had written before and with what I was going to write in the coming chapters. I re-wrote the opening pages at least half a dozen times. The plan for the book was based on its chapters and the detail within these. Each chapter had a message goal that it aimed to achieve. At times, the writing was heart-breaking in terms of the extent to which PD has had an effect on my personal life. This is tempered by anecdotes about me, my upbringing, family, friends and other people who have entered my life. Some are still around, others have moved on.

I used different names for most to protect the privacy of the people in my life or those who were in my life at one time or another. I attempt to explain some cutting-edge medical procedures in layman's terms, retaining the intense nature of the science, which was both challenging and time consuming to achieve.

Going through the publishing process is an experience in itself. I sent my manuscript to a dozen or so agents in New South Wales, Victoria and Queensland. A couple of agents looked like they might go for it but in the end, they missed the opportunity. The time for either an agent or a publisher to get back in touch varied wildly, but most took between twenty minutes and three months to respond. Some didn't bother to reply at all. I then decided to send the manuscript to ten or fifteen Australian publishing houses directly, rather than through an agent, to see if this instigated a better response. This was a bit more risky as I really did not know enough about the relationships between Australian agents and publishers. *Where does the balance of power lie? Is it with the agent or with the publisher?* I wondered.

A couple of publishers pontificated about it but then bowed out graciously. It was disappointing. I knew that the manuscript was good and deserved to be published.

But even that was not enough! It was no longer to do with what 'I' felt that the book 'deserved'. It had come down to what 'needed' to happen.

'Drivin' Daughters and Parkinson's' needed to be published because there was (and doubtless still is) such an enormous lack of positive information from people with PD. It looks at PD from the point-of-view of 'an ordinary man on the street'. Nothing to do with having PD was sugar coated, it was written for the ordinary people of this world who need to be able to relate to other people with PD or those whose lives have in some way have been 'touched' by PD. It encourages all these people to share their unique experiences with one another.

I could put it down to nothing other than what my mother told me, that it was 'very British, even for the Australian market'. The humour was quite subtle and dark in some places – this might have been enough to send it straight over the heads of some Australian readers. Some of my Australian friends have confirmed that this might be the case. The agents and publishers of Australia may have picked up on this although none of them used it as the reason for not taking the book on. There is also the relative market size issue, with the Australian publishing sector being a fraction of the size of that in Europe, North America or the Middle East.

In retrospect, I am glad that I am not represented by an agent. There are pros and cons about having an agent to go between the publishing house and you, which, as a rookie author may have been beneficial. For me, having an agent would put more distance between me and the finished book, it would cause unwanted production delays and I would have had to pay 15% for the privilege.

If the book was that British, well, maybe it needed to be published where it had the greatest chance of being well received.

So, I researched the UK publisher market and sent the manuscript to a dozen publishing houses based in various cities in the UK. Each house had its own preferences about how it liked to assess work for publishing. Every application in both Australia and the UK was different. Some houses wanted to see the first three chapters and an author's biography…others requested the entire manuscript and a chapter synopsis. It was a whole separate project getting material out to publishing houses and with each rejection I was getting more demoralised. No two publishers were the same in terms of what they requested to assess a manuscript for publishing.

Then…success! A major publisher in London, who I had sent my manuscript to indicated that they liked my work and forwarded me a contract in early 2021. I was beside myself with excitement. My mother whooped with relief and joy at the same time when I phoned her in the UK to relay the good news. I took time to read the contract through carefully and asked some questions before signing and returning it.

Shortly after this, I was approached by another UK publisher who wanted to publish the manuscript for *'Drivin' Daughters and Parkinson's'* was rock solid – I was very surprised, flattered and pleased that two UK publishers had shown interest in my work. Everybody had said that I would be very lucky if, for my first book, a publisher acknowledged the manuscript, without committing to publishing, because of the incredibly high level of competition in the publishing industry. To be offered two separate publishing deals, as a first-time author was rare, I was told.

My publisher's comments on the manuscript were that it 'has broad appeal…it is a refreshing approach to a very difficult subject' and 'there is nothing like this currently on the market'. Even the second publisher said they wanted to take it on, 'because it is very well written'.

So, I have done my utmost to write about The Time Thief with the same qualities as *Drivin' Daughters and Parkinson's*. Although they are both books about PD, written by me, mostly about me, they are both very different.

At least, that is what I think.

More importantly…what do YOU think?

Epilogue

I was catching up with a friend of mine, while having a Zoom.com drink with her during the Covid-19 lockdown, in Sydney. She asked me, "So, then. What's next?"

"Well, there's a thought," I said before taking a long swig of Diet Coke, emptying the can. I stood up, put the can in the recycling trash bin and then sat back down in front of the screen.

"I haven't been mining for opal, yet…"